A Poem

I Had A Dream

I had a dream, and that dream became a reality,
And from the reality flowed the emotions of time,
Until the space within was defined, as mine and mine alone, to bring a connectedness to the true self through the Higher Self, of Divine love, a love above all, the one love of Divineness that encompasses all love, in the end.
After one emerges, from the black pit of confusion and despair of self-torture, and collapse of all reasoning of right and wrong, to work out the Karma of the day.
From this reality I found the truth that I am God, experiencing through human eyes all that has been and will be,
That has been created by the Greater energy of timeless boundlessness and limitless all,
I am that, on a universal journey of greatness,
I am an extension of all my past life times that I have been unfolding, up until this life time,
I have chosen to look at the whole truth and not deny my super-being that resides within me,
The all-knowing, wiser, older self of time, and the more loving part of me than can be imagined self.
To open the envelopes in my heart, one by one, to unfold the majesty of this self.
Through the tests, the challenges, the lies and the denials, and the battle between God and ego within.

Christine U. Cowin

My Secret Self: Trials and Tribulations of an Innocent
First published in Australia by Christine U. Cowin 2018
www.christineucowinwriter.com
www.amazon.com/author/christineucowinwriter

Prepublication Data Service details available from
The National Library of Australia
ISBN: 978-0-6484013-0-8 (pbk)
ISBN: 978-0-6484013-1-5 (ebk)

Typesetting and design by Publicious Book Publishing
Published in collaboration with Publicious Book Publishing
www.publicious.com.au

Dedication

I dedicate my book to those who presented themselves as characters in my play of life, and to the God within that gave me the courage and the driving force and strength to awaken me out of my sleeping life, to see my truth from all that was presented to me. This story is my truth, and there is no intention on my part to ever hurt or harm anybody; I just want to tell my true story. Thank you to all who have been apart of my life, and thank you to all who are yet to enter my life.

Saying Thank You

I have to give my thanks to all my family and to all of those who have entered my life and who have played out their various parts or roles to help me unravel myself. People came and people left me, and I'd come in with I will be left, and I accept that fully. I never forced anyone to stay beyond their time limit with me. A few I did allow to stay longer than I should have allowed. All were conveying a message I needed to learn at that particular time. I want to say thank you with all my heartfelt love to those I've encountered, be it a good or not so good encounter. I truly love you all. Thank you for reflecting to me what I needed to learn about myself and thank you to the God within all of us who knows far beyond our physical being's knowings.

A Thought

Each side will have their own story to tell, and their reasons for what they did and why they did it. It's our conditionings that separate us all, and the fact that each feels they are right. Maybe none of us are right.

Christine U. Cowin

My Secret Self:

SERIES - BOOK ONE

*Trials and Tribulations
of an Innocent*

Christine U. Cowin

PART ONE

Introduction

Where do I start: before I arrived here, or after my birth, and where do I begin to finish all of the challenges I have set myself on this path of self-discovery? Many would have thrown in the towel, said to hell with it all, swept whatever evidence they had under the family carpet and said, 'Let's put that secret to rest.'

I arrived here through the channel of my mother. I cry here as I write these words, because I left something more sacred behind somewhere else. There's Reiki music playing behind me, and my heart is touched by the memory of another place more dear to my heart, before I entered this world.

My name is Christine. There was always something I knew beyond this world. My head was always in the clouds, and my mind was somewhere else, much to many people's horror. This happened to me because I was separated from my true world. This is a place to visit, as far as I am concerned, and I've come and gone many times. I'm still labouring over my reasons for being here, and why I've stretched the journeys out for so long, so far. This lifetime, I've promised myself that I'll get it right, and I feel I have been doing so.

Why is it important to look at our past? You may ask this question. What about family patterns? Hmm, now I am beating a path to the door of fulfillment, in a vain effort to understand the reasonings behind the minds of those who had taken on the responsibility to care for me, or play in my world of self-discovery, I reason.

I wasn't the smartest child in our family. I was the aware one, accused of having a vivid imagation. I was the one they'd find talking or singing to herself. I could entertain myself for hours, and not need others' company. I much preferred to be with my pets than people. They knew how to love me unconditionally, and they had no desire to hurt me. I wanted to be friends with my brother and sister, but we were worlds apart. We only got on well when strangers or relatives visited our home. What do I mean by strangers? Friends that aren't part of our immediate clan, so to say. My sister and I fought as children, which caused Dad to run out of the house in a rage when we were fighting. In Dad's presence, we would each bleat out our own innocence. We were all for ourselves, and each was an individual in the family.

My brother puzzled me. I just didn't know him, due to his absence, on and off, in the family. As a child, I didn't understand the full impact he'd had on my life. Dad made us all quake in our boots, Mum was always hiding from us, and my grandma, she had eveyone under her control.

I didn't realise there was a book in me until I'd gone to Turkey to live. There it was all revealed to me. I used to tell myself, I must write a book. I never dreamt or thought I could achieve such a thing, due to considering myself under-educated. My grammatical skills were nil, but living in Turkey, I needed an income. As all foreigners do there, I taught English. Regardless of not being a qualified teacher, just being a native speaker gave me the credentials I needed. My biggest thank you to Turkey was for allowing me to improve my grammatical skills. It wasn't easy living there and dealing with the familiar behaviours from my past; little did I know, I was there for a greater reason: to re-live my life to understand it. On a day-to-day basis, getting around the whole of Turkey for me was simple. However, I knew nothing about Turkey or Istanbul, and excuse my ignorance, I didn't even know it was an Islamic country, so I came to Turkey blind. Blind to the now, but on a deeper level, and not of this time frame, I knew I had to go there. The enormous city of Istanbul was never daunting or frightening, and was always easy to move around in. I always felt safe in that country; it was a homecoming.

Turkey helped open my eyes to the truths locked away in me, truths I wasn't aware of, and some truths that I was in touch with. I had to face aspects of myself, and Turkey unfolded those beautifully for me as I reflected with and mirrored those who crossed my path to say, hey, I am in you. Many of the experiences were hard, and so were the lessons behind them. For me, living there was like being in a relationship with my family, or a man where I either loved him or hated him, and there were never any inbetweens.

For myself, I would say to those who ask, how can I find myself and find my dream: I'd say, walk your path and do your journey, and allow your Soul to guide you safely to wherever it is you need to be. Let your Soul drive your body to do as you must. Many say that the personality drives us; I feel our Soul does, and it takes us to our destinations to heal the self. God only gives us what we can handle.

The world is full of mysteries, and the mystery is you. Life is about learning of the self, and the journey is to remind you what you're here for, and what you need to do to complete it, and become whole.

The personality can't be relied on, and it will throw in the towel and take an easier option, but not your Soul. It pushes you until you comply, and the Soul is eternal and loves you in the flesh. The Soul will allow the personality to rule, and this is when the body may fail us in health, or in illnesses, or even suicide, which may be an option to cease the journey, when one doesn't respond to their calling.

All people in your life, be it family or strangers, have keys, and they have come, or will come into your life, to unlock memories in your subconscious mind for you to work through. They're the players in the game called life. On many occasions you will step off your path. However, once on a path, you will always return to it. The rules of the games are to be able to distinguish the truth from the non-truth, and we need others to experience through to do that. No one can be an island and evolve, because alone one can't learn of the secret hidden self without the reflections of others; it's always up to you if you want to read the messages - if you can stand to look at your own reflection in others.

Experiences in life foretell many aspects of the self, and you cannot journey completely if you avoid the experiences, which many do, and don't want to take any risks by meeting up with strangers. People are catalysts, and if you're bored with life, or you're a workaholic, working until you drop, you're in avoidance. You're not growing. You're not taking a risk. You have patterns in your life, and these can be hidden from you, and for you to realise them or see them, they have to be played out to you. If you are in tune and in awareness, and realise you can clear genetic behaviours that stem from the greater family, you are on your way to change.

The emotions are energy in motion, and if you don't express, move or change, but stay stagnant, then your emotions become suppressed, and you can be tormented internally until the right mirror comes in to make you look at yourself; or an illness may beset you to slow you down, to make you look at yourself. Your mirrors are your biggest gifts. I have a saying: those who nark us the most are our biggest gifts, and what narks us from them is within us.

You are not only from this lifetime, and you carry, in your celluar memory, memories of other lifetimes. It's also important to ask your own mother about your birthing. Get your messages from every source you can to help you unfold the clues to you. I came in with, 'I will be left.'

When you suppress information that comes to you, you block your ability to assess who you really are. You are not what you seem to be, and you're a product of conditionings by others: by community, by culture, by society, by religion, and the beliefs of those closest to you. You learnt many behaviours that may not necessarily be yours. You carry, in your genetics, family patterns and behaviours of this lifetime separate to the now person.

You have brought in lots of secret, hidden knowledge about you and about what you have been, and what you're to do in this lifetime, and even information on what you never complete in other lifetimes.

Social conditionings, and behaviours of others, in the now life suppress us, and prevent us from finding ourselves and/or discovering what it is we need. Families don't like family members to stray out of a perceived image of what is acceptable in their family line. Communication is so important, and none of us want to tell others about our hidden secrets, and/or show our true self; so many of us wear masks to make us presentable or acceptable in our groups, in order to not lose face, or more importantly, the big love or little love we receive from those within our groups, or those we choose to bring into our life. Hence, we are always suppressing our real self.

In doing this, many of us stifle ourselves with bottled-up true feelings, unexpressed and unlived. In doing this, we never become the full human beings we're supposed to be. We sabotage ourselves constantly through fears, and block those fears to not expose ourselves. Secrets must be revealed to free the Soul.

Take a risk, and relieve yourself of supressed pain and sufferings. If your loved ones can't deal with it, it's because you're bringing up their stuff as well; because what we see in others is in us to a lesser or higher degree, or similarly connected without being identical. We each have memories of issues we'd agreed to play out and work through together, so it depends on how buried that information is. Remember, it's your quest for self.

A loving person will never judge you, and will only respect and support you through any ordeal, if they are aware. For many of us, there is a lot of retaliation and fighting as stuff surfaces, and in the battle, each will gain something positive from any negative situation.

Shame and guilt are the killers of life. Release these, and stop imprisoning the self. To let my secrets out is, for me, a blessing. If we don't or can't release to move on, we will constantly draw in many who will cause us to face the self being reflected to us, until one day someone will really press our buttons extra hard and make us explode. In the explosion comes release. In the release, you will be angry, sigh, cry, laugh - but I do guarantee you will be renewed when you face a secret part of the self. It disappears when dealt with for what it is, and for the first time in your life, you will feel lighter as your burden is lifted. You will have exposed a secret part of yourself to another, or told another a secret, or showed yourself to another to reveal to them, and yourself, a truth, and you will have freed the Soul from one of its chains.

Patterns within us will draw us to people who carry the same pattern or similar patterns. People who carry the same energy, as those we need to deal with, will keep entering our lives until we acknowledge that energy from the past, and deal with it in the present to heal the self of a taken-on belief from the past. This belief could be a subconciously taken-on belief that's not even yours on a conscious level. Many of us are unaware of family patterns, or secret stuff families carry, that a child who is sensitive can tap into and claim as their own. There can be an instant hate or love with another, and you don't know why. This can be related to a past life issue that needs to be realised and resolved. Your Soul knows you and loves you, even when you send it to hell or heaven on this Earth. We can become very in tune with some people, and not understand why. It's that they carry familiar energy. Freedom comes with self-knowledge.

I had to dig up many lifetimes in many countries, and I actually had to re-live situations from past lifetimes, and my own immediate lifetime stemming from my childhood, adolesence and adult life. Many stages of my life were under-developed and incorrect, and I knew from a young age that I wanted to change. I also knew, with my own children, I must change the way my family brought me up, and I was willing to change all that.

Life is like a jigsaw puzzle thrown into a large pot. To put it back together again, we can only pull out one piece at a time, to learn the truth and rid the self of learned fears and phobias. When the secrets are out, and seen for what they are, and as one family member heals and clears, all family members heal and clear. Should they continue to create these patterns, it's for them to heal what they must do personally, and it is usually done to a lesser degree. So the genetic structure of our future family members can change. We choose our parents, and those who will help us to solve ourselves; we know on a higher level.

I feel I'd taken on the pains of my whole family, unbeknown to myself. I was also the one unlocking the family secrets that were hidden in both my parents' families. It's amazing, when you start this work, how everyone in your family will open up to you, consciously or unconsciously, and seemingly willingly.

I couldn't fully change until I accepted everything in life that was me. Living in Turkey gave me that opportunity. God is all things, and God created all. We are all things, and nothing is separate or outside us.

We can project the familiar onto others, and blame, and as the other plays out the familiar, we become unhappy and say it's you, not me. An honest person will say I know I am upset with you, but it's me; I haven't as yet seen it for what it is. We've all learnt our roles and behaviours through the eyes of a child, and are playing them out now through the eyes of an adult. The child buried things it didn't understand, and it quickly got on with playing or living. As an adult, we can't remember much of our childhood, so the information is blurry and buried deeply within. Others come in to break the code of the puzzles within: so search within to claim your freedom.

When I first came to Turkey, I walked around the streets thinking these words: with love in my Heart, there is no room for fear. I walked fearlessly and searched, and I conquered the created self, and I knew I was on an inner journey of self-discovery.

Written in November, 2007.

Telling The Truth

By writing of my life, I am sure I will be able to help many people to understand themselves and their families, and I can also help my own family line to change and rid us of any undesirable behaviours. The secrets are out. I love and forgive all, and especially my father, and I am grateful to him. Because of him, I had to go deeper within myself and ask many questions in my loneliness: who am I? What am I here for? What am I to do here? Where am I going to? When will this all be through? What I had to do was understand my life, and understand why I was as I was, and why these trials and tribulations happened to me.

Through recognition of what I'd experienced, and accepting how it was, I could move forward; letting go as I healed, and most of all, love and forgive all, and myself.

Even though Dad abused me, the experience could have helped him to move forward into his next stage of life, and helped him to stop repeating the patterns deeply entrenched within him. My telling my dad, 'You abused me,' made him confront himself; to give himself redemption to claim his true self before his death.

My biggest joy is that my father learnt from our experience that God exists, and there is something greater than we know; and he also learnt, through his spiritual daughter whom he never understood, that there is something greater outside of us.

I love my family, and how I experienced my life may not be how they viewed it. However, we will learn what we need to for the benefit of the healing we need.

Being Spiritual

Many people fear spirituality, but there is nothing to fear. Being spiritual isn't all about meeting spirits and seeing phenomena. Being spiritual is being honest about who you are, and being yourself. Some of us may encounter phenomena; that will depend on what stage of evolution you're at, or what you need to know.

The spiritual journey is about self-awareness, self-growth and self-understanding, and understanding of your role in life: to find the true self out of all the learned behaviours and conditionings. My books will convey to the reader the mystical and magical components of life.

A Phrase That Came To Me

I will sit in my being and smile as you play out your scenes, for I know the dance of your drama.
Through the mirror of your eyes, I see the tests that are mine.

Christine U. Cowin

Chapter 1

The Reminder

My sister and I returned home from a day at high school. We got off the bus and walked along the dirt track that ran through a cleared area, until we reached the only house along the track. Passing the house, we went through a gate where the dirt track and the bush met each other. I loved the silence and the serenity of the bush; there was a feeling of awe and peace that emanated from nature. There was magic in the bush, and I could feel it; it was like it was living, and I was sure that there were eyes watching us. Maxine was ahead of me, nattering on to herself, probably annoyed with me for daydreaming and dilly-dallying. She could go ahead if she wanted to, but she wouldn't; she kept an eye on me to feel safe. I had no fear in the bush, but I felt Maxine was scared of so many things.

It was July, and it got dark quickly, and there was a storm brewing; but I was too busy daydreaming to really worry about the storm.

I'd be sixteen in September and I'd get my L plates; I was getting closer to my freedom. I was a strange person, and no one could really fathom me. I was silent, and I saw without seeing somehow; I was taking it all in without questioning. For me, there was no reason to question my situation. I couldn't change it, and what'd been done was done.

Sometimes, I didn't understand what I was seeing. It was like I was seeing through people, without even knowing what I was doing. They were all so fearful, but I felt no fear. I often spent days and nights in town at my friend's house, and no one questioned it. I had freedom to come and go. When I was at home, I spent a lot of time alone.

I felt old and wise, yet I was young. It was like I'd experienced many things, and I didn't know what; some of my dreams took me to far-off lands, and I knew the places, but I'd never been there.

I saw my mother as young and childish, my father as angry and unpredictable; my grandma as ancient, old and sad; my sister as distant; my brother seemed to be living in his own world; and me - I just was. I didn't know anything about life or things; we had no books, and no one told us about life or the world. I learnt off the TV. I loved shows about other cultures, and I loved documentaries on those cultures.

I heard my sister demanding that I hurry.

In the midst of waking me out of my daydreaming, I heard *Christine, Christine, where art thou? Have you forgotten we have a meeting? It's time.*

I looked over my shoulder, wondering where that had came from. I'd never heard a command like that before. Then I realised, *those words had come from my own mind* - but I didn't recall any meeting. I walked with my head down, kicking my feet in the loose sand that gave me the feeling of movement, as it slipped from the sides of my shoes. I loved the splendour of nature, and I was intrigued by the movement of the soft grains of sand that were concaving into the shape of my shoe print, and disappearing under my foot, filling the gap to leave no trace of me, as I took my next step.

I looked into the bush, and admired its beauty as we walked; it was always more mysterious in this type of weather. I could see lots of different shapes as we walked. I saw the blackboys swaying in the pent-up wind. They were beautiful plants. They had long, black, slender bodies, and a crop of green hair made of fern, like grass. There was the kangaroo tail, so straight and tall. My imagination ran wild; how I'd have loved to have seen people come out of the bush to greet us. The smells of the bush were changing as the weather gained momentum; it was winter, and you could see so many changes. All the birds and insects seemed to be leaving, and they were not as plentiful. There were less noises, and the bush flowers had died off. Things looked a little duller. I loved the little flowers, especially the purple, cream, and red ones. People don't realize how beautiful it is. I looked at my sister and I thought, I do, but maybe she doesn't. I didn't think Maxine ever looked into the bush like I did. Maxine and I didn't see eye-to-eye, and we didn't have much in common with each other. We were worlds apart, and we didn't relate. We only seemed to come together when we argued or fought. Thank God for those situations; they at least allowed us to talk to each other.

It was getting colder, and the rain was getting closer.

'Come on, Christine, walk faster,' I heard her plead.

I quickened my pace in order not to infuriate her, but I loved the changes in the weather, and I wanted to stay in it and feel the cold, crisp, change, and let the rain drench me; but we had to walk a bit faster, at her insistence. Sometimes, I wished we lived in town. This two-and-a-half mile walk to the bus each morning, and two-and-a-half mile walk home in the evening, isolated us from town events. I would have liked to have learned ballet, and I know Maxine would have loved to learn to play the piano. I did admire my sister's strength though; she could demand what she wanted and seemed to get her own way. She played in a netball team, but me, I was the compliant one - don't rock the boat - I'd already done that in a big way, and I was treading on eggshells in that house of fears and secrets.

My stomach was encouraging me to hurry up, because dinner would be ready by the time we got in the door, and I was always so hungry after a day at school. I looked up towards the sky. I felt a feeling of unrest in me as the weather became more threatening.

'Come on, Christine!' my sister screamed.

My sister was running; she was really scared of the approaching storm. I liked storms and lightning. I loved to see the flashes of lightning strike across the sky, giving the sky life. It made me feel like I was never alone. Nature did that to me. It was my life connection. I looked above once more as we ran. I loved it. I heard her voice, like in a distant tunnel.

'It's not funny; you're strange. Come on.'

No one understood me. I was not like Maxine. She had so many friends, and I found it hard to make friends; I often found myself crying because I was not understood.

15

She was really afraid now. 'Come on, Christine. You're so slow, and you don't care if we get caught in the rain. Wait until I tell Mum.'

I couldn't care less if she told Mum. There was an enormous crack of thunder, which made her jump. I laughed, but I didn't let her see me laughing, and I ran behind her, chuckling. My main concern was dinner, and to sit and watch TV. It was my favourite thing. I was the only one who really watched it; I couldn't get enough documentaries and information about people from other countries. I wanted to know how the world worked. I loved cowboy films, and funny shows - but I didn't like the scary shows. Those I couldn't watch. I hid or closed my eyes at the scary bits.

As we came over the crest of a small incline, we ran down the green, grassy slope to the bridge that crossed the creek. There was the pipeline, now exposed to us; it had been running underground to our right, and now it had come out of the ground to greet us. It ran across the bridge to dive once more into the ground on the other side. It was like a big snake, awakened and coming out of the earth to greet us, then to once more descend into its underground home, back into the bowels of the earth. This pipeline fed the pit at Lachlan Main Colliery and gave us our water supply for washing. The bridge crossed a deep gorge called Nelson Creek. The pipeline travelled all the way to the big lagoon that we lived near, which they called Kinread's Lagoon.

Nelson Creek was a long, winding creek. It had the most beautiful, golden, clean sand. I thought of summertime, lying on the sand and soaking up the sun.

'Come on. Stop daydreaming,' I heard as her voice disappeared into the wind. She stood at the start of the bridge.

'I am coming,' I said, irritated at her insistence on making me hurry. As I said this, I realised why she wanted me to hurry. So she could step onto the bridge and run across it, but she'd stopped at the start of the bridge.

I got to her; the wind was blowing a gale, and I thought I'd better hurry. I could see the worry etched into her face; she seemed to be old before her time. Maxine was like that; she worried incessantly.

'It will be okay,' I said to reassure her.

'Of course, it will be,' she snapped, as if she wasn't afraid, and to show me she was strong and that she was just waiting for me.

The bridge was a narrow, wooden bridge, just wide enough for a person and a pushbike to cross it. Some days we rode our bikes to the bus stop, and other times we walked. I guessed that the bridge was made for the pipeline, and not for us. There was a handrail to grip onto, which was good in this weather. As we crossed, the wind was blowing so hard, the bridge swayed. I had never liked heights, but strangely, this was the only bridge I could comfortably cross over. The creek below was low in water, but by the look of the storm clouds, we were going to get a heavy downpour. The wind whipped up and howled around the poles. The bridge reminded me of those on the Westerns, and just like them, our bridge stood high up over a trickling riverbed.

I had to admire the weeping willows as they swayed and rustled in the wind. I heard them say, 'Child, we know you.' I smiled and saw the cows in the paddock ahead.

Then I heard my sister's fading voice as she screamed out, 'Come on!' Maxine was again way in front of me, and she'd crossed the bridge.

I stopped to look at her face, and I stared, mesmerized by the expression she pulled. Her face told me of her feelings. Her school uniform wasn't flattering on her body. I was blessed with a well-developed body and good looks; she with a quick mind and a sharp tongue, and a personality that made friends easily. I was holding onto the railing with one hand, my school bag in the other. I stopped to take another look down at the river, and the cows caught my attention. They started to low in discontent as the storm brewed, then they were running and bowing their heads in disapproval. I realised that I'd better hurry. I ran off the bridge, and my sister and I ran up the steep hill to where our only neighbours lived. Their house sat on the top of the hill, and this part of the land seemed to sit above our house. The cows were more restless and anxious than ever: really lowing and running from us. Fortunately, they never ran at us; only our bull did that, but he'd got us all bluffed. Nonetheless, we never tempted him, and when we saw him, we dived for the wire fence into the next paddock and quickly ducked under to escape him.

I thought of Sherry, who used to walk to school with us. I missed Sherry, because she used to talk to me, but she went to Rosemont to work and live. Maxine and I both missed her. As I thought of her, I saw her pale face and cheeks, always sickly and gaunt. I didn't know why, but Sherry and her mother were always sick, or looked sickly. Sherry's aunt and uncle, Mr and Mrs Newton, lived in the other house across from

Sherry's house. Sherry's house sat closer to the main road, and her aunt's house sat further in from the main road. To me, the land seemed to sweep out and jut towards the main road like an S - S for Sherry.

Sherry's aunt, Macy Newton, petted and protected Sherry to extremes - and that stupid goat she'd bought Sherry for a pet, it hated us, and if it spotted us, we'd have to run because it would chase us and butt at us. That goat only liked Sherry, but now it was gone too. When Sherry left home, they got rid of the goat. Sherry didn't live long on this earth. She died with leukemia.

There wasn't long to go to reach the top of this hill and the neighbour's gate, and we'd go through it and cross the main road to our gate. We'd see Mum at our front gate. She'd be looking out for us in this weather. At Sherry's house I could see our house: my security, comfort, and safety. The house was so large, and in its grandeur, I felt like I could fall into it, and never die of feeling insecure or alone. However, I didn't feel love from the people in the house. I felt secure, and there was something there in our house looking after us all, and still controlling the family from the grave.

It was a beautiful house, set in a picturesque setting of water and mountains, and it stood like a jewel in a crown, enveloped by the most beautiful sights in nature that God could beset any human eye. How lucky I was to be able to live in such a grand house. I knew I longed for the town, but I knew too that I would not be blessed with such a house.

Even though the weather was all-threatening, the house was saying, 'Come, my child, let me embrace you in my arms of love. I understand you and I know your secrets, and I still love you and welcome you home.' It was like that; that house had its own feelings, and it was as much alive as we were.

I remembered, on many occasions, running home from the top gate just to get into the house, regardless of the many issues that were going on there between the people living in it. My relationship with my parents was strained, and I felt like an outsider, but I still sensed a feeling of comfort and security from the house; just not my parents. It's as if the house held us all captive and entranced us. The house was so connected to the past, and the dead ones that lived there before us. There were many mysteries and secrets that filled the house, and there was an eeriness about it.

I knew something was living there besides us, and it wasn't only me sensing it; my sister's friend, Cathy, she felt it too. I remembered her comments when we took her on a tour of our house, as we left the two bottom rooms.

Cathy surprised me at the archway that separated these two rooms from the rest of the house. She said, 'It feels like someone is living down there.'

Looking at my sister as Cathy said that, I didn't think Maxine understood what she'd meant, but Grandma Kinread did. She knew what Cathy meant, and she quickly changed the subject, but my ears pricked up when I caught Cathy's comment. I was glad she felt something in those two rooms, because I knew the house held something in there. Those two rooms seemed to be connected to another world when you passed through the archway; it was like you had walked into another time zone.

Out of the archway, I glanced at Grandma. She wasn't looking at me. I looked back at the two rooms and the hallway, and I felt its separateness from the rest of the house. I looked to the room on the right, which was the formal lounge room, holding many objects and photos from the past. The other room, to the left, was the bedroom of my grandparents Grandma Kinread and Grandfather Kinread, and their old wedding photo sat above the door you entered to go into their bedroom.

When I was in either of these rooms with Grandma, I never felt we were alone. In their bedroom, I sensed my grandfather staring at me, watching me as I walked around the bedroom.

I stopped thinking of the past as we got to the neighbour's gate, and we climbed under the wires of the wooden pole fence and crossed the main road. Both of us walked to our first gate onto our property, but we couldn't climb through our wire fence; it was barbed wire. Mum had just come out of the house to check on us, and she waved; we waved back, and she quickly disappeared into the house. She knew we were nearly home. I looked over at Maxine. She'd slowed down a bit, and she sighed with relief. I waited, and when she pushed the gate open, I walked through, looking at the mountains ahead, and saw the rain clouds gathering, ready to spill their contents.

The beauty of those mountains was breathtaking. They seemed to envelope our place, like arms around a child, and the hills that came off them fell into this enormous lagoon that was so big, it took nearly all day to walk around it. The pump house pumped our water to our house, and to the pit through the pipeline on the bridge. We walked quickly down the hill to the middle gate. The wind was blowing strongly around the cow bales to our right. Those cow bales were so old, the grass had taken over and grown around the wooden fencing. The wind was rustling the grass and howling through the cow bales and the fence in full force.

Our cows were lowing, bowing their heads and getting restless, some of them running at each other in annoyance. Some retaliated, and others just turned their heads as if to say, 'Don't take it out on me.' From the middle gate, we ran the long distance to the front gate of the house. We entered our house's front yard; the fruit trees were really swaying. The wind was whistling through them, and it made them scrape at the metal guttering with a scratching noise, like a badly played fiddle. We passed the water tank that held our drinking water. I could hear the frogs croaking; they knew it was going to rain a beauty.

As we ran down the path and onto the verandah, the rain came pelting down. The clouds had been waiting for us to get home before they dropped their heavy burden, and it bucketed down.

We looked at each other, and Maxine sighed. 'We made it. Thank goodness.'

I smiled at her. She turned and headed into the house, not even noticing. I stood on the verandah and smelt the freshness of the rain and thought of how many times we hadn't made it home. I placed my school port on the old chair near the kitchen door, went to the other end of the verandah, down near the bathroom door, and watched the rain bucketing down. The cows in the yard were barely visible; I could just see them huddled, sheltering near the outside toilet. The toilet sat to the right of an old coal heap we didn't use anymore.

As I looked around, I thought, our once grand house wasn't so grand close up. It was more like a rambling house. When I was younger, it had been so lovely and well looked after. Now there was no maintenance done to it. The only major change that had been made was the bathroom which Dad built. I didn't know why we had to have the outside bathroom for. There was one inside that never got used, not even by my parents when we were younger, and it was a large, modern-style bathroom, better than bathrooms I'd seen at my friends' houses. About seven years prior, we had used a tin bathtub in front of the fireplace in the kitchen, but Mum said I was getting too old to do that, and that we needed a bathroom.

That lovely inside bathroom held my secrets. I was forever visiting it when no one was around. It had a cellar that looked and felt gloomy when I peered down into it. Uncle Donny's rocking horse sat in there as well. The inside bathroom was converted into a bedroom for Barton, my brother. It was a scary room, but I don't think Barton worried about the spooky cellar. He never seemed to be scared of anything.

Standing there, I sighed. If I lived in town, I could have been the ballerina dancer I dreamed of being. In my bedroom, when no one was looking. I had pretended to be that dancer.

As I soaked in the cleanness of the air, I removed my school tie and glanced over at the old table that sat on the verandah. Tom, the old black cat, started to stir out of his deep sleep on seeing me. He had been curled up in a ball and was uncurling himself out of that ball. He stretched his paws out and up over the box. He liked to sit up high on the table. He gave me a wink, but he wasn't going to move out of his warm spot in this weather. I smiled at him, but he didn't care about me. He stood up, turned to reposition himself, and curled back up in a ball with his back to me. The wind suddenly changed direction, and it was blowing a torrent onto the verandah. I quickly patted the cat on the head and rushed to my port, picked it up, and made my way into the kitchen.

Mum was at the stove, dipping a fork into the boiled vegetables to see if they were done. On seeing me, she told me, 'They'll be a while yet; I got behind with your grandma.'

'That's okay, Mum, and how are you?' I bent over and kissed her cheek.

'Rushed, with your brother home and your grandma needing to go to the toilet.'

Now I was home, Mum had me to complain to; not that she needed to complain why she was running late, because she was always late.

'It won't be long,' she reinforced.

'Great. I'm starved.' I smiled at her to boost her mood, but she never looked at me.

Chapter 2

Barton

In the kitchen, my brother, Barton, sat at the table. He hadn't gone to school; he was sick. He didn't like school and got conveniently sick. Just as Maxine and I didn't relate to each other, nor did Barton relate to us. I found it hard to relate to him, or anyone in this house. Regardless, the house smelt good from the cooking, and the kitchen was warm and cozy. Mum dashed out into the laundry. I moved the bench seat out slightly from the kitchen table, placed my port on it and sat down. On either side of the kitchen table were bench seats that sat three, and at each end of the table were chairs.

As I sat, I loosened the belt of my uniform and let it drop, saying, 'Hi, Barton, how are you feeling?' I placed my elbows on the edge of the table, and put my chin into my cupped hands, so my hands wrapped around my cheeks. I stared at Barton, and marvelled at his tightly curled hair. We both had curly hair; mine wasn't tightly curled like his. Maxine's hair was straight as a die.

Barton played with his cars along the edge of the table as I watched him. He was car-mad. In his croaky, coarse voice he managed to say, 'Hello, Christine,' between the *vrooms* of his car game. I watched him at play. He felt like a stranger to me, because he had been separated from my sister and me for a period of two years. After that, I'd never felt close to him, and he was my Mum's favorite. He was twelve years old and in primary school, but he acted like a kid. Barton was a bit like me; he was always going off with his friend into the bush. They'd camp out there. Barton had been subjected to great pain from our dad, from when he was a baby, and this got worse as he got older.

Barton made many twists and turns with his cars. He made the cars do circles and wheelies and slammed on their brakes to suddenly stop them. He looked up at me and smiled, as if I'd just sat down at the table for the first time, saying again, 'Hello, Christine.' Funny, he often did that. It was like he'd just come back into the real world and seen me. His face had a wide smile, as if he was pleased and happy to see me. But he, too, seemed to look old before his time, although inwardly he wasn't; he was very immature for his age, as we all were.

We all looked old somehow, except Mum; her face was so young. My body form was so well-developed and made me look older, but none of us were able to act our age. It was strange; we were young, but old. My brother's face was badly scarred from having suffered infantile eczema. During that time, he'd had to be strapped to his cot for twelve months to stop him scratching his skin. When I thought about him enduring that year of pain, I felt a deep sadness for him. He was so sick, but I marvelled at his strength and his ability to keep smiling all through it.

At the same time, he'd got chickenpox in the blood stream. He was affected by the ordeal, and of course, it would have had an effect on him emotionally, psychologically, mentally, as well as physically; but he didn't seem to have suffered too badly from the experience.

He was Mum's favourite, and her love for him was so great. It was hard for my father to comprehend her love for Barton. The love she had for Barton was to be to Barton's detriment, because it tormented my father's mind.

I asked him, 'What have you been doing all day, Barton?' as I placed my arms down on the table, leaned in towards him, and smiled.

'Playing cars,' he said with a wide grin as he glanced up.

'But what else did you do?'

'Nothing. I just played with my cars.' Barton's speech was slow; he repeated himself, and exaggerated his stories.

As I sat there watching him as he played in his world, I thought how nice it would be to have someone to talk to, but no one wanted to talk here. Everyone seemed to be in their own world. I straightened up, grabbed my tie and thought, we siblings don't even cuddle each other, so how could we talk to each other? This was the way it was, and no one was going to change it. I had my own problems, trying to make my mother happy and keep her on my better side. I couldn't get her to cuddle me, but she loved to cuddle Barton. I rolled my tie up into a ball and picked up my port. I was about to stand up and go, when Mum opened the kitchen door and revealed the wilder weather outside. The wind had really picked up. It was so nasty, and there was lightning striking.

Thunder crashed as she quickly closed the door to block the true reality of the evening. There only one power point in the kitchen, and it was occupied by the stove, where the vegetables were cooking. Mum was using the power point in the laundry for the frying pan.

'Go and get changed,' she told me. She picked up the salt and headed back outside.

'Okay, Mum. I was just talking to Barton,' I informed her as she dashed off, not hearing or answering me. I slipped out from between the bench seat and table and made my way into the very large, open dining room and family living room, where my grandma sat in her favourite cane chair. I placed my port under the dining table and looked at my grandma as she sat there. Her head was down. I wasn't sure if she was sleeping, or just looking into her clasped hands.

Maxine, already changed into her house dress, came out of our bedroom. She had a book in her hand and she walked straight past me, not saying a word.

When she was out of sight, I went over to Grandma, who looked uncomfortable, and seemed all twisted in her chair. 'Grandma, you awake?' I whispered quietly.

Her face was distorted and old, and it made her appearance seem grotesque. The TV sat in the right-hand corner of the family living room. It was on with the volume down low and was the only modern thing in the house. Grandma didn't stir. She hadn't been well since she'd had her bowel operation in 1966. She'd suffered a fall this year - 1967 - breaking her hip, causing her to prefer to stay in bed; but the doctor and Dad said she couldn't stay in bed.

Kneeling near her chair and leaning my chin on the arm of it, I sat on my haunches, and stared at her old face as she slept. She'd been afraid of falling and breaking her hip. I didn't blame her for being frightened, because she'd been in a lot of pain, and in hospital for a long time. Dad got so mad with her if he saw her in bed, so she couldn't win. As time went on, Grandma ended up on a walking frame. She used it to move from her bedroom to the living room, and those were the only two rooms in the house she could go to. She'd lost her position and was not the ruler of the house anymore; she'd handed that over to Mum.

Mum, on the other hand, had never had to do housework since she'd come to live there when they'd married. Things had changed, and she was doing everything. Mum ended up becoming Grandma's caregiver, and she made her breakfast and helped her get out of bed; but Mum made Grandma wash herself. It was very hard on Mum, because she was so tiny, and Grandma was a tall, large-boned woman. Sometimes Grandma was a bit lazy, and this caused Mum a lot of stress and extra problems. Mum had really had to battle with Grandma, and I thought that Mum had used Dad as a threat. Funny how the tides had changed: once it had been Grandma threatening Mum with Dad's wrath.

I was mesmerized by the movement on the TV with no sound, when I heard my name.

'Christine, I was just dozing,' Grandma said. Her face shone a small light through her tired old eyes.

'I thought you were sound asleep, Grandma.' I smiled back at her. 'How are you?' I waited for her to answer me, and as I did, I searched her face, waiting for the clue which will tell me, honestly, how she was really feeling.

She was lying into the arm of the chair, and she looked very uncomfortable. She told me, 'I'm not too well today. How was your day at school?' she asked.

'It was good, Grandma.' I told her about the change in the weather, and the big storm coming. I tried to bring her into the world outside, telling her how the trees around the creek were swaying, the cows were lowing, and we were so lucky to get onto the verandah before it poured down with rain. I told her how I was glad it was Friday. 'If it's going to rain for days, better on the weekend,' I said, 'and it looks set in.' I giggled and she smiled at me, and then, as if her mind took her somewhere else, she drifted off.

'I'd better go and get changed before Mum starts singing out to me.'

Her frail face looked up at me and smiled, as if it took all her might to do that little task, and she nodded, agreeing.

I stood up and moved away over to the edge of the dining room table and stood there. She was so frail and seemed to be fading away. Grandma wasn't the strong woman I'd once known. She looked so tired and old; but she'd always looked old after the death of both her husband, Grandfather Kinread, and her first-born son, Donny. She'd let herself go.

As I looked around my once beautiful house, there was a realisation that it was not only her that had deteriorated; the house had too. It was not the same house I knew as a kid. Nothing was the same after Mum took over the household duties; everything was in disarray, because she didn't know how to maintain a house. Mum had been only allowed to do some small things with Grandma's supervision. The responsibility was great, and Mum couldn't cope.

As I stood near the large dining room table, I ran my fingers through the velvet pile, and forced the pile backwards, which I loved to do. I stroked the old worn and shabby velvet back into its grain. It had lost its lustre; this once brilliant mahogany-colored velvet table cloth was stained, and had patches of discolouration from misuse. The table had become a dumping ground for letters, boxes, magazines, ashtrays, and bits and pieces. Underneath there was still a magnificent wooden table with thick, large, carved legs.

Many Christmas parties had been celebrated at that table, and Grandma would never have had any mess on it when she ruled the house. Under her control, everything had its place and home. The old furniture in this house was over fifty-one years old, and brought here when she first got married. It had never changed - the only addition was the TV - and while she was alive, all would stay the same, or until my parents or Grandma left the house. The family living room sat adjacent to the dining room, and it had a beautiful, large, red, oriental carpet on the floor. I used to sit on that carpet as a baby and stroke the pile. The walls in that room were unusual; they had been painted by an English painter. He'd painted the walls to look like wood paneling, and he'd painted the feature, five foot up the wall from the floor, all around the walls, only in the living room. Grandma was proud of the fact a professional painter from England had painted this feature.

Life had seemed rich to me as a child, when she'd told us her stories about her life in this house; but under her glamorous stories of great times, I felt an underlying sadness, intertwined with grief and regrets, secrets not told. Nonetheless, the works of art on the walls were like new, as if they were painted yesterday, and the old furniture looked good, even though they were her wedding presents given to her in 1917. I'd say they'd been the best quality in their day that money could buy. The large wireless sat near the side door as you entered the dining room from outside, but it seemed neglected since the TV had arrived. The TV had taken over our attention. I remembered some great days listening to the wireless and the serials, and using my imagination to see the pictures of the stories being told. I used to like the story about 'Dr Paul'.

In the quietness of the house, I heard the rain intensifying, and the tin roof made the rain seem louder. The drone of my brother's voice was the only other noise that competed with the rain in the silence of the house. He'd play with his cars, and he'd go on for hours and not get bored. Outside the wind whipped up into a gale, and the fruit trees near the dining room door were scraping and scratching across the roofing and guttering with more vigor. They sounded like their fears made them cry as they were threatened by the storm, which was really strengthening; but in the house, it felt cozy and warm. It always was that way, and I felt secure here, regardless of there being no love shown to us. We knew on some level we were protected, fed, and kept warm.

'Christine, where are you?' Mum shouted from the kitchen, breaking my reminiscing. I rushed off into my bedroom when I heard my name called. My bedroom was off the dining room. I closed the door as I entered. She'd go off if she saw me in my uniform. I got the uniform off and threw on a house dress. At least if she caught me out, it wouldn't be too bad, because I was in my house dress. We were never allowed to eat in our school clothes or good clothes. I drifted off and relaxed, as I placed my school clothes on a hanger, and put them in the wardrobe. I remembered my letter I'd received today from Peter. I unzipped my pocket, took it out and placed it in my secret drawer.

My sister and I had shared the bedroom with Grandma since we were little children. She and I slept in the double-decker beds; I slept in the bottom bunk. My favourite bed was Grandma's big, four-poster bed with its mosquito netting. The mosquito netting on it was the original netting it came with. It was never washed, because it would have fallen to pieces, it was so old. It had some holes in it, and Grandma had some pretty, small brooches pinned to it. In those days it didn't get used for mosquitos, so it didn't matter if it was frayed. The bed was made with wrought iron, and it had a fenced head and foot at each end of the bed that was painted white, and there were two hand-painted, movable porcelain cylinders with seventeenth century English people painted on them.

I headed for the dressing table before my sister came in and pulled out my secret drawer. From it, I took out a shoe box that held all my love letters and placed the letter from Peter in there. I put the box back in the drawer, quickly closed it, and stood up so no one would know. Also in that drawer, I kept my diary and my treasures I'd gathered since I started high school.

I hurried to the kitchen, stopped before I entered it, took a deep breath, and calmly walked in. Mum had set the table, and Maxine had helped her. Mum had got Barton to put his toys away.

'Can I help?' I asked, as if I was not in any trouble.

'Where were you? Daydreaming again?' she quizzed me.

'I've been with Grandma, and I told her about my day,' I said, in an 'I don't care what you think' voice, thinking, I will not tell you what I've been doing. I knew it was a lie, but better to lie than admit I'd been daydreaming.

'Help your brother move his toys and get the bread out for me.'

'Come on, Barton, move. You heard Mum,' I said with a 'come-on, don't upset her any more than she is' tone.

He smiled and was delighted he was the cause of an annoyance; he knew he could cause trouble and Mum would stick up for him, and he could get away with it with us. But not with Dad; he knew who to play his games with, and how.

I moved him physically, and he went off into the TV room, and I could hear him screeching his cars on the bare linoleum floors under the dining room table. I got the bread out of the bread box, placed it on a plate and put it in the centre of the table. Finally, the table was set. Maxine and I passed Mum the dinner plates for her to put the food on. It smelt great as she dished it out. My eyes smiled at the food. I seemed to be hungry all the time. Maxine and I got it all on the table, and we sat down on the long benches. Mum sang out to Barton to come, and he came and sat across from us. We were all hungry, but we said grace first, and then hoed into our food.

Mum couldn't sit and eat her food straight away; she had to get Grandma served first. She put Grandma's dinner on a tray, grabbed a slice of bread and buttered it for her, and then took her tray into her. We had our usual meal of three vegetables and meat. Mum wasn't a good cook, but she tried, and we ate lots of bread with our meals, plus dessert. Mum joined us, but she seemed like she wanted to explode, or cry. She slowly picked up her knife and fork, and daintily took small mouthfuls of food. Not like us; we ate so fast and stuffed our mouths so full with food, we were like wolves. On that night, Maxine was in full voice. With food in her belly, she was ready to natter. She nattered to Mum, but Mum was too exhausted. I could see she tried to look interested in what Maxine had to say but was too stressed. It weighed her down, and she couldn't deal with our childish behaviours. Dad wasn't fair to Mum either. We had free range at the table with Dad away. We could talk and eat at the same time, and do whatever we wanted, and still not get into trouble or be glared at for not being quiet.

Maxine was oblivious to Mum's ordeal and how stressed she was. She kept on with her story. I just ate. If Dad had been home, she wouldn't have been so chatty. I guess she made hay while she could. All the mileage we walked, we had to eat enormous amounts of food, because we burned up our energy as soon as we made it.

Dad had to work back. He'd be home late in the night, and this is what caused Mum stress. Later on I'd get the full story about it. I was the one she dumped on, and I really didn't understand what she was going on about or talked about. It was time to do the dishes, and sure enough, Maxine had an excuse to not help. Mum and I had to do them. Mum reasoned that because she had to do all the cooking, that one of us girls should at least help her with the dishes; but when Grandma had looked after the house, we didn't have to help. Maxine was shrewd, and she always got out of having to help to do the dishes. I could protest all I liked about Maxine not helping, but it would fall on deaf ears. It was true what Grandma said about Maxine; she could weasel her way out of a brown paper bag.

The dishes were washed up in the laundry, built on the verandah. Mum and I tramped in and out of the house carrying the dirty plates. The weather was really nasty; it was pitch black outside, and the rain was pelting down. It came in on the verandah with its full force, because the wind was blowing in that direction. The screen door flew open and banged onto the old shoe box and bounced back into my face. I saw the dogs all huddled under the table. Mum would feed them later on, on the verandah. My heart went out to those dogs in that kind of weather. In all my life, I'd never seen one of our dogs in the house. The cats were allowed in, but not the dogs. The laundry was long, and it had two very big stone sinks for washing clothes at the far end. Where you entered the laundry, there was a stainless steel basin for washing up dishes. With the dishes all stacked, Mum got the hot water from across the verandah, out of the bathroom, where there was a chip heater burning.

Everything in readiness, we washed up with the door closed to keep us warm, and Mum told me her problems. I knew them off by heart: her illnesses and Dad's unfaithfulness to her. I just didn't understand or know what to say to her. All I could do was listen to her talk. I didn't realise the damage it was doing to me, or how it would affect my future relationships. If Mum didn't talk about their marital problems, she'd tell me about her hair, or her face, and the creams she liked to use to keep her skin youthful. These were uneventful topics for me; she couldn't talk about world events, life and its meaning, or science. She seemed so sad and unhappy most of the time; but lately I'd been making her happy by telling her some rude jokes. I heard them at school, told her, and they make her laugh. I really did like to try and make her life happier.

My mum's name was Carol. She told me once she hated that name and wished her mum had called her Carolyn. Carolyn did seem like a prettier name. My father's name was Max, and Dad's mother, Grandma Kinread, told me he was named after Grandfather's youngest brother, Max, a writer who lived on the Isle of Man.

After the dishes were done, we brought the dried and stacked dishes back into the kitchen and put them away in the cupboards. Even when the dishes were put away, the kitchen table still looked choked with clutter. With that done, I could go. Mum fed the dogs and cats, so I headed into the living room to see what was on the TV. My brother and Grandma were watching 'I Love Lucy', and Barton was laughing with his croaky voice. Grandma looked as if she was about to fall off to sleep again. I checked our room. Maxine was reading on her top bunk.

Suddenly, there was uneasiness in my system about the night ahead and I felt moved by the weather we were experiencing. The house was cozy and warm; the lightning had stopped; but the wind was intense, and the rain poured down fast. Trees were banging against the guttering. In the house, there was an unusual calm, but it seemed like a threatening element lurked amongst us. I remembered that I'd left my port under the table. I went back out, grabbed it, and took it to my bedroom to get my homework out of the way.

Sitting on my bed, I placed my port on the floor, bent over, and unclipped the handles to open it up. I pulled out my books, sat back on my bed and leaned on the wardrobe, which was my bedhead. Maxine climbed down and left the room. I wished she'd stayed, because I wasn't comfortable in our room tonight. I got my homework done, and went out to the living room, relaxed, and started to enjoy my weekend off. My sister was with Mum in the kitchen, and I could hear them talking. Barton was in the chair near to Mum's bedroom. Her bedroom was close to the family/living room. Grandma was in her chair, facing straight on to the TV. It felt strange; here we all were as a group, but each of us were alone in this family.

My mother couldn't cope in her marriage, or with my father's temper. I felt my Dad's temper had developed due to his lonely mother's interference in his life and in his marriage. Grandma had chosen to live out here in isolation, away from other people, after the death of Grandfather. She took my parents along into her misery and grief. Grandma had her cross to bear, brought about by the early death of her husband, Don, and her first son, Donny. Nonetheless, she'd been prepared for loneliness prior to their death, because Grandfather had left her alone on the farm for long periods of time during their marriage. Apparently he'd had to go South Australia; it was to do with his work. We all had our own pain and isolation in this house. Each one of us was inflicted with it due to the circumstances of our family.

Love seemed to have escaped us all in some way or another; none of us really understood or had experienced love as a family. We were people in a group, detached and isolated from each other, using each other to get our needs met.

I couldn't rationalise my life; I could only observe it. I tried to understand it the best way I could. In my childhood, and all my life, it'd been like that. I would have to go to the depths of my own hell and rise back out of it to be reborn into my true self; but my family didn't understand this, or give me support, or allow me to grow as a person. I was the different one, and I seemed to know things that weren't everyday things; my family were just everyday people. They didn't wonder how the world was made, or how other people in other countries lived and behaved. I didn't think they knew that there was a world outside our home and home town.

Chapter 3

Once More A Reminder

Grandma was finally taken to bed; the poor old thing was really sore and tired. She walked uneasily with her walking frame, and she panicked as she gingerly took each step. Mum supported Grandma's arm as she gripped the cold, steel frame. Dad had told us children never to help or jump in, or try to stop Grandma if she was falling, because if we grabbed her, we could hurt ourselves. Slowly and steadily, they made it to Grandma's bed. She sat on the edge of her bed while Mum changed her into her nightwear and put her pink bed jacket on her. Mum straightened her night dress around her bottom and down over her legs, then pulled the sheets and blanket up around her chest. I heard them say goodnight to each other as Mum left the room. I'm sure Grandma felt safe back in her bed.

Funny though, seeing Grandma wearing colourful night wear. For many years, she'd only ever dress in black for day wear and wore plain white night wear. Aunty Connie got her to wear greys and grey blue clothes after her first operation on her bowels. We were so glad she changed, but it wasn't an easy transition for Grandma.

There were constant complaints; Grandma didn't like change. With all the family's encouragement and Aunty's determination, and our praises, she changed.

It got late. 'Time for bed,' I heard Mum say. It was close on 10pm, and Dad would be home soon. Actually, I wanted to be in bed before he came in. It was too much of a strain for me with him around, and it infuriated my mother, because she was on tenterhooks - and so was I.

I couldn't cope some days with the separateness of the three of us. The pain seemed unbearable. However, in my mind Grandma didn't know about our situation, and I didn't want her to ever know. I'd begged Mum not to tell her. You see, I was a child of sexual abuse, and this had caused me a life of isolation and separation from my parents through their lack of understanding of their roles. My mother was blaming me, and my dad was not daring to go against my mother. Nonetheless, this whole dilemma was due to Dad's misconduct with me, and the child was now being punished by the parents for their own selfishness. They both were only out to get their needs met, and to be comforted. As much as Dad used me, and Mum hated it, she used me as her counsellor and confidante.

I dashed into my room and put on my pyjamas. They were my blue ones with darker blue, vertical stripes, and well past their use-by date; but our pjs were usually like that. However, our going out clothes were always like new, and in good condition.

Grandma had her eyes closed as I glanced over at her. Her face looked tired, as if all her life had drained from her. I think life had no meaning for her. It was only an existence she had to bear out until her death came.

Once, she had felt there was meaning to life, when we were little children and we relied on her. That was when Mum left us and Grandma had become our caretaker. Back then, Grandma told my sister and I many tales about all the important people she knew, who'd come to her house here on the farm. That was when Grandfather was still alive. She told us tales about the family back in England. At that time, my sister and I brought her a lot of joy and gave her the feeling of being needed. As I looked at her, bedbound, I wondered where that strong woman had gone. To me, Grandma was always independent. What happened to people when they got old? Why did they get old, sad and unhappy?

I made my way to the kitchen to say goodnight to Mum. 'Goodnight, Mum. I'll see you in the morning,' I said. I stood and waited for her response.

'Goodnight, Christine,' she said, without looking up.

I waited. She must have sensed me waiting and came and kissed me quickly with no feelings. It was like we had a brick wall between us, but I was used to it. When I was younger, it really hurt. I guess I felt the effects of it more back then. In the beginning, I used to cry over it, and even thought of dying by taking a bottle of her pills and ending it all, because I felt so rejected, and it was my entire fault. I called my mother *her*, privately. No one knew.

Now I had climbed above those low feelings and learnt to support myself. I stopped those silly thoughts of ending my life. Maybe I was too scared to, or maybe I just adapted to my life's circumstances.

Mum turned from me, rushed off into Barton's room, and her whole face changed. I followed her in there. She went to his bed and tucked him in. I heard them talking and giggling, and she showered him with kisses. I waited at his door.

She saw me and reminded me, 'Christine, I thought you went to bed.'

'I wanted to say good night to you again,' I explained.

'Goodnight, then,' she said in an irritated voice, and pulled Barton's blankets up high around his neck. She got up from his bed and walked out of the room.

As she passed me, I said, 'Goodnight,' and that was it. I went to my room, and I stood near my bed and glanced around the room.

My sister was on the top bunk drifting off to sleep. Grandma was still recovering from her long day in that chair; she wasn't quite asleep yet. She was lying there, allowing each of her muscles to regain some energy. The house was silent, the wind was blowing a gale, and the rain was pinging on the tin roof. I imagined, with all this rain, the creek would be very high and swollen, and running a torrent by tomorrow. I stood for a moment to capture a sense of the rain and looked around the room. I felt uneasy in here tonight. The house felt like there was a change coming over it. I couldn't say anything to anyone in my family, because no one would understand me, and they'd only tell me, 'Stop daydreaming, Christine.' We were never understood. Children in this house were to be seen and not heard, and this ran true, even though my sister and I were teenagers.

My house was so old, the curtains on the windows had never been changed or been washed, and things never, ever got moved, changed or renewed. I went to my secret drawer and pulled out my diary to record the day's events. My life was rather quiet; not like it used to be when I was in the popular group at high school. There was always something happening; that group was mostly made up of friends older than me. They'd all left school, so I had to make new friends. This seemed to be a yearly occurrence for me; everyone eventually left me.

Now I wasn't popular, and I was friends with the not-so-popular girls. These girls came from other countries: Germany and Poland. Mum and Dad had lots of friends from other countries. Strange, though; Dad called these immigrants wogs and dagos, and Grandma, oh my goodness me, she really hated the Chinese and other nationalities. If they didn't speak English, she had no tolerance for them. I couldn't understand it, because Dad's friends were from other countries, and they were so nice and would do anything for you, and my New Australian girlfriends were so polite.

My diary entry was: *School was good. There's a big storm on the way just got home this afternoon, made it in the front door and it pelted down with rain. At home the same old thing. There's not too much to write about.*

I closed the diary, threw it into my drawer and shut it, got up off the floor and stretched. As I did, I turned to see Grandma. She must have been very tired tonight, because she wasn't reading her magazines, *Women's Day* and the *Women's Weekly*. She got an English magazine as well. Aunty Connie sent these to her from Rosemont. Sometimes I read them, but they were boring. I much preferred to read about unusual and strange things. I walked over to Grandma, and my presence made her open her eyes.

She said, 'You're going to bed now, Christine.'

'Yes, Grandma, I'm tired,' I said, as I bent over and kissed her goodnight.

She kissed me back, and I switched off our light and climbed into my bed. I had a kapok bed; it was snuggly, and I made a nest in it to curl up in, and then said my prayers. 'Now I lay me down to sleep, I ask the Lord my Soul to keep, if I should die before morning breaks, I ask the Lord, my Soul to take, Amen.'

In the dead of night, I was suddenly awoken. Sitting upright in my bed, I sensed eeriness in the room; the room felt cold and dark. I noticed the rain had gone, and the wind had stopped, and there was a silence, all-encompassing and smothering. I felt like death was at the door. What was it? Why was I awoken?

I glanced quickly over at Grandma. She was deeply asleep, and my sister must have been too. Then I felt something in the room with me. My skin tensed, and the shock gripped me, then terror took over and I froze. My eyes were guided to the big, old, wooden wardrobe that looked engulfing in the dead of night, and as I moved my eyes slowly to the other side of the room, towards the window, I noticed a stream of yellowish light coming through that window.

'What was that… and who woke me?' I asked.

'By you,' I heard.

'Huh?' I gasped. I couldn't understand that. I wasn't awoken by me. I was woken by something else. I didn't wake me, I thought. My throat tightened and seemed to swell up, and I couldn't make a sound. I nervously searched the room in the dark. I was scared; fear had embraced me. I felt unimaginable fear, like it had a grip on me and was holding me awake, making me feel like a powerless child.

I heard in my mind, 'You're not grasping life and the experiences of it.' I felt unbearable pain, terror and anguish that no one could conceive. Others, I'm sure, would have screamed by now; but no, I didn't even scream. Even though I was terrified, the more the terror was building up inside me, I somehow felt I knew something – and yet I didn't know. There was a smell of oldness in the room, and a greenish tinge in the blackness. I ventured my eyes further around, back over near the old wardrobe, and then I saw it. Terror seized hold of me, and I watched this quivering entity in the corner, between the big old wardrobe and the washing stand. I froze, and my skin tightened and pulled, as if all my senses had gone straight to my whole outer skin. What seemed to be an eternity, must have been only a few seconds. I'd never seen a ghost before and now there was one; a woman, a transparent sheath, wearing a veil on her head. It looked like a negative film, and I was gripped by the fear of her waking me. Then I was released, and I quickly dived under the bedcovers to hide, and I fell instantly asleep.

When I woke, it was raining and windy, but the night before when I was awoken, there was only silence. I heard my sister stirring in her bed above me, and Grandma was already up, reading her magazines. I looked around the room, thinking, what happened last night? I couldn't understand it.

At sixteen, I didn't know about a spiritual world. I knew things without knowing where I knew them from, but I had never heard of the word 'spiritual'. At funerals, I didn't cry, because I knew they'd come back in another body, and because of that, I didn't know why people cried at funerals. I didn't know how the people came back. I thought it must be into a new baby, but how I knew, I don't know, because no one spoke of such things in this house, or at school. I think because of the two bottom rooms, and because I felt things in there. I knew there was something living down there, and I knew it was invisible. No one else in this house told me they felt anything, so I think only I knew about it. As I lay in bed awake, I realised my life was different to other people's lives, and it would be many, many years before I was able to find answers to what I knew, and go and seek myself.

Now for the stories unfolding from this moment on. I'd been told I had a meeting yesterday. Was last night that meeting? Was this the other side getting in touch with me and reinforcing in me that there was another side?

Chapter 4

I Was My Father's Prize As A Baby, However I Will Suffer For Being That Prize

I was born at 5.08am in the spring of 1951. In hospital, I was a quiet baby; I wouldn't cry, and I wanted to die and go back to where I'd come from. *Another journey again, and this one will be a big one. I had Karma to settle, and energies to collect. There are bits and pieces of me to retrieve, and there is a puzzle I need to put together. I must get it right this time. My time is up, and it is my choice to be here, but I am having second thoughts. I am having a change of heart.*

I was visited by many people, who were blowing loving kisses to me, and I peered at them from over my bedclothes. I recognised them, but I didn't want to respond. Our lives were brought together for a reason, but we would not have any idea as to what that reason was. Not until we got further into the story.

Life is a mystery, and we are the mystery - the mystery to ourselves - to solve, and that is done by remembering. We are here to evolve, and it is a long trip full of calculations, of right moves and wrong moves, a perfect game of chess that not many of us know about.

You see, some of us do know what it's all about, because we will have short bursts of remembrance and close encounters with fellow partcipants in our life's course, but it won't be until we get further into our own stories in our individual books of life that we manuscript for ourselves, that we realise this. We realise that this is not just a life to be idle in, to live, work and die; it's a journey to know the self, and learn lessons to evolve and grow through change, and out of it become a better person.

Mostly, it's to forgive the self and others, and to accept who we are through the many mirrors of those who will play their part in our story of our life. We'll help each other to remember, so we can release what doesn't serve us any more, and know ourselves better.

'So let's start the game,' said a voice in the distance. I didn't feel any form of comfort as I moved through the veils of fog. As I spent each moment in this world, I was losing my script.

I heard their voices in the hospital: 'Sister Bloomfield, this child won't eat; it's as cantankerous as its mother.'

'Now, now, Sister Davies, that's no way to speak about a little, helpless baby,' she said, with endearing love for all creatures, humans or animals. This sister, I knew, had a heart of gold. She came to my cot, and I saw her old, heavy face peering down into my face. The face was not soft, yet it had a gentleness. The heavy, metal-rimmed glasses made her lose that softness. Her smile was loving and patient, trying to please. I felt a pull as I was manipulated, drawn up closer and hugged in arms of love. Then suddenly I was raised to her face. I felt like I was going to be dropped, and I couldn't hold on. I had terror in my eyes, but I wouldn't cry, and I wouldn't be fed.

I was bounced down the hallway to the main maternity ward, and taken to the woman that I chose to be my mother. She was soft, and her face was fresh, young, and her skin was milky; but she had no idea of what to do with me.

She panicked and said, 'Careful, she'll fall.'

'Carol! Now there, she won't fall. Take her and hold her,' said the older sister, as she passed me over to my mother with encouraging words. 'Now you can't be afraid of your own baby; you must hold her, and try to feed her.' It was a painful experience for this young mother. I was aware of her thoughts, and had heard lots of her condemning of me in her womb. It was not my fault alone that I was born; it was a choice we'd all made. Sister Bloomfield left me with this woman, and I don't know who I felt the worst with. Carol tried to feed me, and in her awkwardness, she squirmed and shifted in her bed, and placed her enormous breast in my mouth; but I closed my eyes, and pretended the world was not there and that it was a dream.

In her frustration, she called out in distress, 'Sister Bloomfield, Sister Bloomfield.'

'Carol, what is wrong, dear?'

'She won't take to the breast milk, and I can't cope.' Carol turned her head from me and turned away from the Sister. Sister Bloomfield picked me up out of Carol's arms, and she quietly resigned herself to the fact that this woman, Carol, my mother, was not willing to try. I felt the sister's wonderment at what would happen to both of us.

'Alright, Carol, we'll need to express your milk to feed Christine.'

Mother nodded in agreement, and turned her face towards the wall. It was her shame at not being able to cope. There were many concerns in Carol's mind, and she was only seventeen. Her biggest concern was what was she getting herself into, with a new baby and life with Max. How was that going to work out, because it wasn't only him she was to live with; she had his mother, who hated her.

My resistance was great; I even refused bottle feeding. Then, on one visit, I saw a man at the nursery window: tall, handsome, with an air of devilment and anticipation. Ah! This is my father. His violet-blue eyes peered in at me, and he was my reason for being here. I felt excitement. We had karma, and I must succumb to food and nourishment. I took the food, much to everybody's excitement, and the veil closed a little more; and so the journey unfolded, and the veil closed over slowly as the days went by.

My mother and I were to live in this sterile environment for ten days. A man - Max, she called him – appeared, and he had not held me, but there was a strong pull to him. He would stare at me through the glassed-off nursery area, and I'd open my eyes and peek at him. I watched him grinning at me. He was ever so proud of me, and he turned to other people admiring their babies and told them, 'Look at this beautiful baby girl, and she is mine.' Sometimes he was on his own when he visited me, and he always waved goodbye when he had to leave and go back to my mother.

After the tenth day of confinement, my mother and I were to be collected by Max. This was the first day he'd hold me, and this was the day we would bond beyond time and reasoning, for our karma demanded it.

The nursing sister informed me, 'Your father is taking you home today, little one.'

As she picked me up, I moved in my secure blanket and pursed my lips to say, 'Oh well, tell me about it later. I am too tired.'

The sister took me into the ward for the last time, and we were greeted by my father. He took me into his strong arms, and there and then, I felt secure and loved. He walked out of the hospital ward to our waiting transport with my mother's favourite sister, Sister Bloomfield. She was protective of my mother, and allowed her to be the spoilt child she was. Not only did this Sister gain my mother's trust, through care and through spoiling her; my mother also loved her entertaining abilities. She would come into the ward and recite poetry or Shakespearean lines to the patients. My mother loved all of the gaeity of the ward.

We moved out of the quiet of the ward, and into a very noisy area. There was a very bright light.

My mother was fussing. 'Cover her eyes,' she demanded.

I squirmed in my blanket as the light hit my eyes and alerted my senses.

'Carol, please, your baby has to get used to all these elements,' Sister stated in her stern voice, a parent to a child.

My father handed me to the Sister. There a contraption in front of us; it was making a noise and creaking as it swayed, and then it was moved by something, which was sweet to my ears. I heard the voice of nature, a snort, and that smell that waffled into my clean nose. What was it? A smell I had not yet smelt. The only smells I'd smelt had been sterile and clean smells. There was a whinny, and a shuffling of hooves, and the thing was steadied by my dad.

I heard my mother say, in a concerned voice, 'Careful, Max, with that horse.'

'It's okay, Carol. Bonnie is just curious. She's had her own foal, and she wants to check out our baby.'

The horse turned carefully. It didn't touch us; it only wanted to look. Nature was introducing itself to me. This was where I would be consoled and protected throughout my life. The beauty of the world was in nature, and nature would enliven my senses and uplift me to God. However, I would forget all of this very soon.

Max reached to take me from the Sister, requesting, 'Give me the baby.' He took me, and looked down at me with eyes of wonder.

'I'll help you in,' the Sister told my mother.

I could feel my mother's anxieties. She had me worried for my own safety. Was I safe? She got up on the sulky, and the horse stepped back and forward, and she was so scared and cried out to Max.

My father got annoyed with her. 'Carol, stop it,' he snapped, then remembered where he was. The Sister ignored their immaturity, and Dad changed his tone, saying, 'It's okay, Carol. You've been around horses long enough now to know there's movement, and if you're scared of them, they sense it. So calm down.'

The boy (my father - I felt they were both children) passed me to my mother. Her tension and fear passed through me. Father moved around to the other side of the contraption and pulled himself up. I felt the movement and jerking as he did that. His weight shifted our positions on the seat. Mother relaxed with Dad near her side, and we went home. It was going to be a long, long journey to the home I would live in, and it was going to be a long, long journey in this lifetime. The Sister farewelled them. I could hear her as we drove off. The sound of the hooves on the road was like music, and the steady pacing of the horse was like a rhythm that comforted me. The homestead was eight miles out of town. The wind was fresh, it was spring time, and I was introduced to sounds and smells of a world teeming with life. I couldn't wait to sit up and look around. As we moved in this carriage, it was so restful. I felt like we were flying on a winged steed, whose legs strode out, gathering speed and lifting us up into the air to rock me into dreamland. I was soon asleep and contented.

Awakened by barking, someone sang out. I struggled in the tight, enclosed space of the blanket. What was it, all these noises, and who was this I heard?

My mother said, 'Christine, you're home, and here's your grandma.'

I heard the word 'Grandma'. What is a grandma? I thought about these words I'd heard. There was a stronger woman's voice, that of my grandma. She'd be the person to play a major in my life, and have the most impact on me. Her voice was not soft, like my mother's. It was a stern voice of a stronger female that had authority.

She said, 'Max, let me see the baby.'

The horse was still not settled. Max jumped off the carriage, and he took me from my mother's arms, and placed me into the arms of this woman. As I looked through the daylight that made me close my eyes, I saw an old person; that was so scary. She was strong in her eyes, but those eyes were hiding a lot, and I was now with these people.

'Max,' a mousy voice implored, and it was my mother's voice, pleading, 'Get me down.'

He turned to her and apologised, 'Sorry, Carol, so excited to show Mum Christine,' and like a puppy, he tended to my mother, and helped her down off what I learned was the sulky. I'd been taken by my grandma, the person I'd see the most. I felt the energy of this house, cold and sad, as she stepped into it. After I was nursed for a while, I was taken by my mother and father into their room. I heard them talk about a new cot, and Mum lowered me into it and tucked me in.

I was cared for by both women that day, and that night I changed in my nature. I started my demands, and they suffered my pain, and this is how it would be. I didn't want to be here. Why had I chosen them? I cried and cried. Why was I in so much pain? And this pain was so great, so great was my pain, I felt choked, and I couldn't stand it. I cried and gave them my pain.

Chapter 5

Christine The Demanding Child

I was called Christine by my father, and my middle name was one of my grandma's names: Urena. I didn't like my first name, but my dad did. Oh, the joys and torments of my life with the young ones: Mum seventeen and Dad eighteen, too young and insecure to be married, and forever under the wing of Max's mother, Helen. I was living in a hamlet called Lachlan Vale, which was part of the Lachlan Main Colliery.

Pain and hurt prevailed, for I already knew my life was going to be hard, and my tears and fears were for my future. I couldn't be part of this family. It took lots of reassurance for me to come around, and they played into my desire for company. These people bickered, and there was hatred - a strong dislike - for each other, and their seeds were sown into my brain.

The genes of my family held numerous secrets and fears that were unleashed into my psyche. Little did we know, I would be the one to change the genetic coding of this family. It would be a life of many changes -

mysteries and secrets uncovered - that would cause me to become an isolated and misunderstood person.

I slept in my parents' room; however, Grandma would become my second mother, and I'd be raised by this unnatural mother. She'd be the one who'd control my life. Grandma only allowed my mother to feed me, and it wouldn't be until I was three months old that my natural mother would be seen more often. This caused me some confusion; I was not sure who was who, as one fed me and the other attended to my other needs. I learnt early how to control these people with great success, and I had them all at my mercy. I knew how to achieve attention, and I had the family tired and worn out, rocking me in shifts to my full contentment. I had discovered these people were soft in the care of a baby.

Time moved on, and my father had to give up his apprenticeship as an electrician; he needed to make extra money for his new family. Grandma was providing the house rent-free, but Dad had to put food on the table. He had two extra mouths to feed. I'd settled in with these people, but they were not home free yet, not by a long shot.

Dad had to go into the Army Reserve, and this left the two women and I alone on the large property. Mother was in bed most of the day. Grandma took care of me, and she was a lovely old lady under all that harshness. I'd softened to her, and she washed me with care and made sure I was clean in all the right places. I demanded love that couldn't be met by these people. I had a fear of being left alone, and of being left. I felt smothered, and I felt I was unable to breathe. I needed constant attention to meet my need to suppress my fears.

Dad came home on the weekends, and he had to be part of my routine. It was a struggle for them all. As soon as they stopped the rocking, I'd cry and scream until it continued, and this went on for many months. I liked the contraption that had brought me home: the sulky. I enjoyed my sulky ride from the hospital, and the memory of the rocking had stayed with me. I could achieve the same feeling in the arms of these people, or the rocking of the cradle. The motion that swept me back and forth, the dreamy feeling of lulling, and the contentment of knowing I was safe in the movement; and above all, while they had me in their arms, they could give me what I hungered for more than anything else: the touch.

I became so spoilt, and I was given everything. My grandma was more tolerant of me, and she gave me lots more of her attention. Carol was frightened of my grandma, and she wouldn't stand up for herself and demand to take care of me. She and Max fought in their room over this problem, but he was too soft, and wouldn't go against his mother. All he could do was try to put Mum at ease with promises he'd never keep. He promised her they'd leave and move into their own home in town, but they were promises to be broken to keep the peace.

Chapter 6

Baby On The Floor, What Big Blue Eyes You Have To See The World These People Don't See

The people that cared for me looked like giants, as they bent down and scooped me up. My eyes seemed to see through people, and I wondered what they were doing here, and what this was all about. My eyes were questioning eyes. For hours I'd play by myself with my powder tins filled with little pebbles, and sometimes Grandma played with me. I had many toys, but those were my favouite toys.

I was twelve months old when I became aware there was an unsettling feeling in the household. Sometimes I didn't feel safe, and I cried a lot. I was really sad, and I would start to cry. I heard a heavy foot thumping over towards me.

'What are you crying for?' It was the voice of my grandma, and she startled me. Grandma was not like my mother; Mum's steps were light, and I could never hear her until she was upon me, and I'd jump in fright. I had squashed my finger, and my finger hurt. I cried and pursed my lips. Grandma kissed the finger better, cuddled me and picked me up. It was a funny feeling to be raised up so quickly off the ground. I hadn't got over that feeling of being raised up quickly, but the reward of a kiss and a cuddle was all I wanted.

I was taken to Mum's bedroom by Grandma. At the closed door, she stood and sang out, 'Carol, this child is wet.'

I heard a tired voice. 'Okay, I'll change her,' and my mother appeared at the door. She took me, and I felt her irritation. I was bewildered, because Grandma could change me. Why was Mummy going to change me? Grandma threw me into my mother's arms. They avoided each other's eyes. My mother took me to her bed and changed me.

I talked to myself as she mechanically changed me.

She was quiet, and not saying much. 'There you are; you're all clean now.'

My mother had a small, thin frame; she only weighed about forty-four kilos. She was so small next to my grandma, who was like a giant, she was so tall: nearly as tall as Daddy. Mother put me on her hip, and I was bumped along into the kitchen. Grandma was peeling the beans, and looked sideways at Mother as she entered. Grandma didn't like my mother, I could tell. I looked at my mother. She was very unhappy, and tried to be happy and sang. Grandma cleared her throat, as if to say, 'your singing is irritating me'. I cuddled into my mother because I felt her sadness, and she responded by patting my back. She must have been feeling really sad under that singing, because I felt her body; there was tension and trembling in it. She was never calm, and her body was always crying. I felt things around people, things they weren't saying. Mother tired of me and put me down, but I wanted to be held.

I grabbed hold of her and looked at her, but she didn't see me, and said, 'Come on, Christine, down you go.'

My eyes widened, and I let her put me down. The cat came in, and it rubbed up against me.

Mother screamed at it, 'Get away from her, you dirty cat.'

It ran off with its tail straight up. I grabbed the tail, and laughed and pulled it.

Mother screamed, 'Don't do that; it will turn and scratch you.' She shooed the cat away.

I looked at her. It was so quiet through the day in the house. They didn't talk to each other; they only glared at one another, or they didn't look at each other at all; and there was a thickness in the air.

Chapter 7

Mother, Mother, I Loved You, But You Never Loved Me The Way I Wanted You To Love Me. But You Were My Biggest Gift

'Christine, where are you? It's time to change your clothes,' I heard as I looked up from playing with my dolly. It was the voice of my mother. Her voice sent a shiver down me, as I was not sure who she'd be. Her voice didn't go with the person she was. I was learning that she was not a stable person. It felt like she was a stranger in the house. My eyes widened as I waited for her to approach me. Her voice seemed to be drawing nearer to me. I was sitting on the big, old, oriental carpet in the lounge room. It smelt of dust, and it prickled my bottom and my feet. I heard her walking in her room, and I looked at my dolly and brought her closer to my chest. She was a lovely dolly, and she cuddled me. I liked to be cuddled so much, and thinking of cuddles brought a smile to my face, I forgot my mother had called me.

'Mummy doesn't know how to cuddle me,' I told my dolly in my baby talk. 'But you do.' I squeezed my dolly closer, and brushed her face.

This precious moment was interrupted by the voice again. 'Christine, where are you?' This time the voice had more intensity in it, and I felt tense and unsure of what to do, or what to expect from her. She had told me she was going to change my clothes, but I didn't want to get changed. She was always changing my clothes, and I didn't know why, because I was not dirty. Grandma had dressed me earlier, and I had on my favourite summer dress. I liked this dress; it had a bow tie at the back.

I talked to my dolly about my dress. 'It's pretty and I love it and it has flowers on it.' I grabbed the end of my dress with my little, awkward fingers, and I pulled and tugged at the hem, and looked at my frilly panties and sang a song. 'La, la, la, it's pretty.' My dolly listened to me as I sang, and again, I forgot my mother had been calling me.

Then she stepped up behind me. She'd been in her room, and was waiting for me to get up and come in. I froze and clutched the doll, like time had stopped and the monster of the day had just sneaked up on me.

'There you are. Didn't you hear me calling you?' She scowled with her taut face and her hands on her hips. Her long, golden hair flowed over her soft, small face. She scared me, because under that hair were her narrowing and disapproving eyes.

I looked up at her and shook my head. 'No, dolly.' I smiled as I shook my little head, eyes widened in innocence.

It didn't work. She was disappointed in me. I said no, again, to her, and pretended I didn't hear her, because I did not want to get into trouble. I'd learnt denying things wasn't as bad as saying the truth. She bent down and grabbed my arm and lifted me off the carpet, dragging me with her full force into the bedroom. I was unstable on my feet, and felt like I was going to slip out of her grip and fall on my nose, and that would have hurt me. I yelled out, 'Mummy, fall! Fall!' She didn't listen to me. She lifted me up on to the bed. My arm was sore from her dragging me, and I put my dolly down and rubbed my sore arm, while she went mad on me for fussing, and not coming when she'd called me - and because I'd kept her waiting, we'd be late.

She started to tell me things I didn't understand. I watched her face, and she looked a little mad, her grey eyes giving off sparks as each word was driven out of her mouth. I looked into her mouth, and saw her tongue going back and forth; it fascinated me. I peered in to see her tongue, and I watched her hair as it rolled over her face. She pulled my clothes off me, grabbed my arm like I was my dolly, and she twisted my arm to get it out of the sleeve of my dress. She flicked her hair back, stopped and threw her hands down and cried. I was half-naked, and she looked like she was about to throw life in. I felt her life force going out of her. I waited for her next explosive move; the quiet before the storm. I was holding my wrist. It hurt from when she grabbed me. She quietened, picked up from where she'd stopped dressing me, and proceeded to finish the job.

I looked around the room, and saw how she had no idea of being organised. The bed was full of clothes; she couldn't make a decision on what to wear today, or what I would wear today. I pulled at a dress I liked.

She grabbed it. 'No, you're not wearing that one.' She went quiet. Something was wrong. I knew all these clothes would stay here until she went to bed tonight, and then she'd throw them on the little sofa chair under the window. She was telling me how Daddy was mean to her, and she had to tell him something, something about a baby, and she was scared to tell him, frightened of him and his temper. 'And that old witch out there, she'll side with him, and, oh, God, I am being punished again. What have I done wrong in my life to deserve this?' She cried, and pushed me back and forth as she mechanically undressed and dressed me. It was like I wasn't human and I couldn't feel. I was just there - and I wanted a cuddle.

I looked at her, as if to say, Mummy, cuddle me, and she didn't see me at all. I didn't exist. So I played with my dolly as she tried to dress me.

She pulled my dolly from me and snapped, 'Christine, what are you doing? I am trying to dress you, can't you see? You're just as inconsiderate as the others.' Her face looked daggers.

I crouched back, my eyes open wider. She'd got my attention again, and told me her stories. I didn't want my dress changed. She put the blue dress on me, and I didn't like it. The frilly bits stuck into me like pins, and it was hot, and I had to wear socks and shoes when I liked my feet bare. I forced myself away from her, and she grabbed me.

'You're wearing this dress. Now sit still.'

'Why?' I whinged in a little voice, as if I had any say in anything around there. I only got told to be quiet, and to go and play.

She told me, 'Because we have to go out when your father gets home.'

I brightened up, because I liked to go out, and I could take my new purse. I loved purses, and I told my dolly about going out to town and meeting other people and hearing them talk to each other. I laughed. I looked at Mummy, and thought how she was always different in town. She was happier, and laughed and was talking all the time; different to here. Here, she was always cranky, and Daddy was mean to Mummy, and I saw them fighting. When they fought, I hid in my cot, or I sat still and I didn't move; I became still.

I was picked up and put down on the floor and told, 'Now, go and sit in the lounge room and wait, and don't get dirty or get mucked up. Sit still,' she demanded.

'Yes, Mummy,' I toddled off with my dolly. I went back to the old carpet and played.

Mummy never hit me, but she pulled and twisted me. She snarled with her eyes, and they were enough to frighten me. Her face scared me. She didn't realise that I was a baby and not a big person, and I couldn't help it if I forgot.

She had told me she was pregnant and tired, and that there was going to be another baby. It wouldn't be long before it came. Daddy would be cranky with my mother. I was fifteen months old.

Mummy had left it for as long as she could to tell Daddy about the new baby. Finally the day had come. I was sitting in my cot in their room and playing, and then

I heard a scream, and my father said in a low-throated voice, so no one could hear him, 'Shut up, Carol.'

I looked up to see Daddy holding my mother down on the bed, and she was crying.

'Max, don't. Don't hurt me.'

He forced her head into the bed, and it was like he was going to smother her. He punched her and hit her, and threw her off the bed. She curled up on the floor and was crying softly, like she didn't want anyone to hear her. She held her body when my father walked past her. He kicked her. I looked, and as I looked, my lip dropped and I felt sad. I wanted to cry. My father approached me, and he was so big, like a giant, and I was frightened, because when he was cranky, his eyes were glassy and looked strange. He came closer towards me and grabbed me. I felt like I was going to faint. As I was slowly lifted up by his powerful arms, I felt his strength. Daddy was wiry, all muscle and very tall. He wore a lot of hair cream in his hair, and it smelt like flowers. He took me to the kitchen. I turned back to look at my mother on the floor.

She was crying, and she screamed out, 'You bastard, Max. I will have you for this, you bastard. You know it's your baby, and no one else's.'

I was so scared, because he turned toward her, and his eyes grew wider. He glared at her with built-up anger, which I felt in his body. He went back to Mummy and he raised his hand. I whimpered and he looked at me, put his hand on my back, and walked away from her. Mother lay there on the floor and she cried, screamed, and kicked in a tantrum. He shut the door on her. He walked to the kitchen, and I was being bounced up and down by his fierce walk. His temper was still raging, and I felt the heat coming out of his body. I could smell his sweat on his skin, and as I looked back over his shoulder, my little lips touched his body - due to the velocity of his walk - and I could taste the salt on his body. It was a hot, sticky December day. I looked back at the closed door, to hear my mother still screaming in a tantrum. As we approached the kitchen, he stopped, took a deep breath, and held me close to his body, and I felt a calmness come over him.

There was another situation to be faced in the kitchen, and he prepared his body for the onslaught he was going to receive from Grandma. We walked in, and there she was: the old witch in the kitchen, as my mother called her. She was my grandma and a witch, and what is a witch? I got confused. I didn't know what a grandma or a witch was, but she was the one that usually bathed me and dressed me.

Grandma was cooking in the kitchen. 'What's up with Carol, Max?' she enquired, not stopping or meeting his eyes, as she stirred the cake.

'Nothing; she's pregnant again,' he blurted out, as he sat in his chair. I could feel he didn't want to go too deep.

Grandma stopped stirring, and in a calm voice, said, 'Oh, Max, we can't have another baby just yet.' She looked at him with caution. She knew not to go too far with him; not yet anyway. He could turn on her quickly, and lash out at her with his tongue, even though he was frightened of her. As Daddy stood up, she tried to give the impression of caring. In a softer tone, she asked, 'Where are you going to, Max?' She placed the bowl on the table.

'To the shed,' he snapped.

'You're not taking the baby with you, are you?' It was like she wanted to rescue me from him.

He looked at me. I was talking to myself, and playing with Daddy's shirt. I smiled at him, and he said in a gruff voice, forgetting all caution with her, 'Yes, and don't you start.' He diverted from Grandma's eyes, with me as his barrier. 'Come on, Christine, my Christine.' He kissed me all over my face, and cuddled me tight; it was as if he'd forgotten what he'd done five minutes ago. He was now this loving, playful and affectionate person. He decided to sit back down on his chair, and play tickles with me. Grandma resumed stirring, and I could smell the cooking of the first batch of cakes. It smelt lovely there in the kitchen.

Daddy turned me on my back and tickled my tummy, and I laughed and he gooed at me, and he loved me so much. I could tell he loved me, that no one else loved me like he did, and I grabbed his big, powerful hand; it could be so gentle or rough on me. He lifted me close to his chest. I snuggled into his hand and his chest, and tried to put my arms around his wide frame.

Grandma felt safe to talk to him as he calmed down with me. 'What are you worried for, Max?' she stated warily. 'Christine is fifteen months old and...' She stopped the conversation. She could see his mood was changing again.

He was getting upset and aggressive. As he stirred in his chair, Daddy shook himself. He often did that. I felt like it was to re-balance himself. He held me firmly on his knee, but his whole mood changed.

He shouted out, 'I can't cope, Mum, I can't cope with Carol, and it's too much. And the responsibility of this baby, another one on the way. How will I cope?'

Grandma trod carefully. 'I understand that, Max. Carol's a child herself, and Max, I don't like to say this but... Max, I told you, you should never have married her.'

Daddy snapped, 'Well, I did, didn't I? So don't go on about that, for God's sake. Jesus Christ! Why do you have to throw it in my face all the time?' He lowered me to the floor, and shuffled back and forth. The air was tense, and he screamed, 'I'm going! I'll be back later!' As he walked out of the back door that led off from the kitchen, he stopped suddenly, holding the door, and in an irritated voice, turned to Grandma and said, 'You're half of the problem, Mum. You can't understand me; all you can do is condemn me, and I am sick of it. I am sick of it.' He looked like he was about to break down, and I could see that he was nearly crying.

I dropped my lip and whimpered.

He'd let go of the door with a bang, and his heavy body stomped off the verandah. He seemed to make a cracking noise on the wooden boards with the strain of his heavy frame. He disappeared. I looked up at Grandma. She was the only one left to look after me, and I hoped she wouldn't leave the room.

Grandma smirked as she poured the smooth cake mixture into the cake tin, and I watched, mesmerised by the flowing liquid, as Grandma swayed it and curled it. This separated me from what was really happening in this house. The diversion took me into another space. I turned away from the memory of the conflict, and entered my world to play in it. There were some nice people who came to play with me, and I started to talk to them, and they talked to me, and we laughed and played. But no one in my family saw them, and I didn't know why. Maybe they were too cranky to see them.

Chapter 8

My Dad The Boy

The boy was caught up in the madness of his world, living with a domineering mother and a neurotic young wife, each grovelling for his attention to solve their endless hatred for each other, and to fix their unhappy situation. There was a new baby on the way. He asked himself how he would cope in this mayhem with those two women. There was no escape. He couldn't see a way out of the fog and confusion.

His mind drifted into the dream world he loved to live in. He was in a far-off land, where planes and wars existed, and he was the hero of the day: a strong jet fighter pilot. He was conquering his enemies. He shot them down, one by one, and victory was his. He'd be hailed a hero back at base, where he was revered and looked up to.

He'd killed many of the enemy. He smiled as he dreamed. This was one of his many adventure dreams that he often fell into when he couldn't escape the reality of his life. Or was he killing off his enemies here on the farm?

The shed was his place of solace, and where he repaired household items and tinkered with his cars.

In here, he had a sense of himself. He could beat his enemies and be praised and loved by those that understood him.

The planes' engines roared as they swooped and killed the enemies; another one shot down. He sped up to the next kamikaze pilot and *tatter, tatter, boom*! A fireball engulfed a plane, and it fell to the ground. He upthrusted his plane and turned her for home, announcing on the radio back at base, all enemies down… he returned to the here and now.

There was a familiar screeching filling the air as he pulled himself back into his present. What the…? he thought. The hysterical bellowing of his mother drained him.

'Max, Max, answer me. Where are you?'

He took in a deep breath to gather his senses and pulled himself together. Be in the here and now, he told himself, and walked out of the shed, grabbing a bit of rag to disguise the fact that he'd been dreaming.

He rubbed his hands like he was cleaning grease off them and looked into her questioning eyes.

She saw him rubbing his hand on the cloth, and she blurted out, 'Where were you?'

'Here, Mum.' He lowered his head: a boy of nineteen, stifled by a hen-pecking mother; and because of this, he had no courage to put her in her place. Neither did any of us ever question Grandma. The only way people could put Helen in her place, and get away with it, was to leave her - and many did leave her.

'You've got a call to go to work tonight.'

'Oh! Okay, I'll finish up here and go and have a sleep,' he stammered.

She stood staring at him, causing him to fidget.

Dubiously, he turned his back to her to go into his shed. He always felt he had to wait for her to give him permission to move. He tried to be pleasant to this mother, who demanded too much from him. He felt like he was being eaten alive. He knew who his true enemy was - the one who birthed him - but he felt he was held captive on that farm, and many times he'd ask himself why.

She turned from him and walked to the house.

He returned to the safety of the shed. Placing his hands on his bench, moving back and forth, he tried to work it out. He questioned why his mother didn't ever send Carol to the shed with his messages, and why did she have to bring him his messages. He had too many questions in his mind. Thoughts plagued him around why he was still out there on the farm, and not living in town where Carol wanted to live. He thought about his sister, Connie: a soft, gullible, and innocent woman; but she escaped the farm, thanks to our strong-minded warrior, Aunty Beatrice, who lived in Rosemont. His brother, Mitch, lived here a couple of years when he and Kimberly got married. Kimberly got Mitch out because she hated his mum, and had a strong mind as well. Max could understand why Kimberly insisted on them leaving the farm.

Anger overtook him, and he cursed the old, controlling bitch that just wanted to keep them all near her, due to her own fears. *God, what am I here for? Why don't I have the strength to walk away from her? I take her crap, and I can't answer her back. It's not out of respect for her. I hate her because I fear her*, he confessed. *I hate her meanness, and those cruel eyes. I hate her threatening words telling me if I don't do as she wants, I'll be on the streets.*

Here I am, with a wife needier than I can manage, and a baby, and another one on the way. I just want to die, and I am too afraid to move out, because what if I can't support them, Carol and the babies. What if I don't really want to be with Carol, and what if I leave Carol? Where will she end up? Probably at her mother's house, and with my child. No, I couldn't do that to them. I hate my mother, and she hates Carol, and I hate this life, and I hit Carol at my mother's command. I'm a puppet to my mother, and I've seen her glee. Why do I allow her to do this to me? I've trapped myself here.

Max took the hammer and banged it on the table as he cried out in silent pain. *I'm condemned to be chained to my mother.* He breathed in as he felt life force leaving him. His heart ached, and his beautiful, deep, violet-blue eyes pooled up with rivers of tears, and the rivers cascaded down his stubbled face as he sobbed in his shed all alone. He had his head bent between his stretched arms, pushing himself away from what he'd just confessed to through his bench.

He was protected by the private walls of the shed, his only safe haven from hell and dread. As if pulled to turn around, he turned and moved to a crack in the shed. Peering out of the crack, he saw his small wife: a stupid girl with no backbone, meek and mild. *We're both the same; we can't stand up to my mother. Carol's not like Kimberly, who's strong-minded, and wouldn't let Mum control her.* But Kimberly could be just as demanding as his mum was.

Watching Carol at the clothes line, he wondered why he had married her. He whispered, 'My baby Christine.' He smiled, thinking, she is my all, my sanity and comforter, my joy, and only she can make sense of this mayhem, and I am here for her.

Guilt overtook him. He thought if they told his mother that they were leaving, she'd get ill and would have to go to hospital. Then that would cause him both grief and guilt, and she'd tell him she was dying, and she'd put on a bigger performance. *All my siblings have escaped her, but I can't. I'm trapped, I'm trapped...* and he stepped back and placed his back on the wall and slid down in defeat.

Max came back over to the house after a while, and I could hear Grandma and Daddy fighting, but it seemed far away. My friends were with me, and they were gentle and nice, and they took me into their arms and held me. Next thing I knew, I was getting up off the floor, and walking to the big sofa. I climbed up on it. I curled up and fell asleep.

Later on, large, strong arms picked me up and carried me off in a soft, swaying motion, and the movement of being carried put me into a half-and-half feeling of being asleep and awake. I could barely open my eyes, and when I did, I could see my Daddy's face.

He entered our bedroom. It was dark, Mummy had closed the curtains, and was in bed asleep. He went to her and looked down at her. As he did, I half-looked up at him. He was sorry for what he'd done. He seemed to have had too many problems, and he wasn't coping with them. He was too young for this responsibility.

He brushed my mother's hair back, and said, 'I'm sorry, Carol,' and turned from her, and took me to my cot. He lowered me in, ever so gently, and he swept my face with a kiss.

Soon I'd need another bed. This was one of the problems, because Max still considered me a baby, and he wanted me in their room, but the new baby would have to use this cot. I heard I had to go to my grandma's room. I didn't know why, but Daddy didn't want me to be with Grandma in her room. I drifted off into slumber.

Chapter 9

Maxine And My Brother Enter Our World

I was one of nearly three children, and my sister, Maxine, who I called Siggy, was there with me, she was a cute little girl with hardly any hair on her head. She was born bald. I used to like to touch her bald head, and I'd laugh because it was slippery.

I'd say to Grandma as she bathed her, 'She's got a slippery head,' and I'd roar in laughter. Grandma loved me and my laugh.

I also loved to tell her my own little stories in my own way. Grandma was patient and liked to listen to me. My mind was vivid, and I imagined invisible friends. I'd tell her what they'd say to me. What was good was that Grandma never told me I was silly or doubted my stories. I was a regular chatterbox.

She'd say, 'Christine could talk the legs off an iron pot,' and I'd laugh.

I'd play with Maxine in her cot for hours, and Grandma would leave me with the baby while she cooked. I was a good girl, and loved to help.

However, if Daddy heard me talking to myself, he'd say I was silly. He'd say to me, 'Who are you talking to; there's no one there.'

But I was full of confidence. I'd say, 'There is someone there,' and I'd laugh as I looked at my friends, and they would smile at me.

Things changed, because Mummy was having another baby again. I heard the doctor tell her she was not supposed to have any more children, because she had lost a baby. I didn't know what that meant, but there was another baby on the way, and when Mummy told Daddy, he was cranky with her again. This time, my sister was with me when Mummy told Daddy. We were not in their room when they were fighting. I was getting used to their fights. I cuddled my sister, who looked up at me and wondered what it was all about. I told her not to worry, it's Daddy; he's upset with Mummy.

I was feeling really grown up, and I loved to cuddle my sister and take care of her, but she was starting to pull away from me. I'd just catch her and cuddle her, but she would try to bite me. I didn't understand why. She was just like Mummy, and pushed me away.

In September I turned three. I had been a really happy child, but something strange happened to me just before Mummy had her new baby, and I changed. I became unhappy and started to go inside myself. I became shy and frightened, and I couldn't speak to people, or speak up to my father, or brush off what he'd say to me. I lost a part of myself. I used to like people and I'd talk to anyone, but now I'd become closed. The only person I felt really free and safe with was my grandma. I knew she understood me the most, because she cared for me and my sister the most. I lost my happy ways. I didn't understand what had happened to me, and I was left confused. It had something to do with Daddy, my confusion.

This experience exposed me to a dark side of my world. I am unaware of what I'd experienced at that age. However, I know I left the world to seek comfort in the realms of imagination and dreams.

Barton was born in January 1955. He was a sick baby. Our little brother had infantile eczema. My parents had to take him to see the specialists in Rosemont. At the age of four months, he got chickenpox in his blood stream. This was very dangerous and they kept him in Kendale Children's Hospital in Rosemont for a long time. Sometimes, my sister and I would go to the hospital with Mummy and Daddy, and we'd see our little brother all tied up in his cot. He seemed quiet, laying there, but when Mummy took him out of the cot to hold him, he'd cry and scratch himself. My sister and I couldn't go to the hospital all the time, because the journey to Rosemont was too long for us, and there were long periods we'd have to sit. Sometimes Grandma would come with us to Rosemont, and Maxine and I would go with her to see Aunty Connie, who lived with Aunty Beatrice.

I remember the hospital, its smells and its cleanliness. The nurses seemed really busy there. They were always running around from one patient to the other. My parents were there all the time, and this caused lots of problems, because Maxine and I were left with Grandma. Sometimes we didn't see our parents all weekend, or if we went to Rosemont, Daddy sometimes took us back home without Mummy. Many times, Mummy stayed in hospital at Rosemont for long periods of time. Daddy couldn't stay with her because he had to go to work, and he missed our Mummy.

Chapter 10

Barton Returns

Barton was eight months old when he came home. I was almost four. Gradually, his stays at home were for longer periods of time. Once a month he was taken to Rosemont hospital for a check-up, and he and Mummy only had to stay down in Rosemont for a week. He was so sick, and he was strapped to his cot at home. This puzzled me. His little arms and legs were tied to the cot bars.

'Mummy, why is he tied up?' I'd looked in his cot when Mummy was preparing his clean dressings.

'You know why, Christine. I've told you. He will scratch himself and bleed, and we have to tie him up, and his feet too.'

'Naughty boy, isn't he, Mummy?'

She never answered me, and her explanations didn't answer my questions. I was still puzzled about why he had to be strapped in his cot. Why did he cry, and then smile a moment later?

I used to wonder what Barton was feeling. I was confused by his feelings. I'd ask again, 'Mummy, why is Barton like that for?'

'Because he's sick. You can see he has sores on him.'

'Why does he cry and then smile?' I swung on his cot bars.

'Because he's in a lot of pain; that's why he cries.'

I was swinging too hard, and she checked me. 'Christine, don't swing on the cot. You're moving it.'

I wasn't able to play with him. I could only look at him as he laid there. When I looked at him, he always seemed to manage a smile in all his agony. I'd just stand and look at him for long periods of time, and wonder about him. Mummy said he was in pain, but he smiled at me. I saw no pain in his smile, as I smiled back at him.

'What is pain?' I questioned, infuriating my mother.

She gasped, and I went quiet.

We weren't allowed to touch Barton, because Mummy told us we'd give him germs and make him really sick. Sometimes, as I stood near his bed and when Mummy wasn't looking, I'd put my arm through the bars and touch him, and he'd smile. But I wanted to cuddle him. No one could cuddle him, only Mummy.

One day, Mummy caught me touching him and she screamed at me, 'Don't touch him! You'll make him sick with your germs.'

I wondered, could germs run down your arm? From then on, I didn't touch his skin. I started to see him as yucky, and I didn't want to see germs on me either. I could touch his clothes, because sometimes when Mummy had him in her arms, she'd let me touch his sleeve, but I could only touch his clothes, not his skin. I didn't want to make him more sick or get his germs.

He was trapped so badly in his body that itched and bled. His sores were like monster blobs that oozed watery pus. He smelt like dead flesh as his scabs dried and peeled off. His eczema was the weeping type. I don't think they expected Barton to live.

I had to leave the room when Mummy did the dressings. Barton seemed to sleep a lot. Now I think of it, this must have been his way of escaping his body. The room smelt like a hospital from the ointments and dressings my Mummy used on him, and they also smelt of dead skin.

By the time Barton was twelve months old, he was getting better, and he stopped having to stay in hospital. At eighteen months old, Grandma could bath him too, and we were allowed to watch her bath him.

He was different to us, and I'd point and ask Grandma, 'What is this?'

Grandma informed us, 'It's his donkey.'

'His donkey?' I laughed, as I knew what a donkey was.

Mummy said, 'It's his little willy.'

Both sounded funny and made me laugh. I was much happier with my brother. Especially now he didn't smell and was not strapped to the cot. He could walk around. Barton let me cuddle him; he was nice to cuddle, and he had no more sores. I quickly forgot how he used to be, and forgot about his smelly sores and smelly body.

My sister and I loved our little brother, and I loved to take him by the hand and walk him around the house. He was so cute, and I could pick him up and kiss him. He liked that. He was such a little thing for a boy. He loved to laugh, and we'd tickle him and play with him for hours until he needed to sleep. Sometimes we were allowed to watch him go to sleep.

Mummy's room smelt fresh because she always kept her window open, and there was always a breeze coming in. Sometimes, I stood on the little lounge under the window and smelt the fresh air. Grandma's room, where Maxine and I slept, was always shut up, and she never opened her windows.

Mum put Barton to sleep, and when he fell asleep, I ran and jumped up on her bed, and waited for Mummy to come to me.

She said, 'Go and play now, and no noise, so you don't wake your brother.'

I put my arms out for a cuddle, and she gave me a quick cuddle and lowered me to the floor. I held on to her and gave a little giggle.

'Christine, shh! Come on now: go and play,' she said in a whisper, as I released my hold from her and walked to my brother's cot.

I watched his little face twitch, and I giggled at his twitching. 'Mummy, his face is moving.'

'Yes, he's dreaming.'

'Dreaming?' I asked, surprised.

'Yes, you know those pictures in your head when you sleep.'

I knew what she meant when she said pictures in my head, because I had lots of pictures in my head when I was sleeping - and not sleeping. I had learnt they are dream pictures, then I found out everyone had dream pictures in their head. I smiled and touched his head. 'My lovely brother.'

'Mummy, where do I come from?' I asked.

She looked at me startled, and said, 'You fell off a star.'

'Did I?' My eyes lit up, because I knew this wasn't my real home and I didn't belong here.

She smiled. 'Yes, you did.'

I was so happy to know I'd come off a star. I loved to sing my favouite song and sang it as I left the room, 'Twinkle, twinkle, little star, how I wonder what you are. Up above the world so high, like a diamond in the sky.' Grandma used to sing that song to me all the time, and now I knew why. I was so happy - I knew I didn't belong to this family or this world.

Chapter 11

Starting School

In Feburary of 1957, I was 5 and a half. I started kindergarten at Hastings Crossing Primary School. I was a very shy child by then. Nonetheless, I liked my teacher, Mrs. Ford. She was a very pretty, softly spoken lady, who had an endearing smile. To me, she was the true face of a mother. I loved the way she smiled at us, like we were her children and she was proud of us. I'd not felt that unspoken love, but I'd seen it given to other children by their mothers.

The walk to the bus stop was along a long and lonely bush track. Grandma and my mother walked me to the bus stop, pushing my sister and brother in a pram because they were too little to walk it. Sometimes, I got into the pram and I was pushed, but I was big enough to walk the four kilometre walk. When I first started school, my mother showed me where to get off the bus in Hastings Crossing, and where to get back on the bus in the afternoon to go home. Mummy couldn't come into school and pick me up every day, so I had to get used to catching the bus myself. Finally, my Mummy and Grandma just walked me to the bus stop, and they were there when I returned home in the afternoon. I was big enough to do it all by myself.

We had our neighbours' children catching the same bus, and they were bigger than me. Many times, Mummy stayed with Maxine and Barton at home, and only Grandma walked with me, there and back. Daddy had the car, and worked shift work; Mummy couldn't drive. Mummy seemed distant, and she wasn't talking very much. She was in her room more often. She never ever played with us children.

Grandma told us stories, read us poetry and sang to us, and we laughed and played with her. I had to say my prayers before I slept, and Grandma taught me 'Now I lay me down to sleep'. To me, those were just words; there were no feelings around these words, because there was no deeper understanding to what they meant; and we had to say grace at the table before we ate our food. Grandma talked to me about God and Jesus, and I wasn't sure who they were. I asked Mummy about God and Jesus, and she told me that I should love them. She told me that Jesus lived on the Earth a long time ago, and he was a kind man. Grandma told me Jesus was a kind man too, and she told me stories, called parables, about Jesus' kind deeds. I really liked those stories.

Daddy was the one to teach us about the Bogeyman, who lived in the dark. As soon as night came, he was out there waiting for us. Daddy had my sister and I frightened. We were too frightened to go to the toilet, which was about twenty metres from the house, so Grandma had to take us to the outside toilet when it got dark, or we used a chamber pot that was kept in a marble-topped hand-washing cabinet in our room.

I liked that cabinet, with its beautiful tiles that had painted tulips on them. I liked the texture of the tulips that seemed to pop out at me, and I'd run my fingers over these tiles. There were hidden things in that cabinet. I'd discovered a bottle of castor oil. Grandma told me never to touch it, but when I got older, my curiosity got to me, and I used to have a drink of the oil out of that bottle when no one was looking. I liked the taste of castor oil.

I liked school, and best of all, I liked to learn my alphabet. The alphabet was on a chart, and pictures explained the letters. I was very good at remembering anything with a picture: A for apple, B for bat, and so on. My mind could remember a picture, but if I had to remember a letter, or a word that was told to me without a picture, it was harder for me. I remember playing with coloured beads, and we used those beads to count with.

My favourite story at school was about the train going up the hill. He had so much determination to get up that hill. I connected with him, and I felt his determination inside me. I wanted to do something, but I didn't know what I wanted to do in those days. I liked school, and I liked being away from our house. It was so good to watch the other children playing. I played too, but I was shy, so I mainly watched them, because it was so hard for me to play with the other children. I felt like I was a stranger. I was a funny, dreamy child, not fully knowing my place in the scheme of things, what I had to do in this life, and where I fitted in. Most of all, I didn't understand my adult caretakers.

Time moved on, and in first class the following year, my mother wanted me to learn to bank money.

The school offered banking. Mummy gave me forty shillings to bank on my first banking day. I will never forget that day; it's still etched in my memory. Instead of banking the money, I decided to spend my pennies at Flint's shop near the Hastings Crossing hotel. These shillings were pennies to me, so I took my friend Kim Pender with me to the shop, and I bought her a big bag of lollies, and one for me. Unfortunately, playing with Kim, I missed my bus. Daddy and Mummy's friend, Fred, saw me on the street, and he put me in his car and took me home.

Fred was my Daddy's best friend. Daddy used to call him Goog; I don't know why, but Daddy did. Fred was a tall, big-set man with dark skin; he looked different to us. I was sitting on the back seat of his car, happily eating my lollies and singing. Finally, we reached my home. Fred opened the top gate, drove in, and shut the gate behind him, then drove to the next gate, the middle gate, opened and shut it. As we drove through, I saw my mother out the front waiting. I could tell by her face that I was in trouble. She had a stick in her hand. The car stopped, and while she was talking to Fred, I opened the car door and the dog greeted me. I threw the lollies so the dog would eat them quickly, but he just sniffed them.

I said to him, 'Quick! Eat so she can't see them,' but the dog walked off.

My mother came around to my side of the car, and when she saw the lollies on the ground, she was angry, blurting out, 'Where did you get those lollies from?' Without me answering or her giving me a chance to answer, she threw another question. 'Why did you miss the bus?'

I was in real trouble and started to cry, hoping she'd feel sorry for me. I said, 'I spent the pennies.'

'Pennies? You stupid girl, they were shillings, and you fed those lollies to the dog, and you never thought of your sister and brother.' She grabbed my arm, and swished the stick across my legs. I collapsed, struggling to hold myself up, but she gripped my arm and smacked me with her full force.

I cried, 'Mummy, you're hurting me. I thought they were pennies,' I sobbed.

She released me, and told me to go into the house. As I went into the house, I could hear her thanking Fred for bringing me home. Sad and hurt, I walked into the house, where I was greeted by my grandma, who asked me what I'd done. I told her, and she cuddled me. I felt so unhappy, and cried in her arms. I was so glad I had her to hold me in my times of need.

Sometimes, Mummy came into town to pick me up from school. She loved being in town and walking around the streets, talking to the people. I'd just follow her around the street in my own little world. Usually I'd be singing 'Twinkle, twinkle, little star', swinging my body around, and I'd skip as she walked. Sometimes I'd talk to Mummy, telling her my stories. She'd smile at me as if she was listening. I somehow knew she wasn't, but I'd keep talking.

On one occasion, while we were in town, we were walking past the stationary shop. In the shop window, I spied a packet of six pencils, with a pink pencil. My eyes grew wide. I jumped up and down on the spot.

'Mummy, Mummy, look! A pink pencil. Can I have one, please?' I asked her nicely. We always had to say please.

She looked in the window, saw the pencils, and without a word, we went into the shop. Mummy seemed happy in there as she asked the man about the pencils. He got a pack from the counter, and Mummy paid him. He handed them to her, and she handed them to me. It was the wrong packet of pencils.

I blurted out, 'There's no pink pencil.' My face dropped. I looked at her, but she was too busy talking to the man. I waited, tugged her dress, and said, 'Mummy, there's no pink pencil here.' She brushed my hand aside, so I waited. Again, I told her, but she was too busy, so I demanded the proper packet of pencils.

I had got her attention. She looked at me and said, 'No, you can't have that other packet.' She grabbed my arm, and dragged me out of the shop, telling me, 'Don't be rude, you naughty girl, and take what you're given, you ungrateful child.'

I screamed and screamed, stopping on the spot, 'I want the pink pencil!'

'No, you can't have the pink pencil.' She walked off, leaving me on my own. There was no way I could win with her. She just ignored me, or she didn't listen to me. I ran after her, feeling that I could be left if I wasn't careful.

The people in my house pretended they were nice around other people, but they acted silent when we were with each other, alone in our house. At this age, I developed many fears and feelings around being unloved. I quickly learned to get the love I wanted. I had to always be nice and allow the big people to feel right.

At seven years old, I got badly infected tonsils, and ended up in hospital to have them removed. I didn't want to go to the hospital, because I didn't like the smell of hospitals. The whole time I was in hospital, I screamed, even though the nurses told me not to scream, because it would hurt my throat. I didn't care; the smell of the hospital made me sick, there were old people all around me, and I felt unsafe. At home, I felt safe, but I developed sensitivity to the colour orange, and whenever I saw an orange colour, it had a horrible smell, like the chloroform they put me to sleep with. So I'd run away from anything with the colour orange in it.

I had many strange behaviours and thoughts, because I was always on my own, so I formed my own ideas of how the people in my world worked. Sometimes my sister, brother and I played together, but it would always end up in a fight. I was happier alone. Many times, I'd sneak into the kitchen, and eat the black tea leaves Grandma had in a tea caddy. Grandma caught me a few times, and I got into trouble. I kept eating them without her knowing. One of my favourite things to do was to eat the red flowers in the garden, the ones with a sack of honey in their stem. I had some unusual tastes.

Chapter 12

My Father

My father was like a hair trigger; we had to be careful what we said around him, because he could easily go off. My sister and I were playing in the living room, and we heard a big scream coming from the kitchen; it was a frightening scream, and then I heard shouts. I had my dolly in my hands. I drew her in closer to my body. My body shook, and my eyes grew big.

'They're doing it again. Why do my Mummy and Daddy do this for?' I asked my dolly.

Again, more shouts; I felt frozen. I couldn't move. I asked myself if should I go and see what's happening. My dolly just stared back at me, and my eyes were as big as hers.

'What will I see if I go into the kitchen and look?' I glanced at my sister.

She was looking at me, and then she cried.

I said, 'Don't cry, you silly girl,' as I hit her. This caused her to stop crying. I pulled a face at her and kicked her leg.

The noises got louder. Turning away from my sister, who was sobbing and clutching her dolly, I watched in the direction of the kitchen door. There was a lot of talking in there. I looked at my sister. I could see she was looking at me, as her big sister, to help her. I could see she was scared. I was scared too. I edged to the kitchen door to peek in. There I witnessed a very bad thing; I saw Grandma telling Daddy about Mummy. She was telling Daddy that Mummy had been bad, and she should be hit for that.

Mummy begged my Daddy to listen to her. 'Don't listen to her, Max; she's telling you lies. What she's saying is not true.'

On my mother's face, I saw her pain, and there were tears flowing down her cheeks. I stood there staring at them all. My heart was heavy for my mother. My little sister was standing behind me. I threw my arm around her shoulders. In that moment, I saw my Daddy push my mother onto the sofa. As if he needed approval, he looked at Grandma. I wondered what he looked at Grandma for.

I let go of my sister, and I ran to Grandma, hiding behind her. My Mummy was crying, and Grandma was smiling. Why was she smiling? I couldn't understand. Mummy was crying on the sofa, and she was all rolled up in a ball, covering her face. Why doesn't Grandma help Mummy, I wondered. They're all fighting. I am so scared. I gripped Grandma's skirt tighter. Maxine was behind me. I looked at Grandma, who was still smiling, and I didn't understand why. Mummy and Daddy both looked sad. Daddy hit my Mummy, and I looked at Grandma.

'Yes, Max, hit her; she's not a good wife, or mother.'
I looked at my Mummy.

She was pleading, 'No, no, Max, don't hit me. Please don't hit me.'

She was scared, and I couldn't move. I could only watch, because I didn't know what to do. As I watched them, my eyes grew bigger, and I was lost.

Chapter 13

The Fight And Mother's Escape

There were too many fights in our house. There was never any kindness or love; it was mainly fights, glares, and hatred, with no words spoken. When there was a fight, we could only look on. As children, we were too scared to intervene, because we could have been hit by Daddy's big hands. Daddy looked so frightening and fierce. It was his power that scared me, the power in his eyes, and his force. We could die from it, or he could hurt us.

Things suddenly changed in my life at the age of seven. My mother appeared at the house with another man she called Alf. I didn't know how my mother met this man. I'd heard Grandma say that it must have been when she was in Rosemont Hospital with my sick brother. On the day my mother left us, she had my brother with her. Mother beckoned my sister and I over to her, but Grandma held us back. It was summertime. I felt stunned, not understanding what was happening, or what my feelings were. I'd become numb to the behaviour in our house, due to all the fights. I'd learned how to not feel anything, but I was fearful for myself.

Mother had our little brother by his hand, and she was saying, 'I am going.'

Grandma was pushing her away. 'Yes, that's right. You're trash, just like your family. Go! You're not wanted here.'

Mother was trying to tell her that her family weren't trash, and how Grandma had never liked her or been fair to her. Mother was crying and pleading with Grandma to see how her son hit her, and how it wasn't normal. Grandma defended Daddy, and told Mother that she was not a good mother for us girls, and that she should leave. Grandma held us closer to her body. I looked up at my grandma; she was holding my sister and I so hard. My mother wanted to take us too, but Grandma told her she couldn't have us girls.

Maxine was still little, but my mother could only take our brother. I don't think my grandma liked Barton, as she didn't talk to him as much as she did with us.

The man, Alf, said, 'Come on, Carol, leave them. She's not going to let you have the girls.'

Mother was crying. She had to go, but didn't want to leave us. She was sad. She wanted to cuddle us goodbye, but I didn't want to cuddle her. I pulled away from her. I just looked at her, feeling nothing. I couldn't cry. Maxine was crying, and she cuddled Mother. I was too confused. I didn't know what was right, or what this all meant. Grandma had us in her grip, and I had to look at her for approval.

Mother walked off with our little brother. The man had Mother's bags in his hands. He was a tall, quiet man, and said little. He only encouraged my mother to let us all go and go with him. Again, he said, 'Come on, Carol,' and nudged her with his elbow. They walked up the paddock through the gates, my mother and brother with the man called Alf Rush. That was the last I saw of my mother for a long time.

I sometimes questioned my grandma about our mother. She told me bad things about her.

She'd say, 'Your mother is not a good person, and her skin looked like the skin on a sausage.'

'Why, Grandma?'

'Because your mother wastes her money and time on creams to make her face young; she only wants to look good. A waste of time.'

I looked at Grandma, and thought, yes, all Mother wanted to do was to look in the mirror at herself. I could not understand why she wanted to do that. I tried to put it in my mind to see her skin like the skin of a sausage, as Grandma did, but I couldn't see that. This put me into more confusion about people: how they saw the world, how they behaved, and how they thought.

When Daddy came home that night, Grandma told him about our mother leaving us. He went into a rage that scared my sister and I, and we ran and hid behind Grandma. I felt terror; my eyes were popping out of my head. He looked at Grandma with hatred, but she stood her ground, defying his glares. She was the only one who could control him. My Daddy's eyes were too powerful, and when he stared at me, I felt his knife-edge stare and his bigness could crush me if I was naughty. He stared at her, as if he wanted to hit her or say something, then he looked at me and my sister, and calmed down. I looked down to the ground to break his stare.

Grandma said, in her confident snigger, 'She went with that man, Alf. I told you she's no good, like her family. They're all the same.'

My father turned to Grandma; his stare was full of hatred. 'Enough, you...' he bellowed. She just smiled in her funny way. She knew she had power, control, over my father, and he didn't have the guts to override her, because she had the same powerful eyes as his. I just stared up at both of them while Maxine sobbed. My father looked possessed, and when he looked at Grandma, he was saying in his mind, this was your fault, but he couldn't verbally tell her that.

He twirled around, forced the back door open, and flew outside. In the open paddock, he screamed out my mother's name. 'Carol!'

We clung to Grandma, and she put her hands on our shoulders, reassuring us. 'It will be alright; you're safe with me.'

I felt scared; it was not going to be alright. My father was sad, and missed my mother.

I was just seven. I was lost, and didn't understand why all this was happening. In the following days, Daddy was closer to me, and he was close to me for a long time since, and we started doing secret things...

Chapter 14

Fears At School

I became very frightened of men at the age of eight. There was a strange man who came to Hastings Crossing Primary School. He was one of the garbage collectors. I was frightened of him, because whenever he saw me, he'd rush over and hug me.

'My princess, my princess,' he'd say.

When I saw him, I'd freeze. He was so taken by my good looks, he terrified me. Fortunately, when he ran at me, his friends would call out at him to leave me alone, and to go with them. I'd breathe a sigh of relief when he went. I hated this school because of this man, and I was scared to go to the school toilet alone, because it was big and dark in there, and I had to hide from him before he saw me. I'd started to see everything as unfriendly. I didn't want to go into the toilets unless other children were in there with me to protect me. I started to hold in my bowel motions, by crossing my legs and stopping it coming.

One day, I needed to go to the toilet so badly, I couldn't see anyone else around, so I tried to push my poo back inside me, but it wouldn't stay there. It seeped out of my bottom, and I dirtied my pants. I looked to see if anyone was looking, I took off my underpants, and threw them under the step. My sister, who was in kindergarten, must have been watching me. I didn't see her go and pick up my underpants. When we got home, she told Grandma what I'd done. Maxine narrowed her eyes, and squealed with delight at getting me into trouble. I felt her hatred of me.

I cried and told Grandma how I was scared to go to the toilet on my own, because there was a man there who chased me.

Startled at that news, Grandma asked, 'What man?'

'The man who gets the garbage,' I said sadly.

'But that's no excuse to dirty your pants, Christine.'

'I was scared.' I looked at her for any sign of understanding, but there was none. Again I told her I was frightened.

'Well, if you're such a baby, get your sister to take you to the toilet next time,' Grandma said, glaring at me.

Maxine sniggered. In my shame, I hung my head.

That night, I heard Grandma telling Daddy, 'Max, I think you'd better put the girls into Fenton School.' He asked her why, and she told him, 'Because Carol could come and take them away from us.'

Innocently, Daddy asked, 'Do you think she'd do that, Mum?'

'Yes, I do. Be best for the girls to feel safe.'

I held my breath. I was not supposed to hear, but I did, and I was glad.

I thought my mother might take me away, and I didn't want to go with that man she left with. I wanted to stay with my Daddy.

Maxine and I were moved out of Hastings Crossing School and put into Fenton Public School about a month later. I was safe from that garbage collector. He wouldn't see me again.

At Fenton Primary School, I was put into second class, and my sister was put into kindergarten. This school was smaller than Hastings Crossing Primary School, and my cousins went to this school.

Chapter 15

Daddy's Comforter

Daddy's sadness was great, and I'd always gone to my Daddy's bed since I was a little girl. There I'd lie with him; but since my mother left our house, the house felt quiet, cold and lonely. Daddy seemed to want to just stay in his bed, so I'd join him there. Daddy was doing some things to me - I'm not sure what he was doing - and he'd been doing this to me for a long time. I remembered it starting when I was seven years old. Daddy cried as he cuddled into me, and I'd lay there, not knowing what to do. All I knew was that I wanted to comfort him.

When I did, he became very relaxed, and he'd touch me gently between my legs, reassuring me. 'Don't be scared. Daddy loves you, and won't hurt you. You're my princess, and you make me feel so relaxed, and I like to touch you. You're an angel, and you're a comfort to me, and I miss your mummy and you are like her, and I am sorry...' Then he'd kiss my little lips. I didn't know what to do.

He rubbed his big hands all over my little body, and pressed his body on me, and I felt something from him pressing on me. As he did this, he looked into my big, puzzled eyes. He told me, 'Christine, this is our secret. You don't tell nobody, not even your sister or your grandma.'

I nodded. I understood that even though it was a secret, it probably wasn't right; but it felt good, because I needed so much love, and there wasn't enough love given to me. I accepted his caresses, and I was happy to make him happy, so he wouldn't cry or be sad.

His breath was soft as he felt my body and lay on it, gently caressing me; but he'd pause, as if he must have lapsed in and out of right and wrong, and between getting his needs met and me being a child.

He'd often move away from me, but then returned, fondling me, and then after a while he would say, 'You can go and play; remember it's our secret.'

'Yes, Daddy,' I slipped off his big bed, skipping out of his room, saying, 'I love my Daddy.'

At the door, I'd stop and turn back and look at him, and he'd be in his big bed. I'd think, when I get big, I want to marry my daddy. I'd skip out of Daddy's room, sometimes bumping into Grandma. Her eyes glared at me when she saw me coming out of Daddy's room. Her eyes were cold, and I didn't know why, so I'd lower my eyes and walk away from her coldness. I could feel her eyes following me, penetrating my back. She'd stand staring at Daddy's room when I glanced back at her. I didn't understand at all why she was so mean to me.

The time came when Daddy wanted to get my mother back. He tried to find her through her family. We went into Mother's sister's house, my Aunty Kay's. She lived close to Grandma Owens' house. Aunty Kay lived with her husband, Pete, in Fenton. They had two children, Lance and Brandon. Lance was born a few days before Barton; Brandon was one year and a bit old. Aunty Kay didn't know where my mother was, so it was going to be a long journey for my father to find her. During that time, lots of things happened between Daddy and I. I became his constant companion; the one to ease his pain in his bed, and to accompany him in his search for my mother.

Daddy started to make new friends. These were mostly single men like him, men whose wives had left them. Some of them had children or a child to raise on their own. I didn't understand these new friends of Daddy's. One day, one of Daddy's friends came to stay at our home over the weekend. It was strange, because sometimes when this man came to our house, my grandma was not home. He was a nice, gentle, short man. He had a daughter about my age. She didn't always come with him to our house.

They lived in Dawson Hill, in a lovely two-storey, wooden, white-painted house; it was such a lovely house, with a picket fence, set amongst trees. I liked their house so much. It looked clean, and I felt that there was a lot of love in that house.

His daughter was nice. She was his only daughter. She had no mummy. Her name was Lucy. Lucy was a lucky girl. She had a lovely bedroom all to herself. I had to share my bedroom with my sister and Grandma. I liked to go to Dawson Hill to visit them. Sometimes, the man came to stay overnight with us, when Grandma went to Mrs Clements' house in Dawson Hill. I don't know if Daddy ever told Grandma the man was coming. One night, I'd got really scared by a bad dream that woke me up. I screamed out and I cried. Then I heard someone coming towards my room, which made me stop crying, causing me to sob. Listening, fear enveloped me as the footsteps approached my room. I couldn't see in the dark, in the dead of night. Then the light went on. I gasped. It was not my Daddy. I looked over at Grandma's bed; she was not there. I whimpered.

The man sat on my bed, and in a soft voice said, 'It's okay, Christine. You just had a bad dream.' He settled me - not my Grandma or my Daddy. He quietened me, tucked me in, and I went back to sleep. We used to go to this man's house for a long time, then one day it all stopped. Daddy got news of my mother, so the search started again.

Chapter 16

Meeting The Cousins

Maxine never came with Daddy and me, because Grandma wanted her to stay with her, and she was easy to keep at home. All Grandma had to do was promise Maxine lollies or chips to stay with her. Maxine loved sweets, and couldn't get enough of them. Daddy and I searched, but we weren't always successful. As time went by, I became resentful of my mother for leaving us, and causing my Daddy to be so sad. My new name for Mother was *her*.

The best day of our searching was when I met my mother's older sister, Aunty Betty, a funny lady who swore and laughed out loud. She wasn't pretty, but she was a very funny, straight-forward and relaxed lady; not quiet or timid like my mother. She had four children, just as rowdy and funny as she was. She screamed at her kids, but they laughed at her. It wasn't like that in my house; you couldn't laugh at your elders.

On this day, I got to play with these wild cousins. I loved it, because I could run wild and be free. We all played and got on so well together; there were no fights. That day, I forgot about the sadness of my life on the farm. I'd loved to have been able to stay with these cousins and run free, and not have to worry about getting dirty. I screamed like them, laughed and enjoyed myself. I really liked Kelvin and Naomi; they were a bit younger than me.

I heard Daddy calling me, 'Christine, come on.'

I stopped, looked at my cousins, and sadness came over me. Then everything came rushing back in. I walked over to Daddy; he pulled me in close to his body.

'Say goodbye to your cousins. We're going,' he said.

I looked at them, and they looked at me. I gave a little wave. We'd been so happy, and I think they would have liked me to stay with them. Daddy chatted with Aunty Betty. Later, I was told to kiss my Aunty Betty goodbye. I liked her, and she cuddled me. Her twins were standing near her. They smiled at me, then I grabbed my Daddy's big hand. He was having his last word with my Aunty Betty.

She smiled at me, and told him, 'She's so sweet, Max. She's like your mother to look at.'

Daddy stared at me, and said, 'True. I hope her life is better than Mum's, though.'

'Well, Max, while Christine's alive, your mother will always be alive too.'

I didn't understand her words, or what they meant. I was too busy looking at my cousins, longing to run free. We walked to our car. At the car, I turned back. My cousins and I smiled at each other. Raising my hand, I waved.

'Goodbye.' I said.

They each said, 'Goodbye.'

I didn't want to, but I had to go. As soon as we drove off, the cousins broke free of the moment, and ran to play. I looked at them, longing to be with them. After this meeting, it would be many years before I'd see them again, and in years to come, I'd find out how unstable my Aunty Betty really was. My cousins were abused too; they weren't as free as they looked. There had been physical and emotional abuse, especially towards my cousin Kelvin. In the far, far future, I would hear that Naomi suffered sexual abuse in that family. She would bury that abuse inside her for many years.

What was perceived by the eye wasn't always necessarily the truth. All families had their masks. One for the outside world, and one for behind closed doors. Secrets and masks; you'd never know what was lurking or going on in a family. Regardless, I really liked my Aunty Betty so much, even though I learned the hard, cold truth about her. In later life, when we reconnected, we'd spend our school vacations with them.

I grew to love her very much. She was my second favourite aunty, after Aunty Connie, Daddy's sister. Aunty Betty's life was a living hell; the patterns ran deep in her life too. It would take two years before Daddy found my mother... *her*.

Chapter 17

Suffering The Polite Child

'Christine, Christine,' I heard.

'Oh, why did I have to be called that name? I don't like it,' I whispered. 'Yes,' I politely answered in response to my elder. I hated having to be nice. Sometimes I didn't want to be nice, or answer their silly questions, or go for a meal. I heard her call me again.

Quickly, I acknowledged her, 'Yes, Grandma, what do you want? I'm playing with my dolly, and straightening up her dress.' In defense of myself, I turned, feeling someone at the back of me. Her presence was so obvious, and I could feel her ice-cold eyes piercing the back of my neck. I knew it was her; her presence was always felt by all of us. She stood in the doorway of the kitchen, with her hands on her hips, dominating me with eyes that glared right through you.

I knew I'd disappointed her, because I didn't run to her immediate call. I had to act quickly. I smiled. 'Hello, Grandma, look at my dolly. Isn't she pretty?' As I looked at her, I knew I was in deep trouble. I quickly said, 'I am sorry, Grandma, I forgot.' This always saved me, because it was nothing unusual for me to forget.

My family accused me of having my head in the clouds. Sometimes daydreaming saved me.

Her sharp voice commanded me, 'Get yourself into the kitchen now.'

'Yes, Grandma,' I put my dolly down on the dining room chairs, and went with her. I couldn't help forgetting what I had to do, because I was always dreaming. I didn't fully hear them calling me. As I entered the kitchen behind Grandma, my sister was smirking at me. She wasn't that brave or game to say anything while Grandma was looking, but as soon as Grandma turned her back, Maxine poked her tongue out at me and rolled her eyes. She looked so unattractive as she made fun of me. I was in trouble, and this seemed to make her happy. Sometimes, I just looked at her and wondered why she hated me so much. We both were mean to each other, and couldn't stand each other. It was like we had contempt for each other.

Actually, we despised each other. She would run at me with her mouth open and bite me, or pinch me with small twists of my skin. I'd stand there screaming. Many times when we fought, we forgot Daddy was home sleeping for his late shifts. He'd come running out of the house to find out why we were screaming. I'd tell him she'd bit me, but he would stick up for her, telling me I was the one who probably started the fight. This puzzled me, because we had a secret.

Silence was a prerequisite to living in this family, and silence was demanded at the dinner table. We had to be polite; we didn't express ourselves. We bottled up so much. This was why we hated each other. We took our anger out on each other. As chlidren, we had a lot of suppressed emotions. We were often reminded: children are to be seen and not heard. The words 'be quiet' rang through our house.

'Quiet. Don't make noises. Stop fighting. Your father is asleep,' Grandma would bellow at us.

Dad was the worst. He insisted on silence at the dinner table and in the house when he was home. All Dad needed to do was just glare at us, and we knew we were in trouble; words were never needed. Dad was a rough, cruel man in play as well. He had no boundaries when he played with us. He would torment us by tickling us to the extreme, to where we would lose our breath. Then when we'd forgotten ourselves by returning the rough play, he'd snap like a savage dog at a dinner plate and growl, 'Enough. Get. Go and play.' It confused us. We tried to start the play off again, but no, he wouldn't have it. Everything closed down; he was angry at us. We could never defy him. What he gave out didn't apply to us to give out, and when we got too rough, all stopped.

For as long as I remember, I had always been the polite child. We'd been raised to be polite, reminded of our place in the house, town or society. We were constantly told to be polite to others. Grandma taught my sister and I how to sit, how to present ourselves in public and at people's houses, and how to conduct ourselves in the presence of adults. Grandma taught us well. We were really good children while we were in her care. I could have been taken anywhere. But deep down in me was a rebellious side no one knew about.

Behind my family's back, I smoked cigarettes. I'd roll up wood in paper, and smoke it in front of the fuel stove. If someone came, I could stuff the cigarette into the grid of the stove. I'd go through Daddy's ashtrays, and pick out the best cigarette butts to make myself a cigarette with his leftovers. I started this at seven years old. I had this desire to smoke, and this desire would stay with me until I was seventeen.

Chapter 18

Make Believe

In my alone times, I'd play house with my dolly. I'd talk to her, and she'd listen to me. 'I don't know what's going on. Daddy is funny with me, and I can't tell anyone.' I told her how he was taking me to the shed to help him to repair his car, but while we were there, he touched my private parts. Daddy was strange; he loved me, but also screamed at me. I was always confused by his actions.

In the late afternoon, after a late lunch, I was playing on the big verandah, enjoying my time alone. The spring air was still. The verandah protected me from the heat of the day. The heat couldn't penetrate the old homestead verandah, with its large awnings. I was in full conversation, and singing to Ginger the cat and my doll. I'd dressed Ginger up in a dress and bonnet. I was singing as I lifted his paw to slip it into the sleeve of the doll's dress. I was singing my favourite song, 'My Bonnie lies over the ocean, my Bonnie lies over the sea, my Bonnie lies over the ocean, oh bring back my Bonnie to me.'

At that tender age of eight, I didn't know my future and what that song would mean to me. The cat let me dress him up; I think he liked to play dress-ups with me. I'd set up the tea cups for the cat, dolls and me. The cat would wink his eye at me. He seemed to approve of me, and he seemed happy in my company. I'd completely forgotten all my worries and where I was. My sister and Grandma were doing some sewing inside.

I loved being outdoors, where I could smell the animals, and hear the cows moving as they grazed around the farmhouse fence. I could hear the bees in the peach tree near the verandah. They were buzzing around the blossoms, and it felt safe to pretend; I just talked and talked. I loved giving orders to the dolls and the cat. The cat winked at me, as if to say, 'Sure, Christine, I'll do all those things for you.' The dogs were stretched out under the table I was playing on. They were a bit smelly, but I liked their smell. Now and then, the dogs would shake. This got my attention. Grandma said they were dreaming. Sometimes, they whimpered like a child. I looked up, and smiled at the old black cat, Tom, who wouldn't play with me. He was asleep at the other end of the big old table. This table held a lot of amazing things: a cupboard, which was an old bread box, holding an array of tools for quick repair jobs around the house, instead of having to go to the shed; and there were pumpkins on the table, and we'd caught Tom gnawing into them. I giggled. 'He's a naughty cat,' I told Ginger. I heard rustling every now and then. It was the birds in the peach tree. I was lost in my fun and fantasy, surrounded with cats, dogs and nature. From out of the blue, I was startled by a roar. It was my father; his voice echoed, a booming sound. The dogs jumped up, and quickly scattered.

I turned to face my father as he walked onto the verandah like a giant. I felt like I was about to be swallowed up. I hadn't seen or heard him coming. He turned on me with eyes like fire. 'Who are you talking to? Are you stupid or something?' My eyes were big, like dinner plates, and I felt frozen as I stared at him. In my weak voice, I said, 'I am talking to my dollies.'

He looked at me like I was some crazy fool. He told me, 'Don't be stupid; if you talk to yourself, people will think you're mad.'

He walked off. As he entered the kitchen, he banged the door shut. All I could think of was that he didn't even stop to give me a kiss hello. I felt like I wanted to sink into the earth. My heart crashed. Both the cats had run off too. Ginger was on the grass, pulling at the bonnet, trying to get it off his head. All the animals were terrified of my father - and so was I.

Tears rolled down my cheeks. I bent my head over the table and I cried in silence, so no one would hear me. As I sobbed, I listened in case he returned, because if he saw me crying, I'd get into more trouble.

This was not a happy house now Mother had gone away. I felt scared and frightened sometimes. All was changing; even Grandma didn't talk like she used to. I found myself more and more by myself. Maxine and Grandma got on so well. Maxine liked to knit and sew. Grandma tried to teach me, but I was so frustrated with it, I screwed it up in anger. She smacked my face and told me to leave her sight.

I was supposed to be Daddy's princess, who helped him to fix his car in the shed. When we were there, he'd tell me that I was his mechanic, and that I was really good mechanically. He told his friends, 'She's a great little mechanic, and can work as good as any man - and knows her tools.' I was like a doctor with Dad. I used to pass him his tools as he called them out. I liked to get in and unscrew the difficult bolts for him. He'd start them off, I'd finish unscrewing them. Sometimes, he left me to clean the car parts.

I went with him when he was looking for Mother; he was nice to me then. But he was touching my private parts, as my Grandma called them. When my sister and I were in the bath and we used to poke at each other there, my Grandma would say, 'Don't do that, you rude girls.' We'd laugh, but that made her very angry. We sometimes splashed each other and laughed, but one day Grandma slapped me across the face, again. I didn't cry; only putting my eyes down as I swirled the water and sang a song, and half-looked at her. Sometimes I hated her, and wished she'd go away. Daddy didn't hit me when he was touching me. He just told me I was not to tell anyone what he was doing to me.

'I won't tell anyone,' I'd reassure him. It felt so nice when he touched me - because he loved me.

I was not sure why he told me not to tell anyone. I tried to touch my sister like Daddy touched me. Daddy could be cruel to me and turn on me. When he did, I got confused. Sometimes I asked myself why he did that: cuddled me in his bed, then was cruel to me. He also would play with my sister more than me. He seemed to forget me, and he screamed at me. This was so confusing.

The dogs gradually came back on to the verandah. Slowly, I packed up my tea-set, went inside to put it away, and came back outside to sit with the dogs.

Late in the evening, Mr Parker called in. He often called in to chat with Grandma. He'd been coming to our house for years. Lately, he seemed to be coming more frequently, now that my mother was away. He was a very kind, quiet man. Grandma liked to talk to him for a long time, because he had a lot of news to tell her about what was going on in the community. My sister and I really liked Mr Parker. We both felt very safe around him, and he used to always buys us gifts. I remember my sister and I getting these big boxes from him. When I opened my box, there was this beautiful blue tissue paper, and as I unfolded that tissue paper, there lay a beautiful biscuit-brown dress. It would be my favourite dress while I was a young girl. My eyes lit up with excitement. I ran over and gave him a big hug and kissed him. He was so kind. I really loved my gift. My sister and I were always dressed in the same outfits, but this dress allowed me to be different from her. Maxine didn't like the dress he'd chosen for her. He'd bought her a royal blue velvet dress with lace around the collar. Every time she wore it, she'd complain that it scratched her. Not me; I loved my biscuit dress, as I called it.

Mr Parker always let my sister and I pat his bald head. It fascinated us. It was so shiny and slippery. He didn't seem to mind us doing that while he was talking to Grandma. We'd be cuddling him as they spoke. My grandma told us he was very much in love with our Aunty Connie. Unfortunately, Aunty Connie didn't love him back. They'd never get together. Fate would deal my beloved Aunty Connie an unfair marriage. She'd marry someone who would rob her of her self-respect, her health and her money, including all her rights as a person.

Mr Parker lived with his two spinster sisters; the three of them would never marry, just like Grandfather Kinread's sisters on the Isle of Man. They never married, nor did Grandfather's younger brother, Max. Max died an early death, like my grandfather.

The only family overseas were Grandfather's sisters on the Isle of Man. Aunty Connie wrote to them, and she'd tell me stories about Grandfather's sisters; but I liked it when Mr Parker visited us, because he made me feel happy inside.

Chapter 19

School Made Me Sad

The year after second class was a sad time for me. I had to repeat that class. I cried because I didn't want to repeat the class, but my grandma was told it was for my own good. Now my sister was only one year behind me. She was in first class, and if I had to repeat another class, I'd be in her class, and that would make me feel ashamed. Now I felt really dumb, because my grandma didn't let me forget that my sister was brainy, and that I was repeating my class. I felt embarrassed to face the littler kids coming up from 1st class, because I was so tall for my age, and I towered over them. I'd look silly sitting with the little kids, and Maxine would poke fun at me. I knew she would. She was a lot like Grandma. Grandma was always talking about people, and telling us about people's faults and failures. I didn't take any notice, but Maxine copied her.

I suffered badly with nosebleeds and earaches. Grandma baked house bricks in the oven for me to lay my ear on. She laid a towel over the brick. One night, the pain was so unbearable, my dad had to take me into town very late at night to see Dr Jones. He gave me an injection, and after that, the earaches never came back. I must have had a bad infection. The nosebleeds didn't stop until I was much older. Grandma said it happened because I had too much blood in my body, but it happened if I bumped my nose, or sometimes if I was picking my nose. I didn't tell Grandma I picked my nose.

My grandma had lots of secrets. She would go down to the two big, scary rooms, and she would stay there for hours. She said she was doing her secret things. When we went to town with her, she'd do her banking, but we were never allowed to go into the bank with her. My sister and I had to sit in the town's centre park, Hastings Crossing Rotary Park, and wait for her to come. She gave us sweets to eat, and we did what we were told. I loved to watch the people. I was so scared of some of the people. They were strange. There were groups of men who rode bikes. They sat around Flint's shop. Grandma told us never to go near them. I wouldn't have anyway; they looked so big, and dressed different to other people. They wore leather jackets, but their faces looked dirty, with beards. My Daddy wore a leather jacket when he rode his bike, but he shaved every day.

Many times I watched Grandma pack my Daddy's leather jacket with newspapers. I asked her why she did that. She told me the newspapers stopped the wind going through to Daddy's skin. When she told me that, I swung my legs under the bench stool and giggled. Maxine looked at me, and I looked away because she'd glared at me, even though I am sure she must have been interested.

The park where we had to sit had a very old rotunda, and sometimes brass bands played there. On ANZAC Day, they'd have services for people who had died in a war, and at school we had to go to these services. People cried. I didn't know why they were crying; no one was saying bad things to them.

There were people with mental illnesses in our town, and I never understood those people. Grandma said they were mad people, and to keep away from them. These people did look scary and walked funny, and had their hands in the air like they were fighting. They kept moving their hands in the air, and there was no one near them.

As we waited for Grandma, my sister always finished her lollies before me. She was a piggy and ate hers really quickly. She looked across the street. I still had some lollies left, but I didn't let her know, because she'd scream for my lollies.

What really scared me were the drunk people. I didn't like them, and if I saw a drunk person, I would run across the road to get away from them. I was very sensitive, and could pick up on people. If I felt anyone coming towards me wasn't safe, I'd cross the road. It was never explained to us why these people were like that. Daddy didn't like them either.

It was good when Grandma returned to get us, even though we'd sat for ages in the park waiting for her. My grandma always made me feel safe, and when we saw Grandma, we'd both run to her and grab her hand. Then she'd take us to a cafe for our dinner; a treat while we were waiting for Daddy to come and get us.

Sometimes I missed the bus after school, because I forgot to catch it. Daddy had to come into town to get us on his motorbike. We got into trouble, but I liked to ride on his motorbike.

Chapter 20

Grandma And Trips To Rosemont

Grandma was my second mother, and she was the person I looked up to in our house. To me, she was my security, and I knew she would never leave my sister and me. She could be kind, loving and comforting, but other times she was mean and short-tempered. In my eyes, she was a strong person in control of every situation, and when she told us to behave, we did. She was scary, but not as scary as Daddy. Our grandma was a strange woman, and had an uncanny knowing about her. She could tell you things before they'd happen, and sometimes our cousins and us thought she was a witch, she was so old. She had always looked as if she was over 90 years old.

In spite of all this, there was a vulnerable side to her as well. She only showed that at night time. How I knew was because I'd heard her crying in her bed.

I asked, 'What's wrong, Grandma?'

She said, 'It's nothing. Go to sleep,' but she had told my sister and me that she cried because she missed Grandfather, who she really loved, and her son, Donny.

We knew who Grandfather was; the man in the wedding photo, down the back in the scary bedroom. Her oldest son, Donny, born in 1918, died at seventeen, and his large portrait sat on a stand in the other scary room down the back. Grandma never got over their deaths. She told us good stories about how kind our grandfather was, and how everyone in town loved him. She said he never swore, and he only said one bad thing: 'Darn my think.' Darn was his worst swearing word. But my Daddy swears a lot all the time, I thought. Grandma was the one that kept us stable, and I am grateful we had her in our lives, because she cared for us, and taught us ethics and values. If we'd only had our parents, I hate to think how we would have grown up. Maybe I'd have been a delinquent.

'Grandma, how old are you?' I'd ask her as I sat with her, while she brushed Maxine's hair.

'I'm as old as my tongue, and a bit older than my teeth.'

'Grandma, that's funny.'

Sometimes, we'd go to those two scary rooms with Grandma, but none of us would go past Daddy's room alone, through the archway that separated the family living room and the big, wide hallway that kept those two rooms apart. In the formal lounge room, there were lots of old things. My favourite table was a small one that held Uncle Donny's scrolls of honours from school, and all his trophies he'd won in his short life. Grandma told us he was an all-rounder and excelled in whatever he did. She told us he was supposed to go to the 1936 Olympics, but he died that year.

'He was too wonderful a person,' she'd say, in her sad and yearning voice. 'His life was snapped from under him. Only the good die young.' She really missed them both so much.

There were photos of people in very old-fashioned clothes. There were also lots of photos of Grandma when she was a young girl. I'd look at the photos, and look at Grandma, and wonder how she got to be so old, because she was so beautiful when she was young. There were so many things sitting on that long cupboard: photos, trophies, plates, medallions, silver wine goblets, and lots of silver pieces and ivory pieces. Many other things caught my interest, and I would stand and look at all the pieces and wonder where they came from and wonder about the old people in the photos: her parents, sisters, brothers, aunts and uncles. Some of the men had on uniforms, and the women were in gowns, not clothes like ours. The old frames that hung on the wall behind the cabinet were beautifully made out of carved wood.

When I was in these rooms, I felt like someone was watching me, and sometimes I felt a chill hit me. If Grandma went out of the room and into the bedroom across the hallway, or vice versa, and I didn't see her go, suddenly I'd freeze and call out to her in a soft, fearful voice, 'Grandma.'

'I am in the other room,' I'd hear. My eyes would scan the room, and gradually I could release the fear and go to her, watching behind me as I left the room. I'd scurry across the hallway, mucking up the long carpet runner as I ran into whichever room she'd gone into, and I'd look to see if anyone had followed me. Then I would cuddle into her as she looked at her papers. I was so frightened of those rooms, but Grandma never seemed to be.

In the bedroom hung Grandma's and Grandfather's wedding photo. Grandma told us she was only twenty-one when she got married. To me, that seemed old. She looked so different; I couldn't recognize her from the photo, and I'd frown and wonder how they could be the same person. I'd look at their picture only if Grandma was close by me, because I was sure Grandfather was moving his eyes in the picture and following me. It was only this photo that scared me; his eyes definitely followed me. The photos of other family members, in the formal lounge room never scared me.

My grandfather was a tall, handsome, stern man, with a very straight back that carried a slim body over a massive frame of six foot four inches. He possessed sharp eyes that pierced you. They had a cloud of darkness surrounding them. It wasn't the skin on his face. It was a darkness emanating from his eyes. His eyes told me he knew all things about us, and nothing we did would ever escape him. No man would be able to outwit him, and he carried the knowledge of light and dark, good and evil, wisdom and control; he knew how to control others, and maybe he was cruel with his strong, forceful mind, determined to accomplish its task. Both him and Donny possessed determination, and I was sure that if they were alive, they'd both accomplish whatever they set themselves to do. Grandfather was the dark one, while Uncle Donny was definitely light.

Donny looked like a silent, gentle, handsome man, the image of his father, and the only one to resemble his father. Donny possessed a softer soul, almost angelic, and his eyes never scared me. They seemed to be pondering on another world beyond ours. Donny had brown hair like his father, and his fair complexion was radiating; he seemed to be radiating a light from within. A highly intelligent boy, and an all-rounder in the sports arena, he had a loving heart and wise eyes for a young man, old before his time. He was unlike his other siblings: my father, Uncle Mitch and Aunty Connie. They were handsome, but possessed rounded, squat faces with broader facial features, and they had black hair, they looked more like Grandma's side.

I wondered about my grandfather and Uncle Donny, and where their intelligence and good attitudes came from, because my father was a dreamer: lazy, and reliant on the women in his life. Uncle Mitch was a wild boy, irresponsible, took from my grandma, and lived his life how he wanted. He didn't care about his family, as long as he got what he wanted. With her diabetes, my Aunty Connie seemed to be sickly. She was a strong career woman who looked well groomed, but weakened around Grandma.

While my mother was away, Grandma dressed us immaculately, and in a way, I didn't always miss my mother. We went to many places, visiting Grandma's relatives in Rosemont, or her friends in Dawson Hill. Most weekends, we'd be off to Rosemont to visit Aunty Connie. I called her Aunty Cod-gee. I don't know why; it seemed sweet to me. Dad would take us down to Jupiter's Corner in Rosemont on Friday after school, but I can't remember him ever staying with us. It was only us girls and Grandma at Aunty Beatrice's house, where Aunty Connie lived, since she left Grandma's house when she turned sixteen to work in Rosemont. Grandma told us Aunty Connie was not lucky herself, but she was lucky for other people, because lottery tickets she'd bought for her friends won the lottery; but to me, my Aunty Connie seemed beyond human. My sister and I and our cousins all loved and admired her.

As children, while my mother was away, we were given many gifts from our Aunty Connie, gifts that our cousins never knew about. I remember getting a beautiful porcelain eskimo doll from Canada, and Aunty bought me my two other favourite dolls, Tootie and Lindy Lou, but I loved Tootie the most. This doll was so dear to me.

Jupiter's Corner was one of Rosemont's better suburbs on the beautiful shores of the bay around it. I really loved going there, and I wished I could live in Rosemont with my Aunty Connie. She was the most beautiful, well-groomed, perfectly dressed woman who knew how to hold herself, and she always wore red lipstick that enhanced her looks. She often changed her clothes throughout the day, and she wore classic lines. Her brunette hair fell long onto her shoulders and never looked out of place, even when she got out of bed in the morning. Aunty had a permanent smile, and she was so cuddly. She treated us like little adults, and she let us get away with more than Grandma ever did. I liked visiting and staying in different people's houses and watching them in their daily lives; their lives were so different to mine. They seemed happy; they laughed, talked and smiled a lot, and cuddled each other. Aunty Beatrice was a character with a strong personality. She would not take any nonsense from Grandma or Aunty Connie, and put everyone in their place. However, she carried a sadness. She was only married for about five years, and her husband left her, never returned to her, and Aunty Beatrice never remarried.

Actually, come to think of it, Grandma was very quiet around Aunty Beatrice. While in this house, the women seemed to be happy and busy in the morning, cooking and talking. Maxine and I were allowed to go for a walk, and this was when the adults had their serious conversations. Sometimes we got back when they were still talking adult talk, and I could listen in, depending on the topic being discussed. I loved to listen to the women talk. We always had afternoon tea, and Aunty Fannie would join us. She was Aunty Beatrice's mother, and lived across the road from Aunty Beatrice. Aunty Fannie was Grandma's sister. Aunty Connie would dash off to her room to re-dress for the occasion, putting on her lipstick and perfume again.

My mum's sister, Aunty Betty, intrigued me with her wild life. She was my second favourite aunt. However, Connie would set the table to perfection, everything neat, precise and in order. All the good china was used, and there were these paper doilies I liked so much. The food was yummy, and tasted better than Grandma's, but I couldn't tell her that. I loved to eat. It was happy times in Rosemont. My sister and I were happier, and we didn't fight. We both wanted to be near Aunty Connie because she knew how to cuddle us, and we often leaned into her side as she drank her tea and talked to the other ladies. She was plain, but somehow she was beautiful, as well as plain. Her voice rang with confidence, and she was a woman of the world, a world I wanted to explore one day.

Aunty Fannie would join us, and when she came in, we'd give her a kiss and cuddle. She was short, fat and cuddly, different to Grandma, who was tall, lean and bony. After they'd all sat and chatted about how great the food looked, and poured their tea and passed the sugar and milk, and all the formal rituals were over, then the topics of the day would begin. They talked about my great Uncle Mitchell, Grandma's and Aunty Fannie's brother. He lived in Aunty Fannie's house. Aunty Fannie's house was not like Aunty Beatrice's house; her house was dark and old, and seemed lost in the eighteenth century. Aunty Beatrice's house was happy, bright and pretty, and it had an upstairs. I felt good there. It was clean and fresh and safe. I loved Aunty Fannie too. She gave us good messages and taught us religion and other interesting things which I had no concept of. Grandma only told us stories about Jesus and his good deeds, but Aunty Fannie introduced us to other ways of thinking and she gave us hymn books and prayer books. We were never given much religious upbringing until primary school, and we didn't attend church with our family, so my understanding of these books didn't go any further than having them in my possession. Nevertheless, I liked to read them, and I was drawn to the *23rd Psalm*, 'The Lord is my Shepherd I shall not want.'

Aunty Beatrice's house was a beautiful terrace house with three levels, and I loved their lifestyle, and the cosiness of this house. At the very top level, where we stayed on our visits, we had a view of the beautiful Rosemont bay. Sometimes, our cousin Patrick was home. He was Aunty Beatrice's youngest son: so tall, handsome and endearing. I couldn't stop smiling and staring at him when he was around, because of his soft and gentle nature. He was my mother's age. Sometimes he and his brother Albert used to come and visit us on the farm, but he and Albert never spoke to us girls, and we were too shy to talk to them.

All my girl cousins idolised Patrick. Normally men scared me and I couldn't understand them, and because I feared strange men, I kept my distance from them, but Patrick was different. You could tell he was a good person. Being shy, I'd missed out having a closeness to my boy cousins. They were in their teens when I was young, so they didn't even notice us younger cousins.

Patrick and Albert came to visit us when Mum was still at home. The four of them, Mum, Dad, Patrick and Albert, would go swimming in the lagoon. Dad was a torment. He'd chase Mum, and she'd scream at him not to torment her. All four of them fooled around, laughing and diving in the water off the jetty. All were very strong swimmers. Watching them, my parents looked like they were free children, and never had any responiblities, and in a way, they didn't, because Grandma cared for us children. My sister, brother and I couldn't go in the lagoon, as it had a dangerous undertow and it was full of reeds. It was too deep, even at the edge, and we were told the reeds could grab hold of our legs and drag us to the bottom of the lagoon, which Dad said had no bottom. My imagination was so vivid, and the vision of being dragged into the dark depths of the water was too much for me to bear. This fear was in any water, even at the beach. I was afraid to go out too far, and in the creek I couldn't be in the water by myself. I had to make sure my brother or sister were with me. Grandma would take us to the Dawson

Hill beach to heal our cuts or sores. She said the salt water was a good cleanser, but I feared monsters in the sea. They were out there, ready to grab my legs and take me away forever. Little did I know then, my fear was that I'd be dragged into the depths of my emotions, but that was to come.

Chapter 21

Death

The ladies were all talking about Uncle Mitchell. It wouldn't be long before the inevitable, I overheard. I couldn't grasp this inevitable. Aunty Fannie thought we girls should pay a visit to Uncle Mitchell, because he may not be there next time we came to Rosemont. The ladies talked about it. Aunty Connie thought we shouldn't go to see Uncle Mitchell. This caused Aunty Beatrice to jump on her.

Aunty Beatrice was so strong-minded, and she shot back at Connie, 'Come on, Connie, grow up. This is life.'

Timidly, Connie responded, 'Yes, but these girls have gone through enough with their mother leaving them.'

The real truth was that Aunty Connie had to face her own reckonings with death, because she was a chronic diabetic, so to see Uncle Mitchell may have caused her to worry over her own mortality; or it could have brought back her own memories of the loss of her beloved father and brother Donny, because she was only a child when they died.

Grandma was upset with Aunty Connie for bringing up Carol. The two ladies bantered over that.

Finally, Aunty Connie said, 'But she is their mother.' As she said this, she looked at me.

I looked at her in admiration, as she pushed my hair back from my face. I loved my Aunty Connie, however I really didn't care what they did, or if my mother returned or not.

Grandma piped up, 'She might be their mother, but she won't come back. Even if he finds her. I tell Max this.' Coldly, she narrowed her eyes and folded her arms across her chest, as if to protect herself.

There was some silence, before Beatrice broke it. 'How do you know that?'

'She won't come back, I tell you. She'll stay with that man she's with,' Grandma said, bringing up her unkind side.

Aunty Connie changed the subject to cut off the bitterness and resentfulness. Aunty Connie actually liked my mother, but Grandma was her mother, and I could see she was trying to both please her and give my mother a small chance, because Aunty Connie got tired of her mother's hatred and unkind attitude towards Carol.

Aunty Connie had been the one to convince Grandma to sign my parents' marriage consent form. She broke the tension by announcing, 'Okay, girls, who wants to go to Jasper Park next time you come to Rosemont.'

Maxine and I jumped for joy, leaping into Aunty Connie's lap, 'Yes, yes. Me, me.' We were so excited, and couldn't stop jumping for joy, singing, 'Yes, yes, we do,' cuddling Aunty Connie. She knew how to love children. I guess we were the closest to Aunty Connie having children, because she never had her own children. Fate can deal different members of a family different situations. My older cousin, Charlene, after losing a baby, decided to never have children. They carried the family pattern of women choosing to be childless. Grandfather Kinread's two sisters remained childless spinsters.

It was decided the next day that we'd be taken over to Aunty Fannie's to farewell Uncle Mitchell. Aunty Fannie's house was a big, dark house, with heavy furniture and drapes that blocked all light from coming in. I don't know why, but her house was always locked up. We were ushered into the kitchen by Aunty Connie. Uncle Charlie, Aunty Fannie's husband, was sitting at the table mending his shoes, like Daddy mended our shoes. I liked Uncle Charlie; he was a very kind man. I smiled at him as he looked at us over his glasses, politely greeting us with a smile and asking us how we were. Shyly we said, 'Good.' Even though he was sitting at the table, Uncle Charlie was a big man. He was Swedish, Grandma told us, and he had an accent that sounded nice.

Aunty Fannie was at the kitchen sink doing some dishes. She stopped, and the two aunties talked about us going in to see Uncle Mitchell. I watched Uncle Charlie mending his shoes. He looked up at us. He was a quiet man who never said much. I knew he liked us, by the way he smiled at us. Aunty Fannie was the opposite to him. She talked so much, she made up for what he lacked.

Suddenly, Aunty Connie gripped our hands. 'Come now with me,' and we went with her, skipping past Uncle Charlie into the hallway.

We were taken to the door of Uncle Mitchell's room, where we were told to wait and be quiet.

Aunty Fannie came up the hallway, and went into the room. I had no idea what this was all about. Aunty

Connie was telling us we were going to say goodbye to someone I didn't know. Uncle Mitchell was Aunty Fannie's and Grandma's brother. He suddenly got ill, and he came to live with Auntie Fannie. She wanted him to die in a house, and not in the hospital. My sister and I got restless, and started to play a little, ending up in a push game. It was done in fun, because we were always happy around Aunty Connie. My sister and I were never jealous of each other around our Aunty Connie. I think that was because she treated us equally. Nonetheless, I was jealous of my cousins getting any affection from my Aunty Connie. I was possessive of her, because she came to our house and never to their house, so she was ours, not theirs. My cousins were always asking her too many questions. Sometimes they'd ask her to come and stay at their house. She would politely tell them she had to go to Grandma's house. I was glad.

Maxine and I got more restless.

Aunty Connie peeked her head around the door. 'Shh, shh, girls.'

We giggled, wondering what it was all about. We stopped and shrugged our shoulders at each other, and made that a game.

Then Aunty Fannie came to the door. 'Alright, girls, come in.'

We walked in next to Aunty Fannie, and Aunty Connie took our hands. The room was a big, big room, and dark, with a small light on a table. Aunty led us to the big poster bed, and our smiles stopped. In the bed was a man in striped pyjamas. His face was distorted, his mouth open. It looked ugly. He was sitting propped up in the bed. I heard him making a rattle noise. I couldn't understand why he looked like he did. The rattle got louder. It started to scare me, so I stepped back around Aunty's body, and I held her hand tightly. When I looked up at my Aunty Connie, she was crying. We stood there just looking at him. As the moments went by, Aunty put us on a long lounge in this room.

I just watched, not fully understanding what I was seeing, but as I sat there, I got used to his noises. We'd not been told what was going on, or what to expect, before entering the room. Later on, when Aunty Fannie sat with us, she explained in a whisper, 'Girls, Uncle Mitchell is dying.' As I looked at the two women, I could see they were very sad, but I couldn't feel sad. Death was new to me, and whatever death was, I felt no fears around it. I knew people didn't die; they went and came back in another body.

This was to be my first encounter with seeing death. I knew the pain associated with death, because of my Grandma. She was forever sad after her husband and son died. Death wouldn't knock on my door as an adult with children, but it would visit my sister, who I was sure was being prepared for death, because Maxine would be Grandma's constant companion at future funerals. I went once or twice. For me, it was funny, and deep down, I'd laugh and couldn't cry. It made me wonder what they were so sad for; the dead were going to come back in another body.

Chapter 22

Jasper Park

Aunty Connie had promised to take us to Jasper Park in Rosemont on our next visit - and she did. She was a wonderful aunty, who always kept her promise to us. At the park, we had such fun. I remember going on these moving floors; they were circles that turned, causing the floor to move up and down and around. We were in fits of laughter. Aunty Connie knew how to give us a great time.

My biggest fascination in Rosemont was going to the toilet. We had to put a penny in the door to open it. There was nothing like that in our small town of Hastings Crossing. Aunty Connie was so kind. I'd told her last time we were at her house about my dolly Tootie's eyes. She had one closed eye, and one open eye. I told her Grandma couldn't fix it, so Aunty told me to bring her with me next time. It was so exciting, because Aunty took us to the doll hospital. I was so amazed at all the sick dollies. A really kind man fixed my dolly's eye. I was so happy Tootie could see properly again.

Aunty Connie gave us lots of presents to take home after our visits with her, and sometimes she gave us books. I liked the books she gave me, even though I couldn't read properly. I'd just browse through them, reading sections of the book I could read. My favourite books were about a group of children who travelled: *The Five Go Caravaning*. They were always travelling off on some adventure. I wished I could go with them.

Not only did we go to Rosemont, sometimes we went to Dawson Hill to visit Mrs Clements. Mrs Clements was Grandma's best friend; she was a quiet lady, who was very close to Grandma. My sister and I were the most disciplined and loveliest of children, who could be taken anywhere. We never caused any bother. We were children to be seen and not heard. I don't ever remember protesting or being naughty about having to go away to someone's house over the weekends. Actually, I loved going away.

Grandma was always fussing with our hair. She loved to put our hair in old rags overnight to make ringlets the next day. She and Mrs Clements would each brush our hair and style it. The two ladies would talk and reminisce about their younger days when they were girls. I liked to listen to their stories of their childhood. It was hard to think of my grandma as a child; she always looked so old, although in the formal loungeroom there were lots of photos of a very pretty young Grandma. How could someone so pretty be so old?

Mrs Clements told us Grandma's sisters adored her and were always dressing her up. She said to Grandma, 'Remember how they were always doing your hair up,' as if it was yesterday.

Grandma smiled as she remembered those days, and she said, 'Yes, I loved those days.'

By the sound of it, the two ladies had a happy childhood. We gave both ladies a lot of pleasure as they curled our hair; I guess it was bringing back memories for them. At home, Grandma was very rough when she brushed our hair, and sometimes she'd hurt me; but here at Mrs Clement's house, Grandma seemed more relaxed and kinder, as if all her meanness melted away.

We weren't always good; we had some bad habits that caused Grandma to be really upset with us. My Aunty Connie knitted me a jumper, and when I put it on, the jumper was too small for me. I don't think Aunty realised that I was growing very quickly. Grandma insisted I should wear it. When she tried to put that jumper on me, it was so tight that I couldn't stand it, because I lost the sleeve of my blouse in the jumper. I screamed in a temper tantrum. It was really a bad fit of temper, and I received a clip over the ear for my drama. I hated poorly-fitting clothes, and I always seemed to get clothes that were too small for me. No one realized I was growing and maturing quickly, so they weren't allowing for my growth spurts. I had to feel free in clothes, not restricted like a tightly-fitted cocoon.

I had my secrets. No one knew I was smoking, but smoking relaxed me. This seemed to ease my stress. I could always hear Grandma's heavy, trudging steps, and I'd disguise the smoking by putting more fuel on the fire. She didn't mind us building up the fire or stoking it with the poker to separate the coals.

Chapter 23

I Wanted To Understand Life, Its Workings, And This Family

As a child, I was always trying to work out how the world worked. If I couldn't understand something, there was Grandma. She was the only one I could ask questions off. She didn't have all the answers, but she told me certain things. Many times the answers I got weren't what I wanted to hear.

If I found dead frogs, I'd pick them up and bury them. I don't know why. I really didn't understand why I had this urge to bury the dead. I'd make them a wooden cross before I started their funeral. I'd dig a deep hole, place the frog in it, then place dirt over it in the shape of a mound. The cross was put on the top of the mound. After this, I'd kneel and pray over the frog. It wasn't just frogs I'd bury. If I found other dead things, they got buried too. The dead interested me as well as the living, because I could see things grew and things died.

Coming home from school, I found some corn on the road as we crossed it. Grandma said it probably fell off the back of a truck. She told me it could be grown really easily. I cleared a patch of grass away to reveal the dirt, then planted the corn. Each day I'd check the garden bed for a sign of growth, and watered it. I loved to run out each morning to see if it had shot through the soil. It had only taken seven days. I was surprised how quickly it grew. Grandma was right. In no time it was growing beautifully. I loved to watch this plant grow, and I'd sit by the garden bed for ages and marvel at its shoots of beautiful green colour. It was getting taller and taller. Sadly, one morning when I ran out to the garden, the shoots were gone. I was so sad, because I wanted to see it bear fruit. When I asked Grandma what had happened, she explained to me that when the cows see any green shoots, they can't be stopped. They'll do anything to get to them.

Our fence around the house had fallen down, so I understood. I knew the cows were determined beasts, and you couldn't keep them out of our yard. I accepted this, and decided not to plant any more corn.

I loved nature. She helped me to stay connected to the earth, pulling me out of my daydreaming world. Admiring her, I stayed awake. Death, to me, was part of the process of nature. I knew nothing stayed forever, and things came and went. All died eventually, so I accepted death. It seemed the natural course of things.

I'd already seen lots of death with the the cows, frogs, rabbits and chickens, and plants got eaten. It was all part of my life here on the farm. I remember when I was four, Dad killing the chickens and hanging them upside down to drain their blood. When I was seven, Dad used to go rabbitting at night with his friends.

Sometimes he'd take me along, and I saw men shoot the rabbits. It was amazing how the rabbits were stopped in their tracks by the car lights or strong torches. They seemed to let the shooters shoot them. After they'd stopped shooting, I'd follow Dad as he collected the dead rabbits. After that, he'd check his rabbit traps that he'd set the previous night.

I had mixed feelings sometimes about them being trapped, because they couldn't escape their captors. Shooting them didn't worry me. Some of the rabbits looked really pretty and I wanted to pat them, but when I did, they'd kick and scratch me. After collecting the trapped ones, Dad killed them and cleaned them. I liked to watch Dad clean them. He peeled their skin back and opened them up. I was so interested to see inside them, and I wanted to study their insides, but Dad told me to get back. Some had a watery bag inside them, and Dad told me when you saw this, you never ate that rabbit. He told me it had myxomatosis, and if we ate that rabbit, we'd get sick too.

My sister couldn't deal with death, so she never came on these trips with us. If I buried dead things, she was never there, but Grandma was preparing her in another way for death, by taking her to funerals.

Farm life was good. I could explore my world on the farm. There was a lot to do. We never worked as children, but we were free to roam. Many times we'd just walk our paddocks and the surrounding paddocks. I found mushrooms and an array of flowers that grew wild, dandelions and little purple flowers that I didn't know the name of. We found yams; they were great to find, because we ate them. They had a fruity, sweet taste. Grandma told us that the Aboriginal people used to eat them, and one year, when the lagoon was very low, they found a lot of Aboriginal artefacts in the mud. This really intrigued me, and I wished the lagoon would show me these things.

Nature loved me too; I could tell. It showed me its beauty, and I loved it in return. Life outside nature, like people, never understood me. I was regarded as a slow, unintelligent dreamer, and was constantly reminded how bright Maxine was. They told me she was as bright as a button, and she could run rings around me. I didn't have much to say to my elders, especially Grandma, who had formed her point of view of me. Sadly, the adults in my family didn't realise that I was a very smart child, who was in tune with nature. Their rigid belief couldn't be changed, and Grandma seemed to be always analysing me. Once I was quick and happy, like my sister; how could they compare us? They didn't know what I knew. I was precious. Daddy told me that, so why was something so precious, so dumb and slow?

Grandma would laugh as she said, 'Christine has the looks, and Maxine has the brains.' I didn't understand their way of thinking, because they were laughing as they said this. It made me feel embarrassed, as well as ashamed. I'd bow my head, because something pretty and precious was stupid and dumb. I felt a lot of guilt for not being perfect, or not being what they defined as perfect. It could be so confusing. In Daddy's eyes, I was beautiful - in his room - but he pushed me aside around my sister.

I didn't have my sister's gift when I was little, and she didn't understand nature. Nature never interested

145

her. Drawing was one of my favourite things to do. I'd draw pictures of people from around the world: Chinese, cowboys, Indians. I'd draw animals: lions, dogs, cats, elephants' heads or horses' heads. They didn't turn out real-looking, but this was my gift. My favourite thing to do was to create beautiful, long gowns for balls; I drew dresses with bell skirts or mermaid skirts with low-cut tops. I must have seen these types of dresses in Grandma's magazines. I don't remember; who knows where my dress ideas came from? No one asked about them. As far as I know, I was drawing from my own mind. We had no books to copy from, and there was no TV at that time. These gifts in me were never nurtured or encouraged, so I was left to draw, not understanding my gifts. Anyway, I was stupid, and couldn't read or add up like Maxine.

Even though I wasn't good at school, it didn't stop me liking school, because there, at least, I was learning many things. I loved storytelling time at school; it was my most favourite time. Listening to the stories, I would place my elbows on the table, cupping my chin. I'd stare at the teacher as he read to us. *Aesop's Fables* gave me much needed strength. I loved the good values and ethics of the characters. The story of the crow, using his determination to get to the water at the bottom of the pitcher in the desert, by patiently placing one stone at a time into the pitcher until the water rose up to the top so he could drink. I could never forget that story. I was so amazed at the crow's determination to get that drink of water. I loved the song about the little train - 'I think I can do it, yes I can' - and its determination to pull its heavy load up over the hill. The mother chicken and her determination to plant food to care for chicks. She'd plant and tend her crop to have food on her plate. I liked how the chicken was able to see the laziness of other chickens, and she told them so. I should have really listened more carefully to that story, to apply it in my own life.

Maxine was an unpleasant child to me when she was little. I felt she delighted in seeing me defeated, so she could sneer at me. Her face seemed to show me this. Many times she'd be walking around the house with her lips pursed. Maxine would provoke me by tormenting me. My problem was that I'd get so angry and start screaming. We'd done this forever, and we were still fighting the same way, forgetting Dad was home. He'd be just as angry as us. I don't think Dad could stand to hear our squabbling.

As we got older, we'd help each other, telling him there was no problem. We learned to profess our own innocence. Sometimes we'd freeze, and other times we'd run for cover. If Dad was really angry, he'd belt us. His temper was short. Many times I'd run, and keep running round and round the house, until he became tired and gave up. Then I'd wait outside until he cooled down, before I'd venture back into the house. By then, he was calm.

Most of the time, I got the blame for it. Being a shift worker made his and our lives difficult, and he'd throw it onto us.

'Can't a man get any sleep in this place?'

I felt bad for him, a bit ashamed, and guilty that I woke him. I just wished Maxine and I could get on. Many times I wondered why we couldn't be friends, when there were only the two of us.

Maxine was Grandma's favourite, and she'd go everywhere with her. Maxine had a lot of talent for sewing. I think Grandma liked that, and it cemented their relationship, because Grandma had been a seamstress when she was a young girl. Maxine could sew and knit, but not me; I couldn't stand knitting or sewing, and my work seemed to turn out terrible. Grandma would remind me how impatient and stubborn I was. Frustration at not being able to do things they liked made me scream, causing me to rip or pull the thing to pieces in my temper tantrum. Grandma would be really angry with me, stating how I was a lazy, self-centered little girl. Little did she know, these activities bored me. I hated Grandma telling me all the time that I was lazy and stubborn.

I'd tell her, 'I don't like you calling me names.'

That set her off on a patronising song. 'Sticks and stones may break my bones, but names will never hurt me.'

I looked at her, not understanding what she meant. 'What do you mean?' I asked.

'Christine, people in this world aren't always nice. You have to get used to the different people. You will meet some people who will like you, and others who won't.' She stopped what she was working on, and raised her eyes over her glasses as she glared at me.

I lowered my head to avoid her glare.

'And you will be called names by people, but if you can remember to say this little song, you won't get as hurt.'

I frowned, because words did hurt me. I was so sensitive to other people's words, and all I wanted was to be liked by people. I couldn't understand why people couldn't be nice like me. I was always nice to people. Unkind words hurt me; being hit by Dad hurt me for the moment, but the words stuck. I'd always remember the words said to me; somehow words were stronger than a hit.

Dad wanted me to ride our horse, Bonnie. I loved the horses on our farm - Bonnie, Dynamite and Star - but I was afraid to ride them. Dad didn't understand my fear, and he insisted I tried to ride Bonnie. I was terrified of the vibration, bumping up and down, and the horse moving under me. I tensed as Dad put me on Bonnie. She was our quietest horse. Bonnie knew I was fearful. She turned to look at me. I sat on her, unable to relax, whinging to Dad that I didn't want to ride her. He insisted. I'd never been on the horse before. Dad let Bonnie go. I had the reins. I sat there trying to listen to what Dad was telling me to do. My ears closed down, and I fell into deafness. This happened because I was fearful. I couldn't hear him. He patted Bonnie. The ground seemed a long way down to me. Bonnie waited patiently for us. Her chestnut coat was very shaggy, and her girth was wide. I seemed to be rocking side to side on her big, fat belly. She was really old: nineteen.

Dad moved the horse by tapping her bottom. She seemed to be like a jelly on a plate, wobbling all over the place. I couldn't handle her movement and the ground moving. I screamed. Bonnie was startled. She started to run, her mane flowing. I hit the ground crying. The fear had got to me, but what hurt the most was Dad's disappointment in me. He grabbed the horse, calming her down by patting her. She was upset; I could see it in her eyes. They were bulging with fear. She baulked with Dad. He hushed her and got her settled. Meanwhile, I'd stood up, waiting with my head hanging, brushing my sore bottom. There was one good thing to come out of it. Dad never tried to put me on a horse again. Thank goodness for that.

I could listen to stories for hours. I loved stories. Many times as Grandma brushed my hair, she'd stroke my head. 'You've got two crowns, and you'll live in two countries,' she informed me.

My eyes would shine. Eagerly, I replied, 'Really, Grandma? Can you tell me stories about other countries?'

'Your grandfather came from the Isle of Man, which lies between England and Ireland, and his two sisters still live there. His brother, Max, whom I named your Daddy after, was a writer, but he died also.'

I knew what she meant, because her beloved husband, Don, had died. I was all ears, begging her to tell me more. I asked, 'What type of houses did they live in?'

'The two sisters lived together because they never married. Their house was a mansion.'

I was enthralled by the thought of these relatives still living overseas. Both Grandma and Aunty Connie wrote to these sisters. Not only did Grandma have Grandfather's sisters overseas, she also had her sister, Emma, living in Canada. Emma had married a Canadian called Jeffery. When Grandma spoke of Emma, she was sad. I felt she missed her. They were the closest, because Emma was the second youngest and Grandma was the baby of her family. They constantly wrote letters to each other, and I loved to collect the stamps. Grandma wanted to take Maxine and I to Canada while Mother was away, but Dad wouldn't let us go. He wanted us here in case Mother came back.

I was so disappointed. I really wanted to go travelling to see other countries. Poor Grandma was upset because she missed Emma, and she knew in heart if we didn't go then and there, she'd never go. I guess she realised she'd missed her chance of ever seeing Emma again. I felt sorry for her, as well as myself. I'd have loved to have spent six weeks on a boat travelling to Canada. Grandma wouldn't fly there. She'd not long lost Mitchell, her brother, and Emma was getting on in age too. This refusal by Dad, giving preference to our mother, only gave Grandma more reasons to hate Mother. She wasn't secretive with her feelings about our mother, and she told us she hated Mother. Our grandma never retracted her words; once they were said, they stayed said.

Over time, I got a small snippets of family history from Grandma. She told me a story of a rich family member whose daughter fell in love with a poor gardener, much to the family's horror.

'Why, Grandma?' I asked innocently.

'Because he was poor, and she ran away with him, never to return home,' she stressed.

'What were they angry for, if they liked each other?'

With an angry face, Grandma blurted out, 'Because her family was rich, and he was poor.'

This puzzled me. 'If they loved each other, why shouldn't they be together?' I was fascinated by other people's stories and their adventures. She had told me enough on that, and it was dropped.

Grandma told me that when Grandfather was alive, he had very influencial people come and stay at our farm. These were political people. They came because the house Grandma was living in wasn't her house.

When Grandfather died mysteriously, she was given the house to live in until she died.

The house was owned by Michael Davies, the owner of Lachlan Mine. He and his guests stayed in rooms beyond the two bottom rooms. In our house's early days, there had been additional rooms on the outside of the house. You got to those rooms through the archway and that hall to two big doors that open out onto the verandah. However, these doors had never been opened all the time I lived there. When you got onto the verandah, there were steps that led you to a path through the fence, that had a side gate to those rooms. Grandma told me the house was much bigger in those days. At the archway, there had been big cedar doors to separate the two bottom rooms the guests and Michael Davies used.

She told me that where the pear trees were, there had been servants' quarters and, yes, there were stone slabs there that must have been the floor of the servants' quarters. They lived there, and their houses sat on top of the slope that overlooked the lagoon.

I was so excited. 'Huh! Really, Grandma.'

She had servants to help her with the guests, and Grandfather had men working for him on the farm. Back then, it was big business, coal mining. When Grandma told me these stories, I was in awe of our house. This made me want to know more about my grandfather. When Grandfather died, she'd told Henry Davies, the brother of Michael Davies, who had also died, that she didn't want to have servants anymore. My curious mind was thristy for history about our family, and I asked her why she got rid of the servants. She explained too many of her things went missing.

Without Grandfather, she had no control over the help, so the servants were dismissed.

Grandma was happy telling me her stories about the house and about Grandfather. He'd been a very important man in the district. She told me that when Michael Davies was alive, he admired my grandfather greatly. As she told me her stories, I felt as if she was being transported back to those days. She loved to reminisce, and I loved to listen.

The house was built in the 1800's, and it had workers a long time ago, who were convicts. Well before Grandfather's days, these prisoners had to go through a trapdoor on the verandah near the hallway's back door. This was where the prisoners went at the end of their day's work. She told me the prisoners had to stay there until they repented.

There was a trapdoor, because we children would climb down through the trapdoor and go under the house. It was so scary down there under the verandah, and we'd never go alone. I felt eyes watching us under there. It made me wonder if anyone had died there. Were they the ones I felt in those two bottom rooms? It all intrigued me. Grandfather had hired help, not prisoners.

I questioned her on the family history as much as I could. Sometimes I had too many questions, so I'd ask her about her childhood, and the stories remained the same stories.

'Grandma, where were you born?' I rocked on her chair.

'In Chider Beach.'

I knew where Chider Beach was. 'What were your parents like, Grandma?'

She told me her father was Scottish, and her mother was Welsh.

My eyes lit up.

'And your great-grandfather, my father, was a merchant seaman. He travelled to many countries, and we lived in Chider Beach, where he worked. Your grandfather was from the Isle of Man.'

'Tell me about the Isle of Man,' I'd insist. I was told they were called Manx people, descended from Vikings. 'Vikings!' I squealed.

She told me that they were fierce warriors from the Scandinavian countries, who sailed in longships. I was fascinated, and imagined these ships on the seas. She told me it had been said that the people from the Isle of Man were from the Picts.

'The Picts. Who were they?'

'They were natives of the island.'

'Natives?'

'Yes, like the Australian Aborigines who were here first in Australia.'

I nodded.

'The Pict People were small, dark-skinned people who painted their skin with pictures, and that's why they were called the Picts. Of course, there were fairies and pixies on the island.'

My mouth gaped open. I closed it, and bit my bottom lip. I was enthralled by her stories; I'd look at her in wonder. 'Oh, Grandma, tell me more about the Vikings,' I'd bleat.

'Oh, Christine!' she declared.

'But I must know,' I pleaded, stamping my feet gently to show my eagerness. I was impatient to hear everything she knew.

'They were fierce people from Norway and the other Scandinavian countries, like I told you. They sailed in longboats to many far off lands, conquering those countries. They were great fighters. Your grandfather was a very strong man. Everyone respected him in the town. He was feared, and stood six feet four tall, and he could lift a man sitting on a shovel.'

'Grandma,' I'd gush, bedazzled by her stories, 'oh, Grandma, I wish I could meet Grandfather.'

'So do I,' she'd say, and she'd tell me to go and play, as she was tired of me and my endless questions. Talking too much about Grandfather or Uncle Donny made her sad. Somehow I understood her grief and loss.

Sometimes, Grandma told Maxine and I stories about Jesus, and how he helped the people who were sick, but I loved the parables. My favourite was to build your house on a rock and not the sand. I could relate to that story, because the sand at the creek could change in stormy weather. And God? God was good, but nothing more was said about God. I was never a good reader, so I preferred to listen to real life stories about real people's lives.

Stories told about my mother and her family, they weren't nice stories. There was no pretty picture painted in my mind. Grandma loved to belittle Mum and her family, telling me they were poor and from the wrong side of town. This puzzled me. Where was the wrong side of a town? Grandma Owens and Mum's sisters had bad names in town. I was too young to understand what a bad name meant. These words left a mark on my memory, nonetheless, she'd never say anything bad about Mum or her family around Dad. She knew he'd go off at her.

Grandma hated the Chinese people. I found out why. My mother was descended from a Chinese bloodline. Grandma would tell my sister, our cousins and I, of the Yellow Peril that would one day invade Australia, and take us all over. We had to be careful of those Chinamen; they would come and take our land, she said. My mind was fertile as I envisioned Chinese people everywhere, in hordes, ruling our country, but it wouldn't work because I liked people from other countries. We learnt about people from other countries at school. Mainly people from England. They didn't tell us stories about the Chinese like Grandma did. My dreams showed me that these people were friendly. I'd draw pictures of their costumes that interested me. I learned about the Taj Mahal in India, and I wanted to go and see it. I was so drawn to other countries as a child.

Whatever Grandma said about my mother, it didn't faze my Dad. He still loved her. Well, I didn't know what love was, because he hit my mother and made her cry. I guess that's the way he saw love, to abuse the ones he loved to show them that he loved them. What was love? I didn't understand what that word meant.

Chapter 24

The Lonely Child

Often I felt nervous in the house, causing me to bite my nails, which infuriated Dad. He tried everything to stop me doing it, but I'd still bite them, even with bitter aloes painted on them. No one loved me. I was not loveable. How could I be loved, when I was constantly misled by those who were to teach me how to cope with living in a society. I had no confidence, and I was extremely shy; too much had happened to me.

It was a very hot and sticky day in the house. The air was so thick, it was hard to breathe. It stifled me, I think, because somedays, there was no one to talk to. Maxine was dressing up her dolls, and Grandma was too tired and had to cook.

The silence in the house was deadly, so I decided to go for a walk. Even though our house was big, I felt caged and trapped. I didn't understand why I felt like this. Passing through the kitchen, Grandma was preparing to cook. I didn't say anything to her, just looked and left. Outside, it was even quieter. You could feel the thickness in the air. Stepping off the front verandah, the heat of the day hit me, and as I walked on the cement path to the front gate, the sun glared into my eyes. At the water tank, I was squinting from the glare. Under the orange tree, the dogs were stretched out, panting in the heat. I felt so alone, but not alone - because it felt like that was a normal part of my life, to be with myself.

Crossing the open paddock that stretched between the main house and my favourite big tree, I walked on the sun-baked, yellowed grass. It crackled under my feet. I couldn't go barefoot that day, because of the heat and the joe-joes. They were really bad that year, and they hurt when they stuck in my feet.

I hurried to my beautiful tree. It seemed to be calling and welcoming me to join it in its solitude. It had one long branch that spread out from the main trunk, as if it was trying to escape from the tree. Dad had attached a swing to it. This tree was very old, so old that I guessed it'd seen many events and things that had happened on this farm. I sat on the swing, and the grass was soft and green. It felt cooler under its shade. Grandma told us that fairies lived under this tree. I'd watch the ground to see if I could see them.

From this tree, I could see in all directions. I was watching the top gate down near Sherry's house, and I heard a car. Looking up, the noise was coming from the Spencer Shire direction, down the long, isolated, dirt road. Not many cars came along this road, so when we saw or heard a car, we wondered who it was. Was it a visitor for us? Or was it going elsewhere? And where were they going? My eyes followed it, but it passed by our top gate, disappearing down around the sharp bend that dipped. It gave the impression that the road had swallowed the car. I stood up, putting one knee on the swing to watch it. I smiled. It had reappeared at the mouth of the bend, and was driving as fast as it could past the lagoon to gather enough speed to climb that awesome, steep hill on the road leading to Dawson Hill. It disappeared over the hill. I sat facing the top gate in anticipation of another car coming. None came, so I swang and sang to myself. I was used to the quiet. I don't think I realised how quiet our lives were.

My life was so mixed up. I was either with Dad in the shed when he was home, or on the outer, living in my own world of dreams. Maxine had Grandma, and they were constantly talking and doing things together. My salvation were my pets and nature. Both brought me lots of peace. Dad worked long hours through the week, and on weekends he was looking for Mother - with me.

Days later we were visited by Mr Dodds. He was a friendly man, always laughing. He amused me. We'd all gather to listen to him. Dad allowed us to stay with Mr Dodds, and join in. This man had known us since we were babies. He asked Dad how Maxine and I were doing at school.

Grandma informed him, 'Maxine is our star here. She's as bright as a button. The teachers tell us she'll go far but--'

Dad stepped in and said, 'Our Christine is okay too.' Dad winked at me. He could see I was about to cry, as I lowered myself into my seat. I knew I wasn't good at school, but Dad did the worst, unthinkable thing. He grabbed a newspaper and said, 'Christine, show Mr Dodds how well you can read.'

I froze, turning red with embarrassment as Dad stretched out the newspaper across the table for me to read. Holding the paper, I tried to read it, but couldn't.

Mr Dodds noticed my agony, and said, 'Very good, dear.' He started to talk to Grandma and Dad. I was so humiliated, that I slowly got up off the bench from the kitchen table to go to my room.

Chapter 25

Mother Returns

I had just turned nine. It was in the later part of November. My mother returned. I remember the day Dad brought her and Barton home. Both of them felt like strangers. I honestly didn't know what to say to her. I'd grown bitter towards her since she'd left us, and I was secretly calling her *Her,* and referring to her as 'my mother', instead of Mum. I didn't want to go near her or say hello to them, so I stood next to Grandma, who had her arms around my sister and I. Grandma was just as shocked as us at Mother's return. There was no show of affection from my mother. There never would be.

With them back, there were a lot of adjustments to be made. Mother was back, and Dad seemed to be a lot happier. He still saw me as his princess, but I had to be second or third. Dad had no time for our brother. I felt that he hated him. He constantly told Barton he was stupid or an idiot, slow and a drongo. The words that rolled out of his mouth weren't nice. He'd belt Barton for no reason at all. I watched, wondering what he was hitting him for. Barton would try not to cry, to show his braveness as he was flogged. I'd see his face silent as a mute, unable to express the pain that was being inflicted on him. After he was flogged and Dad had walked off, Barton would smile and say, 'It didn't hurt', but I knew it hurt because I felt it. As he was flogged, I was flogged.

Mother would always jump in to try to protect Barton from Dad. Sometimes she could, and other times she couldn't. Barton was five, going on six, when he returned, and Dad never showed him any fun or niceness as he did with us girls.

As time went on, I got used to Mother in the house and I wanted to talk to her, but I couldn't. If I did, Grandma's eyes threw daggers at me. I had to talk to Mum when Grandma was not around. If she entered the room, my face would go red in embarrassment, or was it guilt for betraying her, talking to Mum who she hated.

I don't know why, but my father wanted us girls to have our hair cut really short. He just said one morning, 'You're getting your hair cut off,' and that was it. No asking us or having a say in it. Dad took my sister and I to the local men's barber. He got the barber to saw through our plaited ponytails with his scissors. We asked that could we keep our plaited ponytails. They were given to us. What upset me the most was that Dad took us to a men's barber. I wondered why we couldn't go to a ladies' hairdresser with Mum.

I don't think I realised how resentful I was of Mum leaving us with Dad and Grandma. I had softened to her, and started to call her Mum. Nonetheless, I felt Mum had no regard for my sister and I and our suffering under Grandma's control, and taking the brunt of Dad's anger. My secret with Dad was creating issues. This became painful, as well as upsetting for me, because I had to watch out for jealousy. There were more deceptions in my life. Many things changed, including our weekend trips. We stopped going to Rosemont to see our lovely Aunty Connie, and to Dawson Hill to Mrs Clement's house. There was another benefit to Mum's return: my father insisted that Maxine would go out with us, because she was always with Grandma.

The only one truly happy was Dad. Other than that, we had to endure tension between the two women. The Christmas of Mum's return in 1960 was very big. Our family was together, and I finally got a part in our Christmas play at school. I'd always wanted to be in a school play, but I was never picked. That Mr Clark, our principal, used to pick his pets for the parts in the school plays. That year, Maxine and I scored parts as fairies. We needed fairy costumes, so Mum took us to her good friend Del's house in Fenton. I had never met this lady before. I instantly liked her. She had a beautiful, beaming smile. She was genuinely happy. She had long, black hair and olive skin. She was a bit plump, with a prominent mole on the side of her face under her mouth.

I stared at her in awe as Mum said, 'Del, these are my girls, Christine and Maxine.'

'Hello, girls.' She beamed at us.

We had to call her Aunty Del. We had been told we were never allowed to call an adult by their first name. This lovely lady made us these truly beautiful fairy dresses. As they were being made, I thought they were too flash for the part, because we were only going to be on stage for a few minutes, but Mum insisted that they be the best outfits for our part.

163

On the day of the school play, we dressed up and went on stage. I was so embarrassed, because we were the only ones who had on beautiful costumes, and the only ones who were on stage for the shortest time. Mum must have thought we looked great, because as I watched her from the stage, she was all smiles as she sat with her friends.

Our Christmas was big. Dad always got a pine tree from the creek, and we'd decorate it. I loved the smell of the pine in the house. It gave the house a fresh, clean smell. It was a lovely time of the year. Christmas is summertime in Australia. Our big house was cool in the heat of the day. It was a double-brick house with a concrete floor, which was unusual in those days. Most of the houses were made with wood.

Christmas time was the only time we used the massive dining room table. There was lots of laughter and happiness, and Aunty Connie was home. Grandma always prepared the Christmas pudding two months before Christmas Day, and hung it on the verandah until the day, when it was re-cooked on Christmas morning. The pudding contained threepences, sixpences and trinkets. Finding them in the pudding was better than getting presents for me. Seeing what I got out of the pudding was a great surprise.

This year was our parents' most generous Christmas. We all got many gifts: a new bike each, jewelry for us girls, and an engraved watch with love from Mum and Dad. A gold signet ring with a pretty design with our initials etched into it, a heart locket, and lots of new clothes. I felt Dad was trying to make up for the lost time we'd missed as a family. Even Barton was given a new bike, and lots of great toys and clothes. Grandma had all the family brought together to the farm to celebrate, and this Christmas, for the first time, our cousins Charlene, Gerry and Hope came out for Christmas lunch with their parents, Aunty Kimberly and Uncle Mitch. Uncle Mitch was Dad's brother. Uncle Mitch didn't seem to have much to do with his three girls.

Grandma told me he was a wild boy in his younger days, and used to get into many fights, which she had to bail him out of from the lock-up. Dad said he was still wild. Uncle Mitch was a Union man. He favoured the Communist Party, Grandma told me, and he still got into fights. In our house, we were with the Labor Party. Uncle Mitch was not very nice to my Aunty Kimberly. He was what the family called a man's man. Aunty Kimberly worked as a sister in the Wentworth Public Hospital; she was a very good worker. My cousins were lucky that their mum was a good person, and a good provider. There were many rumours about my Uncle Mitch being all for himself.

Uncle Donny, who was killed at seventeen, it was speculated Uncle Mitch accidentally shot him. He was considered the black sheep of the family, Uncle Mitch. Our beloved Aunty Connie always came every Christmas. This became a tradition from that Christmas on. Maxine and I became closer to our cousins. We all fought heaps, but somehow, I loved Gerry and Hope; they were my soul sisters. Not Charlene; I couldn't connect to her.

That year, Grandma bought me a cooking set. I was never very good with crafts like Maxine. I guess Grandma was going to teach me something. I baked my first cake; it was flat to look at.

Even so, I will never forget Dad's reaction when Grandma told him, 'Max, Christine baked her first cake today. Are you going to try some?'

Dad stared at me, smiling. 'I will, and I'll eat her cake, even if it kills me. I will die for her.'

I looked at Mum and Grandma. I felt so embarrassed. Tears came to my eyes. He'd die for me! He tried my cake, and I waited for his comment.

'Delicious, my princess.'

I was so happy he liked it and didn't die. However, it was also good he would die for me.

Barton got presents for Christmas and his birthday in January: the latest toys for a boy. Barton was inquisitive, and soon had all his toys pulled apart, including a watch he was given on his birthday. He'd wanted to see how they worked. He'd tried to put them back together, but of course he couldn't, much to Dad's horror. Barton was only trying to bring out his creativity, which I didn't know existed back then. We were creative; Barton and I, but no one saw our talents. Barton and I used to like to play under my favourite tree. We'd roll a forty-four-gallon drum down the slight incline as we laid on it. I was wearing my locket I'd been given at Christmas and lost it in the grass. We both searched for it, but the area was too big. We children lost many things around the farmhouse. Mum lost her wedding ring not long after she was married to Dad. She was near the clothesline watching Dad chop wood. She'd flicked her hand at him playfully, and her ring flew off her finger. They searched for it but could never find it. Even in the future, it would never be found. It must have fallen between the piles of wood in the wood heap and buried itself straight away. My sister would lose her wedding ring while on her honeymoon; it would slip off her finger into a lake.

This was the year Dynamite, our old horse, died. It was Uncle Mitch's horse. No one could ride him other than Uncle Mitch. It was said that Dynamite was like a stick of explosive in his younger days. He played calm until you got on him. He'd look at you, and his wick was lit; he threw his tantrum and threw you. You could walk past Dynamite in the paddock, and no problems. He'd just lift his head as he watched you pass him. Then, when you'd passed him, he'd continue grazing. When he was taken to the shed to be saddled, he was fine until you placed your foot in the stirrup. That was it. He flew into a manic thrust, and no one could calm him, only my Uncle Mitch. When Uncle Mitch left home, the horse had been waiting out his days to die. Dynamite died in his favourite spot just down from the middle gate, alongside the middle fence facing the dirt road leading to Dawson Hill. No one was too sad about his loss. We kids hadn't had much to do with him in our lifetime.

This was the year I started to go to the movies. Mum and Dad dropped me off. I loved the Hollywood movies. Mum and Dad were going out, Maxine was with Grandma, and Barton went to stay with Grandma Owens.

Christine U. Cowin

Chapter 26

Services To The Farm

I really loved the experiences we had on the farm. I got to see the old ways of life, when services such as the baker, butcher, ice man, fruito all came to the house in their trucks, all the way out to our farm, which was eight miles from town, with their fresh produce. And I even got to see the ice man deliver us big blocks of ice for our ice chest in the summer time. We didn't have a fridge until I was older.

In my lifetime things were slower, life didn't seem to move very fast, and it was nothing for these services to come out so far to service their customers. People were so much friendlier, and if I think about it, people were more innocent back then, and took the time to socialise. It was as if each knew their role. Grandma used to cook scones or cakes before they'd arrived. On arrival, she'd have a large pot of tea waiting. These social events seemed to carry on for hours as the adults talked. No one was in a hurry. I hung around to listen to the gossip and the community news.

The butcher was having a nice cup of tea and a chat, and while he was inside, a very funny incident occurred. I was inside, listening to the grownups, although I wasn't always allowed. Mum would join in with Grandma on these occasions, and it was as if Mum had permission to. Both women acted as though there was nothing wrong between them. They were talking and laughing, and it was time for Mr Lent to go about his business. We always walked our guests to their cars or trucks; it was respectful and the nice thing to do. We were taught many of these values by Grandma, and I still use them in my life. We were walking up the path to the front gate and they were still reminiscing as they walked. Mum and I were hanging on every word.

On reaching the front gate, with many farewells between him and Grandma, Mr Lent turned to go to his truck. He stopped in his tracks, gasping, 'Oh! My God, what have those kids done?'

My sister and brother had painted his truck red. Grandma raced over to his truck behind him. I laughed to myself.

Grandma was all apologies to Mr. Lent. My sister and brother got a roasting, followed by a smack on the backside as she told them to get in the house. Mr Lent was speechless. You could see it on his face; the poor man didn't know what to say. Grandma was so embarrassed, because they had been friends forever. Mum just stood there like an innocent child struck mute. Grandma kept apologising; this helped him to snap back to reality. He managed to tell Grandma not to worry, children will be children. He was good about it, but Grandma wasn't so happy. My sister and brother got a good dressing down later. Our parents were good at dressing us down, and many times I suffered through their words of humiliation. Nonetheless, it didn't dampen Mr Lent and Grandma's friendship. She reassured him it would never happen again.

Grandma and my parents were always going mad on me for been clumsy. I was always tripping over my own feet. One day we were in the kitchen, and we heard a croak.

'What's that?' asked Grandma, as she poured hot water from the kettle into her cup.

My sister, Mum, and I looked. Then we saw it: a big green frog.

'Grandma, a frog,' screamed Maxine.

Grandma rushed around, forgetting she had the kettle in her hand. She put it on the floor as she looked under the cupboard. My sister and I were behind Grandma, jumping up and down. I loved frogs, but Maxine didn't. I was laughing, and she was whimpering. Mum was holding the kitchen door open for Grandma to oust the frog, but Grandma stood and moved, telling us to be quiet. The frog hopped out from under the kitchen cupboard, and Maxine was screaming and pulling on my clothes. I pushed her hand away from me to break free of her. I didn't see the kettle on the floor behind me, and I tripped over it. As I fell, the kettle tipped, and the boiling water poured down the top of my leg. I started screaming in pain.

Now there was another drama. Grandma grabbed me and rushed me up to our neighbour's house as I screamed. The skin was hanging off the top of my left leg. We were lucky that Mr Dawes was home, and he drove us into the hospital.

Around my thirties, I still had the scar, and had forgotten how I got it. When I asked Mum about it, she told me I was burnt when I was about ten years old, when we were chasing a frog in the kitchen. As soon as she told me, the memory of the day came flooding back. Eventually I lost the scar, because once we recognise the trauma behind a scar, be it visible or invisible, and we feel and recall it and assess it and accept it, the trauma can be felt and remembered, then the scar can leave us. And it did.

Dad had favourite names for us. He called me Ten Ton Tessie the Elephant, because I thumped around the house walking on my heels. I lacked the grace of a lady. He'd jump on me for doing it, humiliating me. He was still abusing me. I was so confused. How could he love me, and then humiliate me? As a teenager, I became more graceful, learning to walk softly.

I loved to sing and I'd get, 'There she goes, singing like a cat on a hot tin roof.' He'd snigger and poke his tongue out at me. I was too sensitive to understand when he was playing and when he was serious. All had to be suppressed to not be humiliated. I was also getting really big boobs by nine, and sometimes Dad slipped and called me Titsy. Then I'd cover my breasts, and step back shyly to avoid his eyes on them. He could be good fun, and he'd rough us up. We three would jump on him, pulling at him. He'd tickle us as he poked his false teeth out at us, and we'd go 'yuck' and laugh, jumping on him. If we got too persistent, he'd growl like a dog, and we'd back off and scatter. We knew how far we could go, and when he'd had enough, all stopped. Grandma and Dad were sticklers for politeness, although he lacked good manners himself. His biggest demand was that you don't tell someone you want something, you ask for something. I don't know why, but it infuriated him.

It was time for me to wear a bra. Mum decided to take me in to get my first training bra at a special ladies' shop. I was maturing very quickly. I was five foot tall at nine years old with big boobs. We both walked into the shop. My mother, who was four foot nine and a half, and I stood at the counter. A mature-looking lady wearing glasses with well-styled blonde hair came over to assist us.

'Can I help you?'

Mum looked at me and said, 'I would like some bras for my little girl.'

I looked at her like… what! Sweetly, I said, 'Mum, I'm not a little girl.'

She looked at me and said, 'You are; you're only nine.'

I felt like a child as well as a woman at the same time. It was too confusing.

I felt my mother hated me, because I looked good in anything I put on, and I was developing a good figure. She wouldn't let me wear pretty shoes with my good dresses. I had to wear my black school shoes for going out. Her excuse was that my feet were growing too fast for pretty shoes, and I had to stop standing in cow manure, she joked. So I had to wait until I was twelve to get my first pretty shoes.

The older I got, the harder Mum was on me. She was always throwing her opinions around about me, calling me Miss Prim, and every time we went into town, she'd laugh at me, poking fun at me because I'd dress up, wearing pretty clothes, even with my black school shoes on. I just loved to dress up when I went out. When we were in Grandma's charge, she insisted that we dressed up.

Mum tormented me. 'We're not going to see the queen, Christine, we're just going shopping.'

I'd never change and would stay in my pretty dress. She was careful when she rubbished me; she would not do it around Grandma. Mum's other pet words for me were 'you're too big for your britches' and 'come down a peg or two'.

Around this time - I don't know how or why or what for - my parents had met a family who belonged to the Jehovah Witnesses; maybe they were trying to seek something beyond themselves. These people, the Dastur family, were from India. They had a daughter called Miranda. She was a very pretty, dark-skinned girl with deep, dark eyes that stared at you. She kind of gave me the shivers, and she made me dizzy when I looked at her. She'd glance at her parents to see if they were looking. If they weren't, she'd stare back at you. She was creepy. We used to go into their house quite often. I loved their food. One day, Mrs Dastur served us honey-roll cake. Oh, my goodness me, I loved honey cake. It sat on the small table next to me. As the adults talked and sipped their tea, I completely forgot myself with this delicious food, eating nearly all the cake on the plate. I forgot it was for everyone, until I felt Dad's eyes on me as I went for the last piece. He glared at me. I sank back into the chair and waited for home time. When we left their house, Dad let me have it. He dressed me down, telling me how disgusted he was by me, and I was never to do that again. He said I'd embarrassed him. I don't know why he was embarrassed; I was embarrassed enough for all of us. He didn't have to tell me he hated me. I sat back on the seat of the car, listening to them rambling on. I cried, the cake was so delicious, and I just forgot. Even my sister and brother shut up and said nothing.

Mum and Dad must have invited the Dasturs to our house. Grandma didn't like strangers in her house. However, she actually didn't mind these people. They were visiting us over a period of a month. Gradually, they allowed Miranda to go and play with me while they talked. I asked her to come into my room, and she agreed. We left the adults in the kitchen talking.

My sister came with us, and we looked at my toys. Miranda got bored and wanted to see more of our house. We told her we weren't allowed into the front rooms, but she ran down there.

I looked at Maxine, and said, 'Oh no, you can't go down there,' my hand over my mouth. I ran after her. At the archway, I looked over at the lounge room. I couldn't hear her. I didn't know which room she'd gone into, and I was scared of those rooms. Then I heard her. She was in Grandma's big old bedroom. I braved up, and went in.

She was standing there, amazed at the room, because this room was truly a picture from the past, with its big four-poster bed, fireplace, and velvet curtains on the old French doors. She swirled around, and then jumped up onto the bed and started to bounce on it.

I warned her, 'Don't do that; my grandma will be angry.'

She sang out to me, 'You're a chicken. Come and jump with me.'

'No,' I squealed.

'Chicken.'

With that, I climbed up on the bed, and started to jump too. We were laughing and I forgot all about the trouble I'd be in if I was caught. Next thing, Grandma was at the door with her hands on her hips. I froze, stopping the jumping, pulling Miranda's dress to stop her. Grandma came over, pulled me off the bed and smacked my legs as she screamed at me, telling me I was a bad girl. I knew I wasn't allowed in this room and had to get out of her room now. Miranda had run off to her mother. On entering the kitchen, Grandma told the Dasturs that they had to leave her house, and to never bring their daughter back out here again.

Everyone was surprised. After they'd left, Grandma told Dad what we girls were doing and that she'd already punished me. We stopped going to the Dasturs' house, and I never saw them again. Their daughter was so naughty; she was going to be a lot of trouble for them. Her parents would have died if they'd heard her talk about things. She talked about men's private parts. I didn't miss the Dasturs, but I did miss their honey roll.

Chapter 27

Facing Sexuality

Mum's friend, Susanne, came out to visit her, to let Mum know her mum, my Grandma Owens, hadn't been well. She brought her two kids with her, Timothy and Penny. I knew them from school, and they lived next door to Grandma Owens. We often played with them when we visited Grandma Owens. I knew Timothy liked me. He'd bailed me up over in their house before. Grandma offered Susanne a cup of tea. We were told to take her kids outside to play, so we took them to the shed. They saw the blackberries, and asked could they eat some, so we ate the blackberries growing on an old, disused shed.

Timothy asked, 'What's in the big shed?'

I looked at him, and said, 'That's where Dad puts his car and the horses' bridles.'

'Can I have a look at them?' he asked.

'Yes, go and look.' I nodded my head in that direction, while eating berries.

'Come with me?'

'No, you go.' I picked fruit to eat.

He stood there looking at me, and I kept eating. My sister was talking to Penny.

Timothy asked me again. 'Can you show me the shed?'

'Alright.' I took him to it.

'Wow! It's very big, and there are lots of things here.' He was poking around the bits and pieces hanging on the wall.

The smell of old bridles and harnesses captured my senses. This was an open shed next to the blackberry vine, and there was an old sulky still sitting there. I loved these old things from the past, and I started to touch the horses' gear, bending in to smell the leather.

'What's this?' he asked.

'Dad's old boat he made.'

'Does it float?'

'No, it doesn't.' Dad had tried to float it on the lagoon, but it sank, and it'd sat on the old storage cabinet across the back of the shed ever since. Next he was up on the cabinet and into the boat, but I took no notice of him.

'Come up here, Christine?'

'No, I don't want to.' I sneered at him. He was such an ugly boy; I didn't like his face, and he looked sneaky.

'You're a chicken,' he taunted.

'No, I don't want to go up there.'

'Come on.'

He annoyed me, so I climbed up into the boat.

'Lay down here with me,' he demanded as he lay down in the boat.

'No.'

'Yes, come on, or I will tell everyone you're a chicken,' he threatened.

'I am not, and I won't lie down.' I folded my arms.

'Come on.' He smiled, sat up and touched my arm.

The same feeling came over me as it did with Dad. I lay down next to him, and he made me touch his willy, then he was playing with my private parts. While we were doing this, I didn't hear my sister and Penny sneak into the shed. They'd been listening to us talking.

Maxine burst out screaming, 'I'm going to tell Grandma on you.'

I pushed his hand away from me and stood up quickly, pulling my pants in place, but Maxine had run off to the house, singing out to Grandma.

Penny stayed with her brother, telling him, 'You're in big trouble.'

I was so angry, and quickly got out of the boat. So did Timothy. I stood guiltily at the back of the shed.

Grandma came into the shed, glaring daggers at me, and yelled, 'What do you think you're doing, you dirty girl?'

Those words hurt me, because I wasn't dirty; it wasn't me, it was him. I pleaded my innocence. 'He said to do it, Grandma.'

She grabbed me by the arm and belted me as she took me out of the shed and into the paddock where Mum and Susanne were standing. She told me to go to the house, threatening me with telling my Dad when he got home. Mum never said anything. Timothy and Penny had run to their mother when Grandma grabbed me. Grandma was so outraged, she told Timothy's mother to get off her property. I heard Susanne apologise to Grandma and going mad on Timothy, as I clambered up the incline to the house. It turned into a right old screaming match between all the women. Susanne piled her children into the car and left. I went straight to my bedroom and hid in my bed.

Later on, Mum came through the house. She was angry. She stopped at my bedroom door, telling me off.

'You think you're smart. Well, my dear, your father will hear about this. You're not too big for your britches yet. You won't get out of this one. We'll fix you very soon.' She stomped off.

I turned over onto my back and looked up at the wire that zigzagged across the base of my sister's bunk bed above me, and I thought about what had just happened, and how Grandma was so disgusted by me. I felt so ashamed. I was dirty, she'd told me. Worst of all, she'd tell Dad - but he was doing the same thing to me.

When Dad came home that evening, Grandma told him what I'd done. He looked at me as I hung my head.

'Did you belt her?' he asked.

'Yes.'

Dad walked away and said no more, much to Grandma's horror.

Back at school, Penny was on the top step as I walked in the front gate. She was telling her friends what had happened. From then on, she would point her finger at me. I knew she was gossiping about me. Her hatred of me was evident, right up until there was an incident that pushed me to the edge. The pain I was bearing alone was so great, but I bore it. Again, women hated me.

As a child, I was exposed to lots of separation at school and in my family. I don't know why, but even before that incident, I could never fit in, spending much of my time alone, or tagging behind my sister and her friends. Maxine made so many friends so easily. This separation taught me how not to upset people. I became nicer, learning to be nice to not cause any problems. I never cursed my parents or defied them in my childhood. I learned if I wanted my own way, I could use tactics to make them like me. Then I got what I wanted or needed. Nonetheless, that year was so hard with all the taunts. They were the hardest to deal with, causing me to break down at school.

Penny had me bailed up down the back of the school, well away from the main classrooms. There was a group of her followers with her, including Maxine. She watched them torment me. The girls were ribbing me and making fun of me. I was poked like I was an animal. I cried to the point of sobbing. Suddenly, it got too much for me, and I cracked up and stood still, and screamed and screamed. The pain of all the abuse in all areas of my life was building up in me, and I had no one to support me or understand me. I knew what I was being subjected to; they didn't, so I just screamed.

My sister stopped her taunts, and shouted at the others, 'Stop it! Leave her alone.'

They stopped. My sister stood near me, putting her hand on me. I looked at her and sobbed. She didn't know why I was so physically distressed and sad.

By now, the teachers had come down. Mr Clark was asking everybody, 'What was going on here, and why was she screaming?'

No one answered him. He was not a kind man, and he hated us Kinreads, because my Uncle Mitch had punched him in the mouth when he'd given Charlene the cane.

'What are you screaming for?' He demanded of me, as he looked down on me.

My sister answered for me. 'She's just upset and sad.'

'Tell her not to do it again,' he said. He ushered everyone away. 'Come on, move on now. It's over.'

The others moved away. I sat and sobbed and sobbed. My life seemed to be falling apart around me. Why were all these things happening to me? What was I going through this for? After this incident, no one tormented me again.

I didn't like Mr Clark. I noticed sometimes that he rubbed his hand in places he shouldn't on his favourite girls in the class. I knew it wasn't right, because what my father was doing to me wasn't right. Mr Clark was always hitching his trousers up, and he made me feel uncomfortable. I was so glad Uncle Mitch had punched him in the face, because at least he wouldn't touch us.

This was also the year my favourite Aunty Connie surprised us all, by bringing home a man she'd met: a Frenchman, Oliver Laurent. Aunty Connie was thirty-five, and all her life that I'd known her, she'd never had a boyfriend. She'd met this man Oliver at her job, where she was a private secretary for the Rosemont Branch of the Save the People Organization. He had a funny sense of humour and we all liked him. He visited us when Aunty did. He had some strange habits. Being farm people, we were all up early, but not him. He slept until late in the day. Grandma was furious and didn't like it at all.

The more we got to see him, the more I saw something about him. I couldn't work it out; I didn't know what it was. Regardless of all our accusations, Aunty Connie loved him. Christmas that year, he'd bought me a fairytale book. He must not have seen me as a grown-up person. I was eleven. Furthermore, I was well-developed. I was definitely not a child. His actions made me wonder why. Fairytales were for children, as far as I was concerned. However, browsing through the book and reading a few of the stories, there were a couple I really loved, especially 'The Matchstick Girl', about a little girl who was unloved, who had no family and died alone in the snow and cold. She was taken up to the light by the angels. This story touched my heart and brought tears to my eyes, because it was my story, and to love is beyond here on earth.

I had no concept of God, due to not being told about God, or angels or beings. I knew about Jesus, but I didn't know about the others at all. To me, there was something bigger outside of us on this planet, than the here and now. Somehow, I did know about life after death, and how life doesn't stop here on earth and goes on, and we return here to the earth to relive a life in another life. I knew others lived on other planets in other galaxies. These things were not uncommon to me. No one else seemed to talk about these topics, so I never talked about these topics to others. I thought everyone must know these things, and that they were common knowledge and didn't need to be talked about.

At this age, I was allowed to go and stay at my cousins' house. They lived in Fenton. They had a three-bedroom home. I loved to sleep over at their house and loved mixing with my cousins. They were great fun.

Chapter 28

I'm Eleven Going On Twelve, And The Hour Has Come When Dad And I Were Caught

There were lots of issues with my sister, and I felt jealousies. Not Barton; we were more neutral with each other. When I fought with Maxine, it was because she'd said something horrible to me or pulled a face at me, or pinched or bitten me. We were never jealous over beauty, or thinking one got more than the other, or even our parents and Grandma, because we all got things equally. Somehow, though, I felt Maxine was resentful towards me. I don't know why. Even when I was denied love from Mum or Grandma, and seeing my siblings getting love, I wasn't resentful. I was longing for the same.

My favourite doll, Tootie, had gone missing for a long time, and I'd hunted high and low for her, but gave up as I got older. I realised I'd never find her, so eventually I let her go.

Barton, Maxine and I were out playing near the old duck pen. There was an old shed near it that was used to store the food for the ducks. As we played, I climbed up onto the shed's roof, and to my surprise, there was Tootie.

'Oh! Tootie.' Joy overcame me as I climbed down and sat on the ground, and put her on my knees. I brushed the dirt off her, bringing her close to my heart. I brushed her hair back. She was so damaged, with mould on her face. She'd been missing for more than a year. I cried out in excitement, 'Oh! I found my Tootie.' I wondered how she'd got up there.

Looking at my brother and sister, Barton blabbed, 'Maxine threw her up there.'

'What?' My face turned serious.

Maxine pushed Barton to the ground. He laughed. I got up with the doll, and Maxine ran. I was angry with her, so I chased her, punching her in the back.

She turned, poking out her tongue out at me, taunting me. 'Ner-ner.' She knew I loved that doll so much; that's why she'd thrown her on the roof of the shed.

I looked at Tootie. It was too late to reconnect with her; I'd outgrown a doll. I took her to the laundry, and tried to clean the mildew off her face. It wouldn't come off, so I placed her in a box, putting her up on top of my wardrobe in my bedroom. Even though Maxine did that to me, I never hated her. I was so glad to find Tootie. In spite of all our problems, I didn't hold too many grudges. I was like that. Problems came, you faced them, and you got over the childhood disputes quickly.

Jealousy wasn't just between us siblings; it was evident between Grandma and Mum, even though it'd been nearly two-and-a-half years since Mum had returned.

The jealousy was mainly over us girls. Grandma had been our caregiver for so long; she could see that we girls were trying to get nearer to our mum. I guess Grandma's fear was Mum might even take over. Grandma's fears were not realistic, because Mum could never take over, simply because Mum was not capable of taking over and caring for us. Mum was the same person who left us. She was still spending the majority of her day in her bedroom when Dad was at work. I can't imagine what she did in there all day. I think Mum was pining for her life, and maybe all the mistakes, regrets and losses she'd made. I think she was dealing with lots of loneliness and sadness, just as Grandma was, and we all were.

Nevertheless, on the streets, Mum was a different woman, displaying a happy, carefree personality, laughing all the time, as if life was a breeze. That was still the same, but I knew different. How could she live a lie, and two separate lives, and put up this pretense? Secret feelings couldn't be shown in our house. I guess back then no one, even in the community, ever knew the truth about people's lives behind closed doors.

I did love my mum as time moved on. However, I couldn't let Grandma know that, so constantly I'd be looking over my shoulder before approaching Mum. Grandma wasn't approachable and had no room in her mind for understanding others' feelings, and the need to be friendly to both my parents. Grandma's demanding personality was questioned by no one in the house. There'd be trouble if you rocked her boat. Despite her tough exterior, she was a loner, living in sadness and grief, which I'm sure pushed people away from her. Closeness was on her terms, if she allowed it.

Dad was still fondling me in his bed, or out on the back verandah. As I got older, I was changing. From the age of eight on, I was wondering why he didn't go further with me. I knew he could, as I'd felt him. It was as if I knew, without knowing, the next step in the intimacy between the opposite sexes. Our time together got more heated. Just as I was starting to feel close to my mum, the unthinkable happened. I was eleven, and as usual, I went to my dad's room in the morning to lie with him. Mum returned to her bedroom, and Dad and I were playing out our secret between us. All was about to change.

In May 1963, I was in Dad's bed, and he was gently caressing me. We didn't hear Mum enter the room. Looking up at the end of the bed, I broke free from Dad. Mum was peering over the back of the bed, and then all hell broke loose. I was ordered out of the bedroom. I ran into my bedroom. I was humiliated and scared. Mum never looked at me. She stayed in her room, and Grandma got us off to school.

In the afternoon, Mum was at the school to meet me. She took me to our GP to have me checked internally. I was checked, and all was intact. I had to tell him what my father was doing to me. I told him he was fondling me. After the doctor's appointment, we went to her mother's, my Grandma Owens' house. There I sat in the lounge room as the two women spoke. I mesmerized myself with Grandma's mats made out of stockings. She was very poor and had very little in her house. As I sat there, Mum told Grandma, and I was so humiliated, because Grandma later looked at me differently, like I was the trouble.

Dad picked us up from Grandma's house. None of us spoke of the incident ever since. I was told to keep away from my father by my mother. Now I was really separated and humiliated. This was to be the way it was until I entered my late forties.

At the time of the incident, and after it, I felt my mother blamed me. She protected Dad and supported him. Even though he'd treated her so badly over their married life, I was never once asked how I was doing or how I was coping or offered support. There was no comfort for me, no enquiry. Even Dad never stuck up for me. He betrayed my trust. I would tell him what he did to me when I was a child before he departed from this earth. After I did, his health would fail, but he had to know that I knew and remembered and suffered; and in my fifties, I would write a ten-page letter to my mother, explaining how I felt unsupported and unloved by her. That would infuriate her.

During this time, there was one person I couldn't bear to know my secret: Grandma Kinread, who'd raised me. If she knew and she didn't talk to me in that house of secrets, or if she despised me, I'd die. Grandma was my only hope of having any human contact, to show me some love, and I was already suffering in loneliness and isolation.

Not long after this, Mum started to make demands on Dad, insisting they moved into town. Dad didn't want to leave the farm, but Mum was slowly winning out, with her new-found strength, over Dad. To keep her happy, Dad would arrange for us to go house-hunting, but nothing ever came of it. Slowly, the idea of moving house died. Grandma must have heard them talking about moving out, because she mysteriously started to get sick. The incident between Dad and I had split the relationship between Mum, Dad and I. Mum never ever brought up the topic. Nor did I.

This was to be a turning point in my life, a new chapter I had to deal with: separation, loneliness and isolation. There was to be no more love given to me. It was never the same in our house. The following months were so hard: I had to duck away and hide if my dad happened to cross my path, just in case Mum saw us. How was I to cope in all this mayhem, and with these snarling faces? I had to get out of the house as much as possible. I was lucky I had wide open paddocks to move around. There I lost myself, by staying away from the house. I'd go down to the lagoon and sit there at the water's edge. I'd be feeling nothing but sadness. How would I handle this situation? Mum couldn't tolerate me, and Dad was hiding from everyone when home, yet he was the luckiest one, because at least he had work to escape to. That kept him away from the house nearly all day.

As usual, the animals were my lifeline. They'd follow me, keeping me company. They never judged me, and with them I could have the fun that I lacked with people. There were always lots of dogs, cats and cows on our farm. Each had their own personality. Our cows were the funniest. Some used to bluff us by showing us a fierce face. Under that face, I could see a frightened cow, disguising its true feelings. Grandma had names for some of our cows, the ones with the most outstanding personalities: Strawberry, Daisy and Susie. I loved nature so much; it seemed to ease my pain. The serenity of our farm felt like a gentle caress to my very being.

Rusty the dog was a great comforter; he was a greyhound dog. Dad had brought him home, because his owner was going to put him down. He was a tall, slender dog with a soft, rusty-coloured coat, and the gentlest heart and loving eyes that cared. Rusty was my constant companion. Whoever was on the outer in the family, Rusty was there to comfort and cuddle into.

There was Blue, the protector, an Australian cattle dog. We always had a dog called Blue. This Blue was a grey-blue speckled dog. He had a mean look, but he only used that as a defence. He was so faithful to us kids.

Then there was sexy Rexy, a part-Kelpie. He was a black dog with white markings. His personality was silly. He was always chasing his tail and running around, chasing invisible things and barking at nothing.

Each had their own personality. I truly loved them, and they probably reflected a lot of me. The serious Rusty comforter, who in his kindness just wanted to be loved in return; Blue, the perfect guard dog, who guarded his loved ones with his life; and daydreaming Rexy, caught up in his own world.

We all bonded with our animals. None of them were pure breeds, all mixed breeds, but so faithful, especially Rusty. I remember we kids had gone to the creek with Grandma. Out of the silence, Maxine began to sing out, 'Help! Help!' Rusty ran into the water, swam to her and tried to pull her out to the shore. It was amazing, his action. She'd got bored, and to break the silence, she'd shouted out help. We were all strong swimmers. We knew she was fooling around. This caused us to laugh. Maxine tried to do it again, but no. Rusty was awake to the game, and he wasn't falling for that trick. He snuggled closer to Grandma, who was sitting on the shore, and he barked at Maxine. He ran and snapped at the water. I think he felt humiliated.

As I sat at the water's edge of the lagoon, I rubbed Rusty's head as he laid it on my lap. Blue kept scout, and Rexy was off chasing something. The tears rolled down my face. How would I live in that house? I had to face those people every day. Rexy came over and stood staring at me, looking a bit dumbfounded by my tears. He was moving his head from side to side, a stupid grin on his face as I cried, as if not sure of what was going on. He pounced on me and jumped on Rusty, waking him. Rusty tried to get up, half-asleep after being knocked by Rexy, and Rusty's long legs collapsed under him. He resembled a new-born deer. I helped Rusty up. Rexy was licking my face, as if to cheer me up. I cuddled him, saying, 'Oh, Rexy.' Rusty was up and becoming just as excited. We all cuddled. Blue joined in, barking like he was saying, 'What's going on here?' It got too out of hand as the dogs started to play and bite each other, and in their boisterous play, I was flattened to the ground, and had to get up and move.

I left them still playing. I walked to the pump house, where Blue joined me. While standing there, Rexy sneaked up behind me. He started to bite my hand gently. Moving in closer to the jetty, I looked at it. We were not allowed to walk on it. It was dangerous, and we were told by Dad that if we went into the lagoon, we'd never come out, because the reeds were long, and would entwine us and drag us down into the depths. The water gently lapped at the jetty. This soothed me and mesmerized me. Rexy pulled at my hand.

I said, 'Don't, Rexy,' facing him with an annoyed look.

He backed off, looking at me with big, dumb eyes. I smiled at him, and he sensed it as a signal to continue playing.

'You mad dog, Rexy. Enough,' I pulled my hand away from his mouth. He backed off, jumping on me again. Blue'd had enough and stepped in, his hair raised on his back. He gave a gentle growl, showing his teeth. Rexy knew he'd gone too far. He rolled over on his back in a defeated stance. I walked away from the jetty and followed the edge of the water to the lower gate of our property, then walked back up the hill to the house of pain. There was no escaping; I had to always return home.

Fate took Rexy from us the following summer. Due to his insistence on living in his own world, tragedy befell him. He was lying under Dad's car, his body half under Dad's car wheel and the other half of his body out from under the car. He'd done this to escape the hot summer sun. Unfortunately, Dad hadn't seen him there when he quickly got in the car, started it and drove off, running over Rexy. Dad felt the dog and heard its yelp. Stopping the car, he got out and saw what he'd done. Rexy had managed to get his body out of the way, but not his leg. It had been run over. My parents rushed Rexy to the vet. Dad was gruff to us and the animals, and he'd hit them when they were naughty, but if they were sick or needed medical help, he made sure they got it. He'd take them immediately to the vet. Rexy came back in a plaster. He'd suffered a badly broken leg. The plaster was from the pit of his leg to his toes.

Gordon Knight came regularly to check the pump house. He'd come in his truck through our property, leave it at the house, and walk down to check the pump. We all liked Gordon; he was a great guy. When he came, we kids would go with him to the pump house. We'd watch him work there. The old pump was a fascination for us. It supplied the pit with water, and us with washing water.

However, fate was out to get Rexy. Gordon was doing a pump house inspection not long after Rexy broke his leg. We were home when we heard Gordon drive to the house. We ran out to greet him and Rexy - I don't know why - ran out in front of the truck. He went straight under the wheels. It was terrible, because we saw it. We were devastated, seeing him die in front of us. Gordon felt so bad for us kids, and he and Grandma tried to console us. After this, he never drove his truck onto our property. I think the incident affected him terribly.

Chapter 29

Friends

At school, a girl I'll refer to as Melinda Pike befriended me. She was in my fifth class. She was similar to me: well-developed, big-busted and looked older. Her face belonged to a twenty-year-old, not an eleven-year-old. She had short, blonde hair. Melinda easily led me on; she'd get me to do some bad things. We used to steal ice blocks from the corner store. We'd wait until Mikie, the shopkeeper, went out the back. Mikie was one of the sweetest, kindest men in town. I think he knew we kids were stealing lollies and ice blocks. I felt he was turning a blind eye to it. I didn't know why I allowed myself to do what she wanted me to do, because in my family we were given money to spend. I didn't need to steal. It wasn't to do with money. I was more interested in being loved.

So while Mikie was busy out the back, we'd run in, steal an ice block and run out. I remember the first time I did it. I was egged on by Melinda and a girl I'll refer to as Dianne.

'Come on, your turn. You've got to do it to be with us.'

I looked at them, and then I headed into the big, dark store building, knowing if I got caught, I'd be in big trouble with Grandma and Dad. Checking to make sure Mikie wasn't there in the store, I quickly darted in like a snake in the grass, seizing the prize to win the tournament of the moment. I succeeded and ran out with the goodies. My heart was pounding. We walked smartly away down the street. The girls gave me their stamp of approval. I ate my stolen reward.

Melinda became more daring; she planned to steal money out of the principal's office. This was strictly between us, and no one else was to know. It had to stay between us forever. We weren't to ever tell a soul what we'd done. I was very good at keeping secrets.

Initially, I felt no remorse, fear or wrongdoing. I'd had to stand guard as she ran into his office to take the money out of a tin he kept in his drawer. I did what she said. When she'd done the deed, she walked off. Later, I followed her. Melinda had stolen eight shillings, which was a lot of money in those days. It turned out to be a very bad experience. The whole school was brought to assembly. Mr Clark told us there was a thief in the school. Eyes fixed ahead, I stayed calm and never looked at anyone. After school, as we walked to my bus stop, Melinda told me that she'd noticed how calm I was. She was pleased with me and saw that I was able to hide my feelings well, so well that no one would be able to pick me as one of the people involved.

Remorse did set in later. I saw that I was easily led astray and when I realised what a terrible thing I'd done just to keep her friendship, I thought, never again. I would not do that to keep a friendship. Melinda and I spent the money on cigarettes. It was a foolish act just to get some cigarettes.

These new friends were years ahead of me in their minds. I found out they had similar issues to me. Melinda, Dianne and her cousin, Noeleen, were talking amongst themselves. We were in the school park. While they chatted, I merrily swung around on the swing set pole. I was humming to myself.

Suddenly, I stopped on hearing Dianne say, 'You know that he touched Noeleen the other day?'

'Did he? How was it, Noeleen?' asked Melinda.

'Good.'

'Did you see his penis?' questioned Melinda.

'Yes.'

They laughed. I was not able to follow them, but knew the girls were talking about Dianne's father's thing. I listened, but I never ever told them of my father. I just pretended not to listen or not to understand. I was very good at pretending, and hiding secrets. No one knew from my face what I felt or knew. I learnt to disguise many things, and I learnt not to let my guard down. Most of all, never trust others with your secrets.

My ears pricked up as Dianne said, 'You have to be careful though, now you've got your period.'

Period: I'd never heard that word before. I listened more intently.

'I hate losing that blood every month. I have to be more careful,' said Dianne.

I didn't know what they were talking about. It frightened me. I pretended that I knew what they meant. At home, I had to ask Mum about periods. She never answered me, and later on, took me to see Dr Judy Jones. She explained what a period was, and what the girls were talking about when they said they were losing blood. As she described the monthly cycle, my mind went blank. Nothing seemed to enter it, so I left her surgery still confused. Being with those girls trained me for life. I wasn't being trained by my caretakers, so I started to learn about people through the girls.

In June of '63, just before my twelfth birthday, I got my period. Mum was very unkind to me. On waking, I saw blood on my sheet. I told Mum. She walked off coldly and came back with a packet of Modess pads, and a suspender belt to hold the pad onto my pants. She handed these to me and said, 'Now you had better keep away from your father.' Stepping back from her, I hung my head in humiliation, feeling her hatred of me. I sat on my bed, wondering how to wear these pads, because she hadn't bothered to explain how to put them on, or that I would need to change my pad a couple of times a day.

Melinda invited me to stay at her house. I thoroughly enjoyed my time there, and I never missed my family. I really liked Melinda's mum, Mrs Pike; she was a warm, friendly, chubby lady who had a lovely smile. I liked Melinda's sister, Flora, as well. She was older and seemed different to Melinda: a much more serious, quiet girl. Melinda was so outgoing, and she looked like her mum. The only difference between them was that her Mum had brown hair, and Melinda had blonde hair. Flora was like their dad. Their house was small, but it seemed cozy. There was a good rapport between the girls and their mum. They had lots of affection given to them, completely different to my household, where the people were distant, and we had to be deathly silent amid glares of mistrust, jealousy and hate. Despite all the love Melinda received, she led a secret life of deception.

She had an almost double life that her family never knew about. When I stayed at Melinda's, I actually got to go to Sunday school. I liked going to their church. This was the first time I went to church. I started going away more often on weekends to stay at friends' houses.

At the same time I became friends with Melinda, and while staying at her house on the weekends, I got to meet another girl in my class, Jill Kline. We also became friends. She was a short, fat girl with short, brown hair, freckles on her cheeks, and as game as Ned Kelly, who she said was a family relative. I believed that, knowing Jill. She also possessed a great sense of humour; a funny girl who made me laugh a lot. So now there were two houses for me to go to on weekends.

Jill's Dad was a very sick man; he was always in bed. I never saw him out of his pyjamas. He only ever said hello. His name was Joseph. Her mum's name was Beth, but I had to call them Mr and Mrs Kline. Mrs Kline worked in Rosemont through the week, due to having to be the breadwinner in the family. They weren't well off; you could tell that. When her Mum was away, Jill had to look after her father and her two brothers, Dave and Laurie.

The house was a bit of a shambles, and the boys were sometimes pigs, and drank out of the milk bottles. I guess they didn't have anyone to tell them not to do that. Through all their hardships, they were a happy family. When her mum was home, she'd sit and chat to us girls. Jill and I become really good friends and stayed friends up until our second year of high school. Then she had to go to work.

Chapter 30

I Met What I Considered A Prince

In September 1963, I turned twelve. Things had calmed down after four months had passed by. On my twelfth birthday, I received many grown-up presents. I was allowed to be pretty. Mum changed towards me, and insisted that I should start to take care of my skin. She started me off on Coty products. I also got to wear lipstick, and I got my first pair of high heels that I chose, a pair of hot pink shoes. I loved them. No more black school shoes for going out. No more embarrassment. This was a big thing for me.

My sister had been allowed to wear pretty shoes, and I couldn't understand why I couldn't. I was glad about my high heels; it was a sign I was really growing up. I felt so mature in my body. I had a thirty-five-inch bust, twenty-four-inch waist, and thirty-six in hips. I had a good figure.

We drove into town to visit our cousins, Charlene, Gerry and Hope. We pulled up in front of their house, and Aunty Kimberly, Charlene, Gerry and Hope were farewelling this man. When we got out of our car, Aunty introduced him to us. I was instantly drawn to this man. To me, he seemed like a prince. He was so different to other men I'd met through the family. He was tall, with blonde hair, and very handsome. When it was my turn to meet him, my eyes connected with his beautiful light green eyes. He took my hand and kissed it. I will never forget that experience. He seemed so gentle, like a person with lots of finesse, a person with culture. After a short talk with the adults, this handsome man got in his car and left us. As he drove off, I turned to watch him leave, and wondered who he was.

We went into their house, the parents had tea and we played with Gerry and Hope; Charlene didn't mix with us a great deal. She almost seemed alien to me then. There were some good experiences with my cousins. Actually, it was good having my younger cousins come out to stay with us on the farm now that they were older, because Maxine and I got on better.

As much as I was allowed to stay over, my friends and cousins were allowed to come and stay at our house. If they weren't part of the immediate clan, we showed them a perfect family. Even with this disguise, I couldn't go near my dad. This was so hard for me; I needed a father to talk to. I dared not lose the little love I had from Mum, so I distanced myself from Dad. Having family and friends stay over helped break the non-communication, and created conversation. Staying away from the house was also making my life better.

Mum's sister, Aunty Kay, and Uncle Pete had four children: Lance, Brandon, Leigh and Sammy, who was two years old. There were many problems in my

Aunty Kay's life. She was very fat, but very pretty. We didn't visit her a lot, like we did my cousins on Dad's side. Dad never ever went to their home. Sometimes I went with Mum to visit Kay. I heard the two women talking about Uncle Pete. Kay was saying he had a drinking problem. I remembered once telling Mum, when I walked past Aunty Kay's house, that I saw Uncle Pete with another man on the front porch. They were drinking beer. I saw the beer bottles in their hands. I told her he sounded drunk, and when he stood up, he was wobbling around.

Mum warned me, 'Christine, never ever to go into their house if Aunty Kay isn't home.'

I looked at her and said, 'I was with my friend.'

'That's okay, but promise me you won't go in the house.'

I promised her I wouldn't. No more was said about it.

Not long after, Aunty Kay sent all her children off to Uncle Pete's parents' home. She walked out and left them all. They were raised by their grandparents, and grew up to become fine, upstanding adults with great jobs: a teacher, an air force pilot and a nurse. They were so lucky to leave their parents. In doing so, they got a better chance in life. Aunty Kay found another man and had four children to him, but they wouldn't fare so well in life. They had no opportunities.

At this time, we got our first black-and-white television set. This helped me to learn about life. The transmitting towers sat on Mt Peel, not far from our house. I learnt more from the TV than from the people in my life. I got some answers to questions I could never get from my family. I would spend hours alone watching it, absorbing the information, and lose myself in learning. The TV showed the Vietnam War, and some of our Australian troops were over there, so sometimes I'd watch reports on the war. TV offered us many new and interesting shows from America: *I Love Lucy*, *I Dream of Jeannie,* and *The Dick Van Dyke* Show. This brought humour into our house, and Mum loved these shows. I loved *Rin Tin Tin* and *Bonanza*, especially Hoss and Little Joe.

I loved the documentaries the most and couldn't get enough of them. I learned of other cultures; how people lived, worked, played, and their beliefs and customs. All the weird rituals of Africa, and the wonderful peculiarities of different races; the world was coming into my living room. My mind devoured all, and I questioned why people lived as they did. Why were we all so different? With their primitive ways of life, African cultures intrigued me the most. I wanted to know about their sexuality. I don't know why, but I felt it from the TV. I felt their sexuality. Other shows on other cultures never brought out sexuality to me. The African drumming and the deep darkness fascinated me: the mystery of what lurked in the Congo; its amazing snakes that swallowed whole animals. Feelings were being stirred within me, and they made me think more.

My mind was expanding beyond my small world, moving far, far into a realm of silence, questioning, and wondering why we were all so different.

These questions plagued me, because throughout my childhood, Grandma had spoken badly about other races. If they weren't white, she didn't want to know about them. My house was full of bigotry, prejudice, and intolerance of other races and countries.

Dad was always calling people from other countries wogs or dagos. He'd constantly criticise them for what they ate and how they talked. There was a big lay-off of men at the Lachlan Mine where Dad had worked all his working life. He happened to be one of the men in the first lot to be laid-off. He was told it was a good idea to go early, because the pit would close in time and he could secure a job before the large influx of laid-off workers took the available jobs. Dad ended up working in Dawson Hill for Smith and Sons in the metal works industry. Dad was taken out of his small world of Hastings Crossing, and put into a world of foreigners from other countries we politely called new Australians. There had been an influx of migrants into Australia over the past twelve years. These people mainly settled in Rosemont. Some came to Dawson Hill. Dad was being forced to meet these people he'd criticised all his life. He'd come home and scoff at the food they'd brought to work, saying it stunk. They'd stink of salami and garlic, which we didn't eat in our culture. Over time, Dad befriended some of these people, but still called them names. I witnessed double standards, because some people were accepted, and others weren't.

Grandma constantly warned us of the impending Yellow Peril which would come down and take over our Australia. Her hatred towards these people was so strong, and she openly expressed her point of view, knowing my mother had Chinese ancestry. This probably fuelled her fire. As far as I was concerned, people were people. They fascinated me, not repulsed me. I didn't understand the mentality of my father and Grandma.

My parents struck up a close friendship with Katrina and Serge from Latvia; they were a happy couple with no children. On occasions, we'd go to their house, staying for the day. Mum and Dad's other friends were Glen and Judy; they came from England. Dad even had a name for the English: Pommies.

Mum and Dad used to take food to Glen and Judy's house. We'd all share each other's food. I think Mum did that because of Grandma. Grandma wouldn't allow my parents to bring their friends to our house: even the English ones weren't allowed. I really liked their friends, who were a lot older than Mum and Dad. I wondered why Dad still held his prejudiced viewpoint away from his friends. My parents were their happiest when visiting these friends; it was so confusing to me. I had my own point of view. I found them interesting to be with, especially when it came to eating their food, which I liked, as well as their house décor, what they thought, and how they lived. Later on, my parents made friends with Don and Donna. They were the sweetest couple. Donna was so cuddly. They had no children of their own, and Donna was happy to share her affection with us.

I wasn't the smartest one in this family; I was the imaginative one, the daydreamer. As I got older, I could entertain myself. I was the one they'd find talking or singing to herself. In spite of being tone deaf, I loved to sing, and my untrained voice used to upset others. I didn't need the company. I preferred my own, and the company of my pets.

I was so awkward, very clumsy and heavy-footed, and often didn't see where I was going. I walked into things, causing me to fall over.

But I had really good eye co-ordination for ball games. I played ball up against the wall of our house near the water tank. It was cool there and offered me lots of space to play this ball game. In this game, I was able to master five tennis balls at once, by throwing them up onto the wall and catching them. I could juggle and weave those balls in and out, up and down, between my legs, up and over and under and behind my back, and I could throw one, as all were in the air or bouncing off the wall. One, two, three… coming back into my hands. I sang songs and recited poems that rhymed; this helped me to coordinate as I played ball. My favorite songs I were 'My Bonnie Lies over the Ocean' and 'What Can the Matter Be'. I loved 'Row, Row, Row Your Boat' and 'Frere Jacques'. I'd sing these songs and play these games for hours.

This was how I learned to entertain myself. I'd teach myself these games. It was a source of relief in my loneliness. Hopscotch was another game I could play for hours. Sometimes my sister would join me in hopscotch. Nonetheless, I haven't a clue what Maxine was doing with her time. I think she was somewhere with Grandma and Barton.

Someone always caught me out and tried to embarrass me by telling me that my voice was woeful, and to stop that screeching. Dad was the best at hitting my sore spot, saying I sounded like a cat on a hot tin roof. It was alright for them. My Dad had the most beautiful tenor voice; we loved to listen to him sing. Mum loved Dad singing to her, which he often did. Mum had a lovely voice too; she'd often sing to herself in her loneliness. When we travelled by car, Dad always sang songs he liked, 'He'll Have to Go' and 'Danny Boy' and 'I Can't Stop Loving You', and many others, whereas Mum loved the music of Acker Bilk and the Paramount Jazz Band, and especially their piece 'Stranger on the Shore'. Music seemed to help both my parents lose themselves.

With all their ups and downs, Mum truly loved my dad. Often she'd request a song for him over the radio. The song she requested most was 'I Wouldn't Trade You For The World'. The lyrics were 'I wouldn't trade you for the world or the heavens above; I have heaven here on Earth, dear, since you've given me your love'. Dad was never home to hear the requests, and I wondered did he hear Mum's requests to know she loved him.

If I sang, forgetting myself and Dad heard me, he'd laugh and I'd blush. It never stopped me from singing. As far as Mum and Dad were concerned, I could never do anything right. I was either too big for my britches or walking like an elephant that sang like a scalded cat. All these remarks made me too sensitive, and this sensitivity was to my detriment. More times than one, I was crying to myself when reminded of my failures or imperfections.

Over the Christmas holidays, we'd go to the pictures. I really loved the pictures 'Pollyanna,' and 'Summer Holiday' with Cliff Richard, who travelled across Europe from England in a double-decker bus to Greece. How I wished I could travel to other countries. My parents went to the clubs to enter dancing competitions. Mum was always winning boxes of chocolates, for the Limbo Rock competitions. Mum really loved dancing. Not Dad; he was good though, and let her dance with other men so she could enter the competitions.

After the pictures, Mum and Dad would pick us up and take us back to our house, or we'd go to Don and Donna's home for dinner. Everyone was so happy and talkative. After dinner, we kids would sit and watch the adults dance. I actually liked watching my parents dance; it was like they lost themselves in each other's arms, completely forgetting about us and their lives. Many times we'd be there until one or two in the morning. By that time we had fallen asleep on the lounge, and when everyone had enough talking and dancing, Dad woke us up and took us home.

Mum and Dad had lots of lovely friends, and we went to many places with them for outings. We went on picnics to the beach or the mountains, but their friends could never come to our house. It seemed as if my parents wanted to be away from the farm, and away from Grandma's control, they were different people. Our lives were getting better.

Chapter 31

Connection With Nature

1964 was a learning year for me at high school. I had Social Studies for a subject, and I learned of the great missionaries David Livingstone and Albert Schweitzer. I was intrigued by the thought of going into the dark continent of Africa and living and working in there.

This fuelled my imagination, and so this year, us siblings decided to do a nature study in summer, autumn, and spring on our holidays. The three of us agreed to do this, so it was a botany year. This venture turned out to be very pleasurable. We all loved the bush. Well, Maxine not so much, but she joined us. I loved nature and its beauty. Barton loved the bush to ride his bike in. My sister and I decided to collect details on the plants and animal life. Barton did not want to do this, but he had no option; he was under our control. It was a very relaxing activity. In the bush, we lost ourselves for hours. There was no leader there, and it brought us all a little closer. We got to talk about the things we'd found. We definitely were friendlier towards each other; our rivalry disappeared until we returned home. On these bush expeditions, we were so different.

It was great to do things together. We'd go into the bush and discover and draw pictures of plants, trees, and any animals we saw. We mainly found insects. We'd name them; we picked up debris, examined it, and assessed what it was. We found many dried insect's bodies that looked like soft fragile shells. We wrote about what we found. We'd look for wild animals' droppings and investigate how fresh they were.

For me, this idea was pure heaven. One could sense the silence and the noises of the bush at the same time. The insects were making their various sounds, and then, as if the bush paused, all were listening, all was silent, waiting for the next move. All was in anticipation of something; but no, it was nothing, and we all continued about our work, and the insects started up their choirs again.

I loved the smells of the eucalyptus trees, and the clean dirt under our feet. I was sure I could smell the animals that lived there. Now and then, we'd hear cracking of sticks underfoot. You'd be startled by the noise. You'd stop and turn, looking, hoping to see a kangaroo. You'd wait, but nothing. Maybe it was a stray cow that roamed in from the grassy areas around the track. The noises were good, and always brought us back to where we were. We were a bit like the cows; grazing on the beauty of nature, wrapped in the awe of its perfection. I loved to draw as a child, even though I wasn't very good at it, which never stopped me from trying. The bush was so safe. On our adventures, we'd always take a packed lunch to make a day of it, not returning home until late in the afternoon.

Our arguments were about our possessions, mainly lollies. As a child, material things didn't interest me.

I had no desire for them; space and privacy were what I demanded. I think my siblings and I fought because we were angry inside ourselves. We each had our own space in our bedrooms. In my space, I put my little treasures. My space was a drawer. In there, I hid my secrets. My treasures were sacred to me.

Each week, we were given a big, brown paper bag of lollies. Maxine would gobble her lollies down in a matter of minutes, whereas I'd eat a few and put the rest in my drawer for later on. Maxine knew I kept my lollies in my drawer, and she'd go in and help herself to my lollies. Of course I knew every lolly that was there, and if one was missing, there was holy hell. Arguments could be good because, while arguing, we were talking.

Over the course of the seasons, my sister and I filled quite a few exercise books with our drawings and stories of our botany discoveries. Not that we could say the same for Barton. He was only there for the ride. More often than not, he just got bored with our activities and rode off on his bike. In a way, he'd been forced to join us. This activity didn't interest him, and many times he'd sit in the dirt and draw in it. Try as he may, he couldn't get interested in our games. He did a lot of complaining when we insisted. Many times he'd just trail behind us to be in it. He loved his push bike, and he'd make fishtails in the dirt, which upset us because he was upsetting nature. We'd end up shouting at him not to upset the animals or birds. Maxine and I tried to get Barton to do some drawings, but his efforts were very poor, and he could only manage stick trees and people. His heart wasn't in it.

Unfortunately, Barton did not have much of a say in our family, especially with us girls. We'd subject him to many embarrassing moments when he was much younger. We'd dress him up as a girl, telling him his name was Betty. He was one of us then, even though he didn't look like us. It gave us a lot of pleasure to make him like us. I remember one day we were really causing a ruckus dressing up Barton. Dad came home unexpectedly and found Barton dressed as a girl with lipstick on. Dad already had a dislike for Barton. He lashed out at him, calling him stupid, but it was just a game. That day made matters worse for him. We were told to get those clothes off him and wash his face. We were mean, spiteful, unkind children who could hurt each other so easily. We even turned on Barton in his embarrassment.

'Barton's a girl,' we wailed in delight.

Our taunts made Dad's anger worse. He began screaming at Barton, calling him worse names, and he wanted that dress off of him there and then. My poor brother suffered just as much as I did.

I can still hear Dad screaming, 'Get those clothes off and wash your face, you stupid idiot.'

My sister and I couldn't understand why he was so cranky with Barton. It was only a game.

At this time, Dad received an inheritance from the Isle of Man, due to the last sister of Grandfather's dying. He'd had an inheritance a few years back and bought a pink Morris Isis car. With this inheritance, he received a very good sum of money, and bought himself a brand new green Falcon '64, a truly beautiful car.

I think Mum would have loved to have used the money as a deposit on a house in town. With this extra money, it made their lives that more comfortable. This was the time Dad started to buy Mum lots of presents, and Mum was given money to buy herself gowns. She bought some really lovely gowns. Dad continued to buy Mum jewellery over a long period of time: opals, pearls, cameo sets and rubies. This was the time they'd leave us with Grandma and go out for the night dancing. They went to lots of balls that were being held in and around our area. Mum got her hair done at the hairdresser for these occasions. I really loved to see Mum dressed up in her gowns. She looked beautiful, and she was so very happy. It was a happy period for them.

Winter time, Maxine opted to play basketball on Saturdays. Not me; I wasn't into sports. I picked the films which coincided with the basketball games. Around 1pm I would go to the movies for my pastime. I was given one shilling and thirty pence, and with that I bought myself a bottle of Cottees bitter lemon cordial, a bag of chips, and a honeycomb bar, and my ticket into the film. Barton sometimes went to the pictures, but mostly he went to Grandma Owens' house to play with his friends. Out of us three, Barton was the closest to Mum's mum.

My favorite films were the ones about the Mediterranean lifestyles, and about rich American women falling in love with Mediterranean gigolos, who seemed to have an amazing way of loving with sensuality. I loved the films showing the fishing boats coming in after a day's fishing, and the rivalry between the fishermen. I liked the actresses Sophia Loren and Gina Lollobrigida; they were stunning women with strong personalities. They didn't take any crap from the men, until their hearts were won over by a nice man. My favourite personality was Rosalind Russell as Aunty

Mame; I loved her energy and her love of life. She travelled the world and had so many stories to tell her young nephew. I loved adventure stories such as *Aladdin* and *Ali Baba and the Forty Thieves*, *Hercules* and *Jason and the Argonauts*; anything to do with the myths and legends I was never told about as a child. The films of the Mediterranean area intrigued me the most, and I couldn't get enough of them. I liked *Three Coins in the Fountain,* and women looking for love in strange lands. I had no idea why I was so drawn to these places, because my family never spoke of such places, only England or Canada.

I loved musicals, especially *High Society*, or anything with Ginger Rogers and Fred Astaire, Frank Sinatra, and Gene Kelly in *Singin' in the Rain*. I loved watching any type of dancing shows. All Westerns captivated me, and so did the Roman and Egyptian films like *Ben Hur*, and any African films. I liked *Zulu* with Michael Caine the most. My favorite films were about travelling, and any that showed me different parts of the world, other peoples' cultures and how everyday people lived in other countries.

My friend Melinda was also playing basketball. At school, she asked me to join her team. I really didn't want to, but got it into my head that I'd give it a try; if I could do it, I could; if not, I'd leave it. My parents were pleased when I asked them if I could play basketball. They signed me up the following weekend with Melinda's team, 'The Sweet Girls'. Mum arranged with Aunty Del to make a uniform for me. The following weekend, all dressed in the uniform and ready for the part, I had my first and last game of basketball. What a disaster! I played for about half an hour, and after being knocked, jostled and pushed by manic girls set on breaking their opponents' necks, that was enough for me. When they came to pick us up, I told my parents I didn't want to play ever again, complaining how the girls were too rough and mean. My dad was upset with me, because he'd spent money on me for registration fees and a uniform used for one game. He thought I was lazy. That wasn't the reason; sport just wasn't for me. Mum was okay about it. She gave the uniform to Aunty Del to sell to someone else, if she could.

So back to the pictures for me. My final analysis on sport was that somehow, in the long run, after all those years of thumping on one's feet so hard on unforgiving concrete, it was going to be no good for the body. I felt the body would suffer in later life. Somehow I knew it was important to look after your body and not mistreat it.

My passions in life lay in theatre, culture and drawing. I'd draw on anything I could lay my hands on: old books, butchers' paper, old exercise books. I was drawing animals, people, and I was still designing beautiful gowns. I was getting the ideas from the pictures. My loves weren't active like sport, so no one could see anything productive from what I was doing. My passions were ignored. While designing these gowns, I'd daydream of wearing the fashions myself, and being a princess who married a prince. My imagination kept me happy and strong in my mind. Unfortunately, I was constantly accused of having my head in the clouds and forgetting where I was, causing me many problems with my elders. They thought I wasn't paying attention to them. It wasn't that; I was just lost in my dreams.

Regardless of their taunts and snarls, my daydreaming was important to me. They could rant, rave and complain all they liked; they weren't going to change me, and no one could take my private world from me. My private fantasies were vivid, exciting, great, and took me into a space that was safe and comfortable, beyond this realm of confusion, heartaches and sorrows. In my world were stories of intrigue, adventure and love. I wanted to write stories about things, places and people. I even dreamed of other worlds, and I created stories about outer space. Death didn't worry me, and I could have written stories about it. All my stories were in my head because I wasn't good at writing. To interrupt me while I was daydreaming, was like an invasion into my secret drawer.

I was sensitive to my surroundings, feeling in tune and connected to nature. Nature provided me with an inner peace. Spring came, and it was time to head back down to the creek. This whole area was shrouded in mystery and beauty. The creek had crystal clear water running over a soft sand bed. This intrigued me, as it trickled fast, making a gurgling sound while the current drove it over pebbles and larger stones. Some of these stones blocked the water's way and seemed to split the water, causing it to divert around either side of the stone. With other stones, the water easily rolled over them and cascaded along. Some parts of the water seemed to have an easy life, and other parts seemed to be struggling, as it toiled along the creek bed on its long journey to I didn't know where.

I could sit and watch the water run over these stones for ages, while I listened to the wind talk to me through the willow trees, sounding like old men moaning, telling me a story of long ago. The rustling of the water reeds as the wind caught them felt like they were inner beings, vibrating to create a tune, to harmonize with all the sounds of nature that surrounded them. I was in tune with nature, but not with people. It was so different to be with nature; nature understood you and didn't take from you. It gave you something every time you entered its realm; nature protected me and kept me safe. I knew things without being able to name what I knew.

As I searched the sky at night, I knew people lived on other worlds. They lived on planets far away from our galaxy. I found life easier to live here on Earth, knowing we weren't alone. Death and life were important. Death was good; it had to come to all of us, and there was no need to worry about it, because we could come back here again, and that wasn't a bad thing to do. When our Uncle Mitchell died in Rosemont, I wasn't sad. For me, it was okay for him to die; it was better than seeing him sitting or lying in his bed, old, wrinkled and sick. He could come back in a fresh, new skin as a baby. I understood life did not stop here on earth. Life went on, maybe by returning here to earth, or by going on to other planets. I couldn't fully understand what I knew, because I didn't have the words to describe it, but there was no ending here. My family wouldn't have understood what I felt or knew.

Daydreaming was where I could investigate these thoughts. I loved to do this, but it got me into so much trouble. I loved to dream of being a heroine and helping the people in trouble in the world, and it was coming through that this was what I wanted to do: to help people. Most of all, I wanted to help people understand the things I knew about, so they wouldn't feel so scared, bad or upset.

Chapter 32

Seeking Myself

At thirteen, it was important for me to connect with Mum, but the more I tried, the more I felt her tension. Sometimes when Dad was at work, I'd go and knock on their door. She'd allow me in. I'd go and sit near her on the small sofa under the open window. Mum always had the window open in their room, and this made the room bright and airy. It was a big room, holding their large bed and wardrobe, and our baby cot was still there, but it probably was all Grandma's furniture. There was a fireplace with a long mantelpiece, and a sofa for two people. Mum was usually reading her bible or looking through it. It was like her secret bible. In this bible, she kept pieces of paper with special dates on them, and notes of important occasions to her. Her bible was like my secret drawer. We were never allowed to touch or look in her bible. She'd always place it back into her wardrobe and hide it. She never left it lying around. Unfortunately, there was never any depth in my efforts to have a conversation with Mum. So many times I'd just sit there as she read magazines.

Mike Long, a new mate of Barton's, started to come out to visit us. He was a nice guy, older than Barton, who always liked older people too. They were really good friends, so Mike became a regular visitor to our farm. We all liked him too, and invited him to join us on many of our nature trips. Near the lagoon spillway, we'd been surveying what came over the spillway after a long period of heavy rain. On this day, we found a cute little turtle about four inches long. It was a baby turtle, and the three of us fought over it. We couldn't share it and pass it around. With all the pulling and tugging, I became worried for the turtle. It could get hurt because we were all trying to grab it. Being the tallest, I managed to grab it, and threw it back into the water. I got a couple of punches for it, but the pain of the punches soon wore off. Mike never intervened when we fought; he'd just wait until we stopped fighting. He was an only child, and he must have thought our behaviour was strange at times.

When we were much younger, we did some terrible things. We thought we could look after nature better than nature itself. One of my sister's friends, Julie, came from town to stay with us on the weekend. There was a bird's nest on the verandah, and in it were some chicks. Deciding to feed and care for them, we climbed up and took out of their nest. Of course they died. I really suffered with guilt for doing something I knew was wrong. I'd grown up on a farm and been with nature long enough to know that only nature can look after its own.

One weekend we got a visitor. A car with a boat behind it parked near our top gate on the main road. The dogs started to bark, and Grandma rushed out to see what was happening. A tall, fair-haired man entered our property. He walked down through our top paddock to the second gate and came to the house. The dogs were barking madly. Grandma had to hush them, and we kept them back from him. She called out to Dad, who was in the shed.

He screamed out, 'Okay, I'll be there in a minute.'

The stranger was drawing closer to the house. He was tall, a good-looking man about thirty-years old. The dogs were still restless and we were shushing them. Finally, Dad arrived from the shed to greet the stranger.

'Hello, I am Phillip.' He smiled, putting his hand out.

Dad shook hands. Grandma and us kids joined them.

The man asked, 'Do you own this land?'

Grandma replied, 'Yes, I do.'

Dad looked at Grandma and back at the stranger. 'How can we help you?' Dad asked.

Phillip turned and pointed to the road, 'Well, er, um, I have a speedboat, and I was wondering, could I use it on your lagoon?'

Dad looked at Grandma.

She said, 'You're not supposed to, as it's a sanctuary.'

'Oh well, um,' he seemed a bit disappointed as he twisted and turned, and you could see he didn't want to go without another try at convincing them to let him use the lagoon. 'Are you sure I can't use it?' As he stared down towards the beautiful lagoon, Grandma looked at Dad for a decision.

Dad took the initiative and said, 'Yes, you can use it, but only this one time, because it belongs to the pit.'

He was so excited, he almost jumped with joy. 'Oh! Thanks!' and he shook Dad's hand again, saying, 'I'll just go and bring my boat in. I have a mate in the car as well.'

He ran off to the car in case we changed our minds. They came through each of the gates, and when they got to where we were all standing, Dad got into their car with them. They all went off to the lagoon. Dad seemed really excited. Mum joined us, and we all walked to the lagoon to watch them use their speedboat.

Phillip and his mate, Peter, gave us all a ride. When it was my turn, I backed away, fearing the depth of the water. I didn't like fast rides. I declined, thanking them.

Grandma insisted I go for a ride. 'Don't be silly. Go and have a go on the boat.' I edged my way into the lagoon, thinking of the reeds getting me if I fell. I was terrified.

Phillip sensed my fear. He took my hand. 'I won't go too fast.'

I smiled. 'Please don't. I am frightened.'

He helped me into the boat. 'Hold on to the side, and Peter will sit with you.'

'Okay, er.' I sat gripping the gunnel of the boat. Even with Peter near me, I was still scared. I wanted to scream, but I didn't. I just held tight to the side of the boat.

When we returned, Grandma laughed. 'Look at Christine; she's as white as a ghost.'

I didn't care what colour I was. Sitting on the bank, I shook from the experience. I didn't like fast moving things back then.

Dad had told us never, ever go into the lagoon, and we never did. The edge of the lagoon seemed to drop away into a deep hole. To me, in there lurked unknown things, and there was no bottom to it. Not only did I fear the speed, but the thought of the boat overturning, and having to be in that scary water.

Aunty Connie and Uncle Oliver always came to stay with us over Christmas and into the New Year. Aunty was the only one I could talk to. I was so glad of her company. She told me about some good jobs I could think about for when I eventually went out to work. She'd bought me some books on cosmetics to consider a job as a cosmetician. She tried to encourage me to do modelling work, or to work as a masseur. She thought I'd make a great masseur, because I was good at massaging her back. She told me I had the hands to be a good masseur. Connie inspired me to think of a career. Unfortunately, my interest was in becoming a policewoman.

Our aunty was with us when we welcomed in 1965. This year, Aunty announced she and Oliver would be getting married in August. Everyone was happy for her, except Grandma. She didn't like Oliver one bit. When Aunty wasn't around, Grandma told us that Oliver was lazy and allergic to work. She inferred that he would be trouble for Connie. How right she was. Grandma seemed to come out of her doldrums with the invasion called Oliver.

When I asked Grandma if Aunty had ever had a boyfriend before Oliver, Grandma informed me that she did a long time ago.

'He was a lovely man,' she told me.

Curious, I asked, 'What happened to him?' I never got an answer.

Regardless of Grandma's opposition, Aunty seemed to be more alive and happy with Oliver than she'd been for a long time. Maxine, me and our cousins were to be Aunty's bridesmaids. We were to wear blue satin chiffon-covered dresses, which she had made by our Aunty Del. For convenience's sake, they were made in Fenton, not Rosemont. Around the middle of January, Connie and Uncle Oliver had to return to Rosemont.

Not long after confessing to Grandma that I wanted to be a policewoman, we were visited by two policemen. I don't know why they called in to the farm. It wasn't in regard to anyone in our home. The day they came, I was at home with Grandma, and the rest of my family was out. After introductions and putting tea and biscuits on a tray, Grandma and I escorted our guests to our special lounge room, where honoured guests were taken. The adults were talking about Grandfather, because he had been a policeman. I was sitting close to Grandma, listening to the grown-up talk.

Suddenly, she revealed to the policemen, 'Christine wants to be a policewoman when she leaves school.'

One of the policemen looked at me. 'Yes, you could be a policewoman; you're tall enough.'

I smiled, even though I felt very shy. As I sat there in their company, listening to Grandma elaborating on Grandfather's role in Australia as a Special Constable for Michael Davis, the mining merchant who owned the Lachlan Main Colliery, I felt something come over me, causing me to instantly think, no, I don't want to be a policewoman.

They were there for a long time and looked at the old photos of the policemen in our family. Grandma was discussing Grandfather's role on the farm when he was alive. When it was time for them to go, Grandma and I showed them back out of the house to the front gate where they'd parked their car. They got in their car and drove off back to their station, I guess.

At the front gate, as we watched them leave the property, Grandma asked me, 'Well, do you still want to be a policewoman?'

'No.'

She smiled, and no more was said.

Chapter 33

On The Farm In Times Of Drought And Floods

Throughout my life on the farm, we faced droughts, bad droughts during 1964 and 1965. They were so bad.

That summer, we went to Stanmore Beach in Dawson Hill for our summer holiday, in case Dad had to go back home and check the cows. We weren't that far from the house. We'd spent Christmas Day and Boxing Day at home with the family, and the weather had picked up a little with some light rain. There was a very dry period. Dad had to hand feed the cows after the springtime, up until nearly Christmas, when light rains reappeared.

I remember how we sometimes helped Dad distribute the food to the animals; they were very hungry, and came running to us as he brought the food around on a tractor to them. As the hay bales were thrown to them, they dived into them like there was no tomorrow. They became so reliant on us, and they, too, had to feel safe and cared for. Many of our cows were given names, and we were very close to them, but the drought was unyielding. Sometimes some of the cows died. Dad said that we had to burn the dead cows to prevent the spread of disease, so we kids helped him gather wood to pile around the beasts, and then he'd set fire to them. We'd move back, and watch the dead cow slowly succumb to the flames.

The grass was so brown and burnt-looking, and there was plenty of water around us in the lagoon, but we had no irrigation system. Maybe Dad didn't put any in because it wasn't his property; I guess he didn't want to spend money on setting up an irrigation system. However, hand feeding also proved to be expensive.

During this period of the drought, I was reminded of Grandma's stories. When she first came to live out on the farm, after she was married, there was a great drought. So much so that the water in the lagoon receded so far down that they actually found lots of Aboriginal artifacts. As I walked around the lagoon, I thought how I'd love to discover such things. I thought how great it would be to be an archeologist. I was so intrigued to find ancient things, but there was no way that was going to happen. Looking at the lagoon with all its water, I thought we'd have to suffer months of prolonged drought, and I'd not wish that on our animals. I was wanting to find the buried treasures of the past in that bottomless lagoon that could drag you down by its reeds. The reeds and rushes that stood above the water line seemed to sigh, calling you in with their mournful and enticing voice when a gentle breeze touched them. I swear the water was calling you in with its hypnotic moan from the swaying reeds and rushes.

There was so much mystery around our home, and I wondered, did the others feel it?

Many times, I'd just stare into the depths of the lagoon, and what I was seeking was my own inner buried treasures, locked up in my subconscious mind. As a child, I had no idea of such things or what I was seeking. For me, seeking knowledge was my main concern, and to learn of the world that was a mystery to me that I wanted to solve.

Chapter 34

High School And Being A Teenager

In February of 1965, I started my first year at high school, attending Hastings Crossing High School. All through primary school, we'd been walking the track to catch our bus with Sherry and her two brothers, Todd and Steven, who were a lot older than us. Now Steven had finished school, there was only Sherry and Todd walking with us. Sherry was a very special girl, so different to her cranky parents, Mr and Mrs Dawes. I wondered how they had such a precious girl as Sherry. She was the youngest of five children. Her older sister, Nancy, was living and working in Rosemont. Her two elder brothers were working in and around Hastings Crossing. Todd was the last of the brothers to attend school, and he left at the end of that year. Todd had very little to do with us. He mostly walked off ahead, but Sherry was so kind. She tried to keep everyone happy.

I was finding school very interesting. I loved my classes and the teachers. For the first time, I was being offered a variety of subjects to learn about. We actually had different teachers for each subject, which was great. The teachers in high school discussed their subjects at length. I was captivated, hanging on their every word. Unfortunately, I was put into the third lowest class, because Mr Clark hated Kinreads. I think he just gave me any score on my final primary school assessment. In high school, I studied hard and worked my way up to a higher class. Even though I was very shy, I was happier. My two friends, Jill and Melinda, were at high school with me.

I did learn that not all people were nice. On our bus, there was one boy, who was in first year, who was very rude to me. He was supposed to have come from a good family in Spencer Shire. He was staring at my arm as I held onto the bus seat railing. There usually weren't any seats left by the time we got on the bus.

He rudely said, 'Your arms are hairy, and I have none.'

I glared at him with dagger eyes. Holding the railing, I couldn't move on. All I could do was wish I could fall through the floor of the bus and disappear. I was so indignant. He must have realised what he'd done, as he lowered his eyes from my glare. He wasn't a nice-looking boy. He looked like Nero out of the Roman films, and just as fat.

Not long into my first year, we were to go to Rosemont to see the stage musical, 'Funny Girl'. I loved musicals, and Mum and Dad allowed me to go. I was booked in around August. I would be fourteen in September.

I was so developed, and sometimes it caused me to become the centre of attention. My cousin, Charlene, and her friends were always measuring me and themselves. I was thirty-six, twenty-four, and thirty-six. For that time, it was the perfect figure. However, with a woman lurking somewhere in the shadows of this adult body, there was still a child's mind; it was confusing. It wasn't just my cousin noticing me; it was the older boys as well. Some of their looks said it all.

My cousin was a great mentor. She told me to tell my parents to bring me over to her house for the weekend, and she'd cut my hair in the latest style. Mum and Dad were obliging and took both Maxine and I to Aunty Kimberly's house. We spent the day with our cousins. Charlene cut all our hair. She had fashion magazines, and she checked our face shapes and cut our hair according to the style in the magazine that would best suit us. I was given a mod cut, all the rage at that moment.

Not that I knew about fashion, but all my cousins did. They were very up to date with modern styles, clothes, magazines, books and makeup, and knew all about modern music, and even had a record player. I hadn't been introduced to any of these things until we got our TV, so I started to learn about pop groups and singers. Before we got the TV, we listened to Mum or Grandma's favourite radio news, music or stories on their radio stations of choice. Now I was interested in these new styles more and more. Charlene showed them to me in her fashion magazines. Even Maxine wanted to have some of the new, fashionable clothes. Charlene told me I should start to shave my legs now I was at high school. She suggested I start to be more fashionable and cool. I told her I was too shy to be cool. She encouraged me to try to be more open, and to go and introduce myself to other students at school. She asked me to come and see her on Monday at school, and she'd show me how to wear my uniform to look cool.

She was a great mentor and being with her made me think how nice it would have been to have had an older sister. Yet she never invited me into her group. I think she thought she was too old and cool. It was one of our best weekends. I learnt a lot about fashions. When Mum and Dad came to pick us up, they liked mine and Maxine's hair styles.

On Monday, in the girls' toilets, Charlene showed me how to blouse up my uniform over my belt to wear it shorter.

Protesting, I said, 'But Charlene, Miss Gordon will be angry with me, and I've seen her going around pulling down girls' uniforms.'

'Don't worry about her, and if she does pull it down, you pull it back up later on, like everyone else does,' she informed me. Charlene spoke really quickly and seemed impatient. Turning me to look in the mirror, she said, 'Now look; isn't that better?'

'It is.' I was wearing my uniform below my knees. She brought it up to just above my knees and she got me to pull my socks up and told me to start wear stockings to make my legs look better.

She told me I had great legs, and to show them off. 'And tell Aunty Carol to let you shave your legs; they're too hairy, Christine.' We looked at my legs. They were hairy. She had no hair on her legs, and they looked great. She was still adjusting my uniform.

I thought of my legs and said, 'I've been told I'm hairy.'

I was happy and so was she, but she had to go and meet up with her friends. I thanked her and stayed looking in the mirror at my new hair style and shorter uniform. It all looked good.

When I got home, Dad wasn't there. I went and knocked on Mum's door.

'Who's there?'

'It's me, Mum.'

'What do you want?'

'Can I come in?' I heard a sigh and a magazine being thrown down on the lounge, and next thing Mum's at the door.

'Come in, and what is it?'

'Mum, can I shave my legs, please?'

She declined.

'Oh, Mum,' I whined, but still no, so I asked again, begging her, 'Please, Mum, pretty please, can I shave my legs? Look how hairy they are.' I flashed my legs at her.

She looked and walked off.

'Can I?' I followed her around her room, not giving in yet.

'It's too early for you to shave your legs, and you will have to do it all the time once you start.'

'But Mum, I want to shave my legs. That horrible Royce boy pointed out how hairy my arms were on the bus, and I was embarrassed.'

That caught her attention. She said, 'Let me look at your legs, Christine.'

I lifted my skirt and showed her my legs. They had dark hair on them, even though I was fair.

'Okay, I can see what you mean. You can shave, but you have to use my electric shaver; it's better for your hair.'

I nodded, smiling. 'Good. Thanks Mum.'

She went to her wardrobe and pulled out her blue electric Lady Gillette razor. 'Here; you can use this. But first do it here, so I can watch you, and then you can use it in your room.'

I was so excited to get rid of those hairs, and I commenced shaving. The end results were wonderful. I was glad my cousin was helping me.

It was time to go to the musical in Rosemont. The bus was full, but none of my friends went, because they weren't into such things. I didn't care; I went alone. On the way down, I sat next to one of the older girls from fifth form. She spoke to me sometimes. The musical was all that I'd anticipated. It thrilled me, keeping me on the edge of my seat. I had a permanent smile on my face, and goose bumps on my skin.

After the theatre, we were directed back to our bus to head back to Hastings Crossing. It was late. On the journey back, I was sitting in silence, not taking any notice of anyone on the bus. Next, I felt someone near me. I'll refer to him as Stanton. He was in fifth form. Stanton's dad was an important person in town. All the boys in fifth form were from very prominent people in our community.

He asked me to come and join him up the back of the bus.

At first I said, 'No, thanks.'

He bent down near me and said, 'Come on; I won't do anything to hurt you.'

My better judgement said to stay where I was, but an inner part of me said to go.

I went. We were sitting, smiling and making some small talk. He was seventeen and I was thirteen, but nearly fourteen. About half an hour later, before I knew it, he and I were kissing very passionately; so passionately I had lost all sense of where I was, until the bus stopped in Hastings Crossing. It was like reality clicked in. I realized where I was, and the other boys were staring at us.

Quickly I stood up and rushed off the bus. I went straight to my parents, who were standing outside waiting for me. We hurried to our car, and as we drove off, I saw Stanton looking my way. I sat back into the seat of the car. Mum asked me how the show was, and I told her it was the best thing I'd seen so far in my life, and I loved it. The memories of Stanton's kisses were still with me, and also the fact that I would have to face everyone at school on Monday was hitting me hard. Again, I was going to be embarrassed around a boy.

Monday came and I had to go to school; there was no avoiding it. At school I was so embarrassed by what I'd done. I couldn't believe I'd allowed myself to be put into that situation again, but it was too late to retract it. It was done. My first year class was in line, and behind us was the fifth form boys' class. I could have died. I sensed Stanton trying to talk to me before assembly was called to order. I ignored him. Assembly was addressed by our Principal, and news for the week was always announced. He commended all the students who had given rave reviews of 'Funny Girl'. My heart jumped. After assembly was over, we had to turn, and as I did, I saw Stanton looking at me. Shock gripped me and the sound, 'Huh!' came out of me. Then we had to march off, thank goodness. As we marched, I saw him and his friends looking at me. Because they were older students, they were treated like adults. They didn't have to be as disciplined in their line-ups. It was hard for Stanton. I feel now, looking back on the situation, he'd fallen in love with me.

September came and so did my fourteenth birthday. My experience caused me continued humiliation. Slowly, Stanton stopped trying to get my attention. My lack of self-esteem and confidence spoilt my life. I was so painfully shy, to the point of almost hurting me on a physical level. Desperately, I tried to build up my confidence, but all I could do was hide behind my friends' bravery.

Our lockers weren't far from the sixth years' recreation classroom. Almost adults, the sixth formers occupied that room for get-togethers. It was our lunch break, and I was putting my books away in my locker, getting out books for the next lot of afternoon classes. There was a noisy bunch of people coming down the hallway. I had my back to them. On turning, I saw it was my sewing teacher, Miss Ferguson. I stood admiring her for a moment and reflected on her words to me: 'Whatever you do in life, Christine, you should think about doing modelling.' I used to smile back at her and wonder how I could do that, with my parents. They wouldn't understand, and for that matter, where would I begin? The dream seemed unreachable, and the thought of achieving it daunted me, but I wanted it too. I wanted to be famous; it was one of my dreams to be famous, to stand out in the crowd, to be admired, but how could I achieve that fame when I feared it as much as I wanted it.

She was beautiful, our sewing teacher, and she had a lovely figure, shoulder-length blonde hair and blue eyes. She walked with grace and poise. Her loveliest asset was her kind nature and gentle voice, and everyone loved her. She was once a Miss Australia entrant. Miss Ferguson was flanked by the girls from my year; they were on either side of her, talking and laughing.

I pulled my books out and piled them up on top of the lockers to get to the books I needed. As I did, I glanced at them and smiled at her. She paused, slowing her pace, and smiled back at me. I lowered my eyes, still smiling, and wished I could be as open as the girls with her. I couldn't let her look fully into my eyes and see the real me, that was not clean and not as good as the other girls. I really liked her so much, and she made time for the girls at the school and tried to encourage us through the skills she recognized within us.

Then Carmel, one of my classmates, sang out the unthinkable - 'Urine' - and laughed.

My face showed shock as the book I held slipped from my chest to my stomach in my hands, and my body felt dragged down to the pits of hell. I was crushed and felt like I wanted to crawl into my locker and lock myself away forever.

Miss Ferguson checked Carmel, and then I heard Carmel telling everyone, 'It's her second name.'

Sadness enveloped my whole being. Glancing up, Miss Ferguson looked at me as she ushered the girls on. I saw her concern, but to those girls, it was funny. Laughter rang through the corridors as they went off. I was humiliated and betrayed again. Carmel had gained my confidence, and I'd told her my middle name was Urena, after my Grandma, and I asked her not to tell anyone, because I didn't like that name. Trust was broken, and so was my heart. I tried to reason how someone could do that to another person. That is the last thing I would do to any person publicly. Now there was more separateness; everyone knew one of my secrets, and Carmel had taught me never to tell anyone your secrets. I was so glad I'd never told anyone my biggest secret. Imagine if that secret got out.

At the lockers, the tears welled up into my eyes and flowed down my cheeks as warm pain. My secrets will stay with me forever, I thought. From then on, I had never discussed my life with anyone, because it was a burden I would have to face on my own and work through.

My disappointments never stopped me going to school. School was very important in my life. I could learn. I really loved to learn, although it had been a battle throughout my childhood, always being reminded of how intelligent Maxine was and how pretty I was: pretty meant dumb. Repeating second class in primary school reinforced that belief as I got older. My class colleagues were proving to be hard to handle as well.

In high school, I saw changes in me. I was excelling. While studying for my exams, I found out I was a visual learner, and because I couldn't spell, my mind remembered how to see the words visually to spell them. This helped me in my tests and exams. I'd bring up the pages I needed on the topic for the words I couldn't spell, or the texts I had to answer the questions about. It was like I could photogragh everything in my mind, and just re-write. Later on, I could see maps, even sentences and poetry and pages of books I had read from. It was getting easier for me to remember what I needed for the tests or exams.

I later learnt that I had a photographic mind. This was how I passed my exams and tests. It helped me so much that I was able to excel in all my subjects:

mathematics, science, music, art, and history; but not the grammar part of English. It was the most difficult subject for me to remember. I could remember the poems and sonnets. I loved the story-telling in the compositions. All that helped me through English.

Parents' day came. Our parents got to meet our teachers and listen to their praise of us, and their suggestions for our guidance and help. My mum came for the day. She was all smiles as we walked around to find my teachers. As we spoke to them, she listened and looked at me. I was so pleased that day. I was being praised and receiving good comments on my hard work and achievements, and I was going to be promoted to a higher class next year. I was really happy to hear my English teacher, Mr Meers, ask Mum if she realized I was highly imaginative and recommend I be encouraged to develop it. I smiled because English was my worst subject, but I'd just passed it with a grade of sixty-five percent.

I think Mum had no concept of what he was actually saying to her, and she just looked at me and smiled at him. Some of my teachers were fascinated by her and couldn't believe she was my mother. They told her they thought she was my sister. I got so mad, hating their remarks, thinking, she's my mother. My hate for her grew because of her inability to act as a mature parent. This had happened in primary school with my friends too. They thought she was my sister, and now here, at high school, it was the same.

I jumped in and angrily conveyed to my friends, 'No, she's my mother. She just looks young because she uses creams on her face.'

At high school, I couldn't say that to my teachers. Mum liked to dress very young, and she loved to wear these boater hats, looking like an English school child of some rich family attending a rich school. I didn't mind my mother looking young, but she was showing a false self, portraying a happy, loving, and caring mother who was very interested in me, while all along, I knew different.

My parents became interested in travelling around the country. Mum and Dad had bought an old plywood caravan. Maxine, Barton and I painted it hot pink, putting a white strip around it. We did a very good job, and Dad liked it as well. On our first caravan holiday, we decided to reconnect with Mum's older sister, Betty. I had last met Aunty Betty when Dad and I were looking for Mum. It was our May holidays, and they were living on a sheep station out west towards Chapman Plains. Aunty had a new man in her life: Uncle Darcy. He was managing the station.

The journey to Chapman Plains was long; it seemed to take forever, as we drove along flat roads that never ended, with images of mirages in the distance. I was anxious to meet up with my cousins again, and Aunty Betty. She was so funny, and I hoped she was still happy. The weather was very warm. I remember the trip, and we children taking a portable radio to listen to music as we were driven there. It didn't always pick up a signal, but when it did, we had some entertainment.

Dad had to stop on the side of the road for a break from driving, because Mum couldn't drive. We had lunch and then moved on. It was so great to get away from our farm. When we arrived, everyone ran out of the house to greet us. Their house was run down, but what the heck!

This was holiday time. Kelvin, Naomi, and the twins had grown up. Aunty Betty introduced us to her new man. We had to call him Uncle Darcy. We met his two little girls to Aunty Betty, Charlene and Josephine. We all hugged and chatted, then went inside and had tea and cake. Everyone was so happy. Later on, we kids went with our cousins to investigate the area and look around the property. We saw the sheep dogs tied up, but we weren't allowed to touch them. They weren't pets.

It was fun, and we talked to Naomi while the boys did boy things. We'd been there a few days, and I could see problems between Uncle Darcy and Aunty's children to her former husband. He was especially cruel to Kelvin, making him do a man's job, and Kelvin was a year younger than me. At thirteen, he had to cook the dog's mutton in cut-up forty-four-gallon drum tins. His job was to feed all these farm dogs on short leashes, and then the other dogs. I don't know who I felt for the most, Kelvin or the dogs. Regardless, I enjoyed my time there. As we got to know Aunty Betty more, I grew to love her heaps, but I didn't like Uncle Darcy.

While at Aunty Betty's, I again done something I shouldn't have done. I touched one of the twins, and I was caught out. But this time I learned a big lesson. This was not right, and I vowed at the age of fourteen, never to touch another child, and I never did. I had to make that choice, and I did.

In August 1965, Connie and Oliver were married. The wedding was held in Rosemont. For years, my family had been going to Aunty Beatrice's house at Jupiter's Corner, but ever since Mum returned home, we'd stopped going there. We were all looking forward to reuniting with Aunty Beatrice, and we even managed to get Grandma to Rosemont and to the wedding. We got her to wear one of her grey dresses that Aunty Connie had bought her in January, which made us all think Connie'd known Oliver longer than she was telling us.

Aunty Beatrice's house was just as elegant, neat and clean, but she was looking tired and older. My Aunty Fannie was now in a nursing home and would not be attending the wedding. She had bowel cancer.

Aunty Beatrice's house was where Connie and us girls prepared for the day. It was a big day, and we all had to go to the hairdressers to have our hair done. This was a treat, and it would be my first time I'd ever had my hair styled in a hairdressing salon. At the house, it was all laughter and fun as we dressed and prepared, and helped Aunty Connie dress too. She looked so beautiful on her day, a picture of happiness, and we five girls looked beautiful in our blue satin chiffon-covered dresses. Each of us carried a pink bouquet of gladioli, and Aunty Connie carried white ones.

The wedding was held in the Church of England at Jupiter's Corner. It was such a lovely wedding. The reception was held in Aunty Beatrice's house. There were many relatives that we hadn't seen for years. It was a great family gathering, as well as a great wedding. Aunty Henrietta and her daughter, Susanne, who we hadn't seen for years, were there. I remembered we'd met Susanne once out on the farm. She'd fascinated me because she was studying ballet. She was such a beautiful girl, an only child. She'd done all the things I'd liked to have done: ballet, singing, and she went to concerts with her mother. We never had those opportunities, and as a child

I remembered holding onto her every word as she talked about her life. My cousin from Fenton and Maxine and I all admired Patrick most of all, but Patrick was now married to Gerry. His brother, Albert, was there with his wife, Lydia. It was so good to see all these people again.

I managed to embarrass myself. We were allowed to have a drink of champagne, but it went straight to my head and made me feel dizzy, causing me to fall over. This made me feel silly and even more useless, because I'd done it in front of the whole family. My embarrassment was mainly around my older male cousins, Patrick and Albert. I don't know why, but to be silly in front of boys caused me more pain than in front of girls. How could people accept me, when I was so silly?

Aunty's marriage would be the beginning of hell for her, with a man who would wear her down from a well-groomed lady with never a hair out of place, to a bedraggled, grey-haired, rotten-toothed, weak-minded lady, whose only interests would be him and their two dogs, Minnie and Sheba. Her diabetes she'd had since she was sixteen would worsen, causing her to be hospitalized often, and we would see big changes in her as she gradually became a weaker, insecure, and a crying, defeated lady, scared of life. Aunty Connie had not long purchased herself a home in Denton, a very good area in Rosemont in the early 60s. She had money from her inheritance from the Isle of Man, and from working, and she'd lived with Aunty Beatrice and probably saved her money. I heard Aunty Beatrice didn't like Oliver either. When Aunty Connie and Oliver got married, Aunty Connie left her job. She left her security and he didn't have a job, until later on he got a job as a debt collector.

Grandma told us he got that job so he could sleep all day and be up all night. Maybe she was right, because my beautiful aunty was sleeping in, and Aunty Connie never used to do that. She was always up with the birds. Oliver wasn't a clean man. I heard my aunty had to take his underwear away while he was showering; if she didn't, he'd wear it for another week. This gave me the shivers, because in our house, we bathed every day, and sometimes twice a day. Oliver also had rotten teeth. You could see he didn't look after himself at all, and as time went on, I wondered if Grandma was right about him.

Grandma also told us he was a beggar off the street. Aunty had met him as a beggar through her job at the Save the People Organisation. He'd come in as a homeless man. He would drag Connie down to his level eventually and keep her in poverty, until she died in a neglectful state. Not that her money would have been taken from her by him then. No, on the contrary, he wouldn't allow her to spend her money on herself for grooming, only for her diabetic health and her wellbeing. His plan was that when she died, he'd get all her money. This would be revealed in the future. Grandma's words would ring true. He was a master of disguise, and disguised his true self, intent and motives well.

As a fourteen-year-old teenager, I reasoned that Grandma's opinion of Oliver was because he was taking up a lot of Aunty's time, and we didn't get to see her as often as we liked. They still came out to the farm each Christmas, and sometimes during the year. As we got to see them more, we warmed to Uncle Oliver, especially his sense of humour. He had a quick wit, but there was something I couldn't work out about him.

Charlene was always chatting to me at school, giving me the rundown on how to think modern. She'd introduced me to pop music, and she encouraged me to watch *Bandstand* with Brian Henderson as the host. I told Mum, and she agreed we could watch it. It became one of our most watched shows. We all liked the Delltones. Mostly Peewee with his deep voice; he was our favourite. We loved Col Joye, as well as Ray Brown, the Bee Gees, and Helen Reddy.

My favourite pop singer was Normie Rowe, who was extremely popular in '65 with his hit songs 'Que Sera Sera', 'Shakin' All Over' and 'I (who have nothing)', which was my favourite song.

We'd been told the local radio announcers were coming to our school with Col Joye, and if we wanted their autographs, to have autograph books ready. So I got myself an autograph book for the day. The radio announcers came, and we were so lucky because it created a big excitement at school, and it was a great day seeing these people in the flesh. We knew the personalities and had heard them over the radio, and saw them on the TV. Pat was one of the most popular radio announcers of our time. I managed to get Pat's autograph and everyone else's on the day. These radio announcers brought along posters of different pop singers, and I scored a pin-up of Normie Rowe, which thrilled me to bits. There were many pop singers and bands at this time, but I didn't like them all, especially Billy Thorpe and the Aztecs. For me, they were too way out, and I wasn't too keen on the Rolling Stones either, but I loved the Beatles, especially Paul McCartney and George Harrison. I loved the Beatles' songs, 'She Loves

You', 'A Hard Day's Night', 'Ticket to Ride', and their song 'Help', and I even went to see the film *Help*. It was a great era for me. But however many times I saw The Beatles on TV, it puzzled me how those girl fans of theirs could carry on as they did, screaming and fainting and acting really stupid.

On the TV in October 1965, we got to see Jean Shrimpton wearing her mini-skirt above her knees. This was what my cousin Charlene had been trying to tell me about. In London, they were already wearing these clothes. London was way ahead of Australia in fashion. I liked the new fashions so much. Maxine asked Mum if we could get some of these new clothes, and she agreed to it for our Christmas presents. Both Maxine and I were very happy. Charlene had done us a favour by introducing us to the fashion world, but we'd never go to the extremes my cousins went to in their endeavours to be fashionable.

In the December school break, we'd head north, taking our cousin Charlene on this holiday; we did a lot of travelling around, spending a couple of days here and there. Charlene was older than me and more in tune with life. She was also very mischievous. In one of the caravan parks, Charlene and I were in the shower room, and we ended up having a water fight with all the taps on, splashing water everywhere, throwing it on all the mirrors and the walls. The owner of the park caught us. He'd come in to see what all the laughter was about. We were told to pack up and leave the park. We actually got kicked out. Dad had to find another caravan park, which he couldn't. It took us ages to find a nice park like the one we'd just left. I got a tongue-lashing, and Charlene was meant to take note of my reprimand.

We went to a pineapple factory. Again, Charlene was up to no good. She sat near the tap, helping herself to the free pineapple juice. Being a cousin, and Dad's brother's daughter, he couldn't go off at her. In a way, it was funny watching him lose his temper, and having to deal with his own annoyance. He had to keep it all under his hat and not show it, because he couldn't hit her. That was the first and last time she came away with us.

School was stressful, and I was glad it was coming to a close. Finally, it was the end of my first year at high school. Not long after the incident with Stanton, he left school after completing his fifth year. He didn't do sixth form to get his Higher School Certificate, which was strange for someone to do that: to not complete their sixth year to get that higher school certificate, especially being the son of a well-educated and renowned family in Hastings Crossing. I heard later on, through others, he went and joined one of the forces. I couldn't go out with Stanton because Dr Jones' son, Alex Jones, was also in his group. Dr Jones was our family doctor, so Alex's father knew about me and my father, and what he'd done to me. I could have told Stanton the truth about who I was, what I'd done and how I wasn't a good person, but Stanton's father was also very important in our town, and I would have been shunned by them.

Chapter 35

Catching Up With The World

In my second year in high school, I was placed in a higher class. It was so nice to be moved up a class. I'd strived so hard in my first year and became an achiever. I was definitely wrongly assessed in primary school by my parents and the teacher, who never took the time to see my true potential as a student. I had silently won on my own merits. That's all I needed to do, was win for me, no one else. Gaining firsts, seconds and thirds in my class subjects, I was so pleased with myself, and I did excel. I was so pleased, because our school acknowledged those who moved up a class with a book, congratulating us on our achievement at assembly. When I told Mum the good news, her comment was, 'That's good, Christine.' I felt she'd probably thought, and now you've told me, don't bother me.

That year, I took on geography, and became very good at mapping. Maxine was also at high school, in her first year, and she was put straight into the third highest class. I excelled in all my subjects again: commerce, home science, mathematics and science. Not so good in English. English would always be a problem subject for me throughout school. Story writing would save me, and remembering the poems; that was the only part of English I liked. I couldn't grasp the concepts of grammar. My stories told of unseen worlds, and of being visited by people from other worlds, taken by them to their worlds and returned here to Earth. I was highly imaginative, and my teachers let me know this, but I wasn't encouraged to do anything about it. In high school, my teachers were mainly males. I liked them, and I felt safe with them, and they actually praised me; but my happiest time was with my two friends, Melinda and Jill.

My parents always showed two faces. That's the way it was. Outside the house, they had a face, and inside the house, they had another face. Sometimes, their behaviour affected me as a teenager. I could have easily faded away out of everyone's sight. I thought about taking a bottle of Mum's sedatives and ridding myself of them, and them of me. My home life was an issue, not school. School life was too good, and I was coping with what had happened last year with Stanton. This year was going to unfold new strengths within me, because I would discover I could cope in life. I would make sure no one ever knew my secret. I just hoped Doctor Jones never told his son what I was. And I'd be so glad when the sixth formers eventually left school, because if Alex found out about me and my secret was released, I would die. I mustn't cause myself any more embarrassing moments.

In the Easter break, Maxine was allowed to go to a National Fitness Camp offered by the school. These camps gave her many opportunities to try all kinds of sports and games, and meet new friends, but I was never allowed to go. I guess it was because they didn't trust me, due to what happened between Dad and me, which I'm sure Mum was still blaming on me. Mum had never once approached me and asked me how I was going. She never bothered to ask me how I was coping, or suggest we talk about what had happened, or was there someone I needed to talk to, or did I need help. No, it was just as if nothing had happened. It was some sort of dream, a bad memory. Yes, it was a bad memory that left a permanent reminder in me. She knew Dad had taken advantage of me as a child, but she never protected me. She protected Dad.

Boys were becoming more interested in me, but I couldn't get interested in them. There was one boy, Gavin Lacey, who tried so hard to get my attention, that I agreed to become his girlfriend. It was a failure; there was no communication between us, and I had no idea about what to say to him or talk to him about. In the recess break, we'd just sit near each other, staring out at the playground, and not talk. It was too hard, and I hated going to him. Boys didn't interest me. The relationship lasted a month, and then I told him I didn't want to be with him, and I returned to my girlfriends. It was painful having a boyfriend, and painful being in his company. For me, friendship was all I wanted with anyone.

My sister and I wore the latest fashions, thanks to Charlene, and I loved my baby doll dress, because it was a full dress from the bodice down, and it hid my well-developed body and made me look like I had no waistline, and we both had the mumu dresses. These were also straight shifts, with bobbles sewn on the seams of the shift, which my Aunty Del made for us. So we were really into the latest fashions without the hype, but Melinda wasn't. She only cared about the boys, I'd noticed, and she was starting to fancy the boys at school as well. I didn't know what all the fuss was about having a boyfriend. To me, it was a silly thing to want a boyfriend. I much preferred my own company.

My parents invited Melinda to come away with us during the May '66 school holidays. Maxine and Barton would never take any of their friends away. I knew why. Now we had a caravan, we all were in closer proximity to each other. Mum and Dad needed a go-between, and that would be a friend of mine. I didn't mind, because it was good having an outsider on the family holidays. They broke any tension, and it helped Mum to chat.

Both my parents liked Melinda and her bubbly personality, and so did I. Melinda was the type of girl who could fit in anywhere. She knew how to win people over, especially my mum. They got on so well. I was glad, because she was opening my mum up, which allowed us to get closer. Even if the conversations were only about her body preparations to keep her young and youthful, it was chatting.

Mum was an image person, obsessed about keeping her youth. She ensured that we girls also maintained our youthfulness by buying us skin care products, and she was forever pointing out Grandma was old and had wrinkled skin because she had let herself go. For me, Grandma had always looked the same. She looked at least ninety, compared to Mum and Dad, who always look so fresh, young and youthful. Their youth stood out more around Grandma. They seemed like they weren't much older than us young kids, like lost children themselves.

On this holiday, we were off to Ashton, which was near Drovers Shire, a country town in the central northern districts, the sheep belt area. Aunty Betty and her family had moved up there to live on a sheep station. On our journey, we stopped at Port Foxdale for a few days. We enjoyed the beaches, and Dad always took us sightseeing around the old churches and cemeteries. I remember Maxine was bored on one of these ventures, and started swinging her camera, a Brownie 26. We'd both got one each for Christmas the previous year. She hit the camera on the cement and cracked it, much to Dad's horror, so I was the only one left with a camera. On arriving at Ashton, we headed out of town and found the sheep station, belonging to the Bradshaw's, where Uncle Darcy worked. As we pulled alongside this beautiful big house, similar to our own, with wide verandahs around it and trees surrounding that shaded the house, I was in awe. Wearing a big smile, a man, and presumably his son, strolled casually out of the house and through their front gate, like typical country people. This man greeted my dad, and Dad, being of the same mind frame, showed him similar country respect.

Immediately, on seeing the boy closer up, Melinda liked him. He seemed to be a year older than us: tall, with dark hair, thin build, and he seemed a bit shy. In the car, she was giggling and telling my mum how she'd like to meet him. 'Aunty Carol, how can I meet him?' She pestered my Mum.

I giggled, and Maxine wasn't paying attention, hanging her head out of the window. Barton was looking at me and smirking at Melinda. Mum suggested we ask Aunty Betty. The farmer knew we were coming. He and Dad started up a conversation. Dad looked settled in for a yack, because out came his roll-your-own tobacco pouch, and he commenced to make a cigarette and lit it up, folding his arms across his stomach and smoking his cigarette, lifting his arm up for the draw and placing it back over his stomach. This was a sign we were in for a long wait. The boy was nervous, glancing over towards us in the car, and he gently kicked the toe of his boot into the soft dirt. Melinda was holding her heart, gasping.

After a while, Dad returned to the car, and we drove off to Aunty's house, not far from the main big homestead. As we were driving along, Melinda was trying to find out the boy's name from Dad, and of course Dad didn't remember. Approaching Aunty's house, I could see there was a stark difference between the owners' homestead and their house. Aunty's house was run down and needed a coat of paint. It was exposed to the elements, having no trees around it to shade it. There were a couple of small trees on the side of the house, where I could see Uncle Darcy's working dogs. The whole family was outside the house, jumping up and down, ready to greet us, and as soon as the car stopped and we got out, we all rushed to my Aunty Betty. We kissed her and cuddled her, and my cousins also cuddled us, and I introduced Melinda to my cousins. Of course they loved her.

After settling in, having some tea and some of my aunty's famous boiled fruit cake, the men left the house. Melinda asked Aunty Betty about the boy in the homestead.

'Oh, so you're seen our Jules,' she said, smirking in the kindest of ways at silly young girls.

'Jules, how old is he?' Melinda enquired.

'About seventeen,' she said.

Melinda's heart was racing a hundred miles an hour, and her eyes seemed to melt just thinking of this boy, and her fascination for Jules grew. Melinda had a hundred and one questions to ask my aunty about him. To me he was nice-looking, and I thought he was a bit shy. I liked that about him, but nothing more, though Melinda's enthusiasm was stirring my own interest in him.

Try as we might to get Jules' attention, we failed. I think because he was too shy, and he was always with his parents, and it was hard to make a move with them around. Melinda suggested we dress up as really cool beatniks or hippies, so we did. We acted like really cool hippies and walked around with our smaller cousins not far from Jules' house, but he probably thought we were nuts. In long pants, with our shirts outside of them, and wild, long, messed-up hair, we really did look like real hippies.

We went out to the larger town of Drovers Shire to a rodeo, and their show day, and to the town's museum. We got to wear our fashionable clothes, and I got Mum to take photos of us dressed up.

Dad took us to see a famous sheer rock face, and Aunty Betty told us about the area and its landmarks. We spent a day in Goolalong, and another in Owensville at the artesian baths, good for aches and pains, and I thought it really cleaned my skin. While staying with Aunty Betty, we had a lot of fun. It was coming close to the time for us to return home, so one night we were all excited, and we really played up. We were all singing to Jules at the top of our voices. Our beds were on the back enclosed verandah, so as we lay there, we sang. I became asthmatic, and began wheezing from the excitement, and it got worse, tightening my chest.

Maxine got frightened and went and got Mum. Mum and Aunty Betty came to see me, and Mum told me I was too excited and had to leave that room. Aunty Betty suggested I sleep in her room, in Charlene's bed next to their bed, so she could keep an eye on me through the night.

I will never forget what happened to me. I slept very deeply all night. This was my nature; I was a deep sleeper. That morning I woke with a start, to find my Uncle Darcy had put my hand on his penis. Realising what had happened, I quickly moved my hand. Now he, too, had interfered with me, and this left me even more insecure. I turned my back on him, and he was trying to turn me back around. My aunty was sound asleep in the same bed. I moved closer in to Charlene. I eventually got up and went out to the verandah to my bed.

When everyone got up, I couldn't look at him. I was so quiet and withdrawn, not saying anything to anyone. I was outside near the water tank having a wash, when he came around the corner. I quickly ran off back into the house. I couldn't bear to be there in their house, and I was glad when we left. Now there was someone else in my life who threatened me, someone I'd have to dodge and avoid. Thankfully, we only went to their place one more time, and then Dad stopped going there.

After this, I became even more changed, and went further into myself, trying to understand why my body betrayed me, and why these men wanted to touch me. Back at school, I soon forgot about the incident, putting it behind me. Around August, Melinda had to leave school early. She didn't finish her year. As soon as you turned fifteen, you could leave. I knew she didn't like school. Her leaving upset me, but Jill was still at school. We became closer, and I started to spend more time with her, and stayed at her house on the weekends.

For our September holidays, we took Jill away with us. It was a wonderful time, and unlike Melinda, she wasn't interested in Mum. Many times we'd let Maxine join us. Other times, Maxine preferred to stay with Mum. This holiday was at Port Foxdale, a beautiful, coastal town. I was fifteen and feeling very brave. Jill and I were down on the beach, and we met some surfers. Jill was braver than me, and very forward. I liked her braveness. We were talking to these surfer guys. Jill had her hands on her hips. They were all talking about surfing and music, and I was just looking on, not saying anything because I felt awkward. So I crossed my arms across my stomach to hide it. Then it was time to go.

Jill said goodbye, and as we moved a step away to leave, one guy looked at me and said, 'You're a witch.'

'Huh! A what?'

'A witch,' he said.

Jill said, 'Come on. He's joking.'

He wasn't, and he kept staring at me. I was devastated and didn't know why he'd said that. I wanted to tell him off, but I couldn't, so I just reacted to his words and they haunted me for ages. I wasn't able to find out what he meant and what he saw within me, until later in life.

After the September break, Sherry, my neighbour, invited Jill and me into her group. They were older than us, but I liked being with Sherry, and I liked her schoolmates. This was the popular group at school. The boys here were different: friendly, nice guys, just wanting to talk and be friends. I started to love the company of boys more than girls, because I was finding their conversations much more interesting. They talked about political topics, the war, and they gave their opinions, and I was asked for my opinions. Even so, with my newfound confidence with these boys, I was still too afraid to have a boyfriend. Kevin, who was in our group, was into photography, and he was developing our films for us. My sister and I loved photography; we regularly took photos at home.

Our school also allowed us to bring our cameras to school, so I used to take lots of photos of my friends. Kevin offered to develop the films for me at a cheaper price than the pharmacy. Before my sister broke her camera, she'd taken a really good photo of me posing on Dad's car, and when Kevin developed that film, he remarked on how great I looked in a model pose. Because I knew him, I looked at the photo with him and laughed, agreeing with him. I did look good.

There was a notice in the school monthly newspaper, which Kevin organized, and he ran a story about a pin-up photo in the senior boys' room. I wondered if it was my photo he was talking about. Many times I'd still get looks from the guys in the sixth year and I knew they liked me, and some tried to get close to me through the group I was in, but I'd pretend I didn't notice them.

There was one boy I really liked, and I never told anyone. Patrick Fox was tall, quiet and strong, with dark, ethnic good looks. He carried an air of mystery around him. Ethnic men were starting to interest me more and more. I'd seen them in the movies and on TV. Somehow I knew why I wasn't interested in the boys in my own town; I was sure I would meet a man from overseas and marry him. Regardless of all the guys that surrounded me in school, I was a teenager in a woman's body, and I had no idea of what to do with them, or the woman locked up inside me. I still couldn't go out with any of them, because I wasn't good enough. Alex's father knew my secret, and I would die if it got out around the school.

One weekend, while at Jill's house, we decided to gate crash Lance Hargreaves' party. We just walked into his backyard unannounced, and we were accepted into the party. His mum was at home, and she didn't mind us girls staying; we were the only girls there with six guys. We all danced to the Beatles, The Troggs, the Rolling Stones, and many others. Lance put on Chubby Checker's 'Let's Limbo More' and we did the limbo rock under the stick, which made Jeff comment on my big boobs, saying, 'Wow! Great beehives.'

That night I was so happy, I smiled and just felt free in my body, as well as comfortable around these guys. They never put me down because they were great guys, and respectful. I was having too much fun to notice otherwise.

Through this group, I got to meet other girls in my year, but not in my class, and I started to build up friendships with them. Also the boys from various years were starting to take notice of me as my confidence was growing; this allowed me to be able to express myself freely. One of the girls in my year, Vera, got on really well with me. Her boyfriend was Klaus. He was a thin, tall, dark-haired boy with a very handsome face and a smile that lured you in. He knew he was handsome and popular with the girls. Klaus and Vera lived in the same town and were friends from little, and now they were boyfriend and girlfriend, but they had many fights and they'd often break up. Later she'd return him his friendship ring.

I did like this boy, and I thought he liked me too, but I also liked Vera and she seemed to like me. They'd broken up, and I went on a date with him to the pictures. He was nice at first and we kissed, and then he became too excited and was all hands. He wanted to touch me, and I had to fight him off in the cinema. I noticed other boys were looking at us. He never got his way with me. Unfortunately, I'd made a terrible mistake, because Vera distanced herself from me. Nonetheless, Klaus and I had a nice time together and he would meet me at the pictures. However, he was too forward for me. I didn't mind him kissing and cuddling me, but I couldn't bring myself to let him or anyone touch me intimately. Klaus ended up leaving me and going back with Vera.

We all remained friends, and it was easier to be a friend and nothing else, and as a friend we could laugh and joke with each other. I was really happy and having some fun times. I was starting to like the mixed groups. My courage grew and so did my expression. For the first time in my life, I was very popular. Sadness came over me when Jill announced she had to leave school and go to work to help her mum support the family. The girls and Sherry, in the group were so lovely, and they rallied around me and kept me in their group, even though Jill was gone. Second year at school proved to be my best, most memorable year.

Days were long on the farm on the weekends, and I'd draw to entertain myself. The activity was relaxing, and I got hungry. I went into Barton's bedroom, snooping around for biscuits that Grandma hid in there. Instead I found some magazines hidden in a box in one of the big cupboards built into the room. I could see they were magazines forbidden for us to read. I knew, because they were hidden; this meant not for children. Once I knew they were there, I'd sneak into that room, close the door and read them: *Playboy*, *Pix* and *People* magazines. They entertained me for hours. They told stories about people's lives, lives so different to ours. What I read in them totally fascinated me. In Mum and Dad's room, I found newer magazines on or under their small sofa bed. When they went out for the day or night to their dances, I'd go into their room and read.

I read about actors and actresses, pop stars and their lifestyles, models and their lives. I found an article on a supermodel I liked, and I loved her boyfriend, named Julian, and I instantly loved that name. I thought, when I have my first child, I will call him Julian. I read about the darker side of life: drug dealers, murderers, and prostitution. I read about people who took drugs, and the effects of those drugs on them. I read about white slave traders, black people on ships and how poor and mistreated they were, stowaways trying to seek a better life. There was a religion called Islam, which fascinated me, because I read Muslims washed their bottoms and never believed in using toilet paper, so when you met a Muslim, you should remember they washed their bottoms with their right hand and ate with their left hand. Wow! What a fascinating world we live in, I thought. I didn't understand a lot of what I was reading. Sometimes I had to use my dictionary to understand the words. My reading skills were a bit better in high school, but still poor. The photos helped me paint a picture of what I read in the stories. Some of the photos took me to the edge of wanting to know more and more. There was no one to fill in the gaps for me or the missing pieces of the puzzle. My thirst for knowledge, wanting to know how things worked in this world, grew and grew, but of course I couldn't tell anyone I was reading those magazines.

The deviant, bizarre and underworld side of life was fascinating. These stories made me realize how sheltered we were as children, kept away from the true reality of what goes on in the world. It wasn't always pretty. I guess in small towns the people who are polite and nice don't do anything to disgrace themselves. Life had many sides to it. The more I came in contact with knowledge about people from overseas, the more I saw myself somehow connected to a man from overseas.

I liked the *Playboy* magazines as well. These had some interesting pictures of women exposing themselves, and somehow it seemed okay for them to do that. There were some good stories in them besides the naked women. I didn't always understand, but pictures spoke for me.

My body's curves were causing me problems, but I had to take care of it. Looking at these magazines and seeing the effect drugs had on people, I would never take drugs. I wouldn't ever put my body under any risk. I couldn't understand why people let themselves go so low. At showtimes, I'd never go on dangerous rides. I was protective of my body. To me, it was so important, even though I didn't understand my body. Living on a farm, we should have been well informed about the body and life, because the animals on the farm had babies, and we should have been taught about sexuality and how life was produced, and taught to see the beauty in sexuality, as it brings forth life. The birthing of the animals and their sexuality was all hidden from us. However, death was acceptable and allowable for us to witness.

I remember clearly seeing our dogs in sexual fusion after they'd mated, and Grandma screaming at us to get in the house, as if it was some horrible, catchy disease they were emitting. She'd be running to the trough at the bottom of our clothes line to get the water hose to blast them apart. I had no idea what they were doing anyway; even though I had been abused, I still wasn't getting it. Her panic drew more attention to the dogs than if she'd not commented.

I saw the pets with their babies, but how they got there, I never saw. We missed the birthing. We had many cows, and sometimes the cows got into difficulty giving birth. The vet had to be called in. I wanted to go and see what was going on. Once I saw Dad helping the vet. Dad had his arm right up inside the cow. He was too busy with the cow to notice me. They were all worried about the cow. The cow was lowing in great pain. She seemed to be in agony with her mournful moans. My biggest thrill would have been to see the baby coming out of the cow in real life.

Unfortunately, Dad spotted me, and he screamed frantically at me, telling me to get in the house. He sang out to Grandma, 'Mum! Come and get this kid away from here.'

Grandma scalded me for bothering Dad while he was busy, and dragged me off from the scene. I kept looking back, hoping to see something. I wasn't a child, I was a teenager. I couldn't demand to stay, or I'd be belted for disobeying. There were always lots of activities around cows on the farm, and many times, birthing issues cropped up and the vet had to come and help out. Funny, I never seemed to see a birth just by chance.

Even though we grew up on a farm, we never saw many snakes, which was good. Grandma said our dogs were killing them, because she'd found dead ones. Maybe I could have passed lots of them, but I would have been in a dream and never saw them. I did get to see one. It was mushrooming time. I loved to mushroom, and loved to eat them in a white sauce. This day I got tired, and sat on a long log near the water's edge at the lagoon. I was watching my sister and brother bobbing up and down as they cut the mushrooms off at their stems. Grandma had told us since we were little to never pull the mushrooms completely out of the soil, because they wouldn't grow back again next year. We were always given knives and a bowl to collect them in. I was sitting and gazing in my own world, and the silence was so lovely. I felt something near me, and casually looked down to see what it was. A red-bellied black snake was sliding over the log I was sitting on.

'Eek! Snake!' I jumped up off the log, but the snake didn't seem to notice me. I'd noticed it. I guess when it first approached the log, it was probably flashing its tongue out to sense what was around it. It mustn't have felt any fear coming from me, and there was no fear until I saw it. I watched it until it disappeared into the long grass. My sister and brother were still running to me.

'How big was it?' asked Bart.

'Probably six foot, and it was fairly thick around its girth.'

Bart was peering over the log and looking into the grass.

I went, 'Rrrr, got you.'

He laughed as he jumped. 'Christine! You bugger!'

It was summertime, and school was coming to a close. Miss Ferguson wanted us to have a fashion parade. The principal, Mr Rogers, agreed to her proposal, so the school maintenance men were hard at work setting up a catwalk for our big fashion parade. Of course, Miss Ferguson nominated me as one of her models. I had to model some of her clothes she'd brought in, and some of my own clothes. I chose my baby-doll dress that was so fashionable, and my mumu dress, and Aunty Connie's wedding gown.

Maxine was doing sewing that year, and she'd made herself a go-go dress. She had gotten boots for her birthday and wore them. During the parade, Miss Ferguson was so impressed by my modelling, that she kept reminding me I should consider modelling as a career. In my shyness, all I could do was bend my head down and smile, telling her that I couldn't do it. At school it was alright and safe, because I knew many people and felt confident in front of them, but to face outsiders was too daunting.

As I walked down the catwalk, I could see the looks on the faces of the older boys from sixth form who didn't really hang around our group. I knew it was because of my body that they were looking at me. My male friends in fourth form were also seeing another side of me, and it scared me. I quickly diverted my eyes from the boys and looked out at the girls. In my mind, I was never good enough for any of those boys who'd come from upstanding families. I did love the modelling part, but how could I do such things, and where would I start? There was no one to talk to. My parents would never understand me having an interest in modelling.

There was also a big pageant. We got to act, and also sing, though miming. It was all pretending, and I got to get up on stage, which I'd always secretly wanted to do. So, Vera, Polly, Milly and I formed our band called 'The Off Beats' and we mimed the music of the Beatles, choosing the song 'Help'. We really had a fun year, and it was time to farewell many of the fourth formers who were my friends, as they wouldn't be coming back next year. Sherry was one of those people, and the sixth formers definitely weren't coming back next year, so this meant that Patrick, who I secretly admired, wouldn't be back. He'd started to date Jennifer, one of the girls in his year.

The sixth formers put on a farewell party. The theme was 'Yellow Submarine' by The Beatles, and they would be playing all the Beatles music on the night. They put out flyers, inviting all the school members to come along, regardless of year. After they'd decorated the hall, Vera, Polly and I checked it out, and decided to go to the farewell. The hall looked amazing. It was like an undersea world with fish, submarines, mermaids and streamers.

Vera invited me along to join her and her new boyfriend, Jimmy, who didn't go to our school. Polly told me she'd bring along her boyfriend, Mike, who didn't attend our school either. I was asked if I had a boyfriend to bring along. I told them I didn't, but it wasn't a problem for them. On the night of the farewell, I stayed at my cousin Charlene's house in Fenton. Charlene was so generous. She wanted me to look good, so she lent me her new dress and her favorite overcoat, and I had my hair styled. On arrival at school, I met Vera and Polly in the lobby, and we had our photos taken by Kevin before going into the hall. Seeing the girls with their boyfriends, I realized I was lonely. Everyone seemed to have a boyfriend or girlfriend except me, and the boy I liked, Patrick, was with Jennifer, and they were really lovey-doves together.

It was a great party. I stayed almost all the night, and my friends were good. We talked; even though they had partners, I was included in their group with their guys. Late in the night, I felt a bit sad, so I sneaked away from the party. I walked to the main road, and as I walked up to the road, I realized I'd forgotten to go to the toilet before I left the school. Suddenly I needed to go, and it was getting to desperation point. I turned to go back to the school. I was busting. A taxi came from nowhere. I was feeling very uneasy as the taxi driver stopped.

He stared at me, asking, 'Do you want to go home?'

'Yes.' I jumped into the front seat.

On reaching Charlene's house, paying the cab driver and getting out of the cab, I peed myself. I quickly walked into the house and took off the coat. I didn't know what to do and began to sob.

Charlene heard me sobbing and came out of her room. 'What's wrong?'

I started to cry more. 'I'm sorry I wet your coat.'

'How?'

'I wet myself.' I turned my eyes from her.

'Christine! How could you?' She grabbed her coat, leaving me crying. There was nothing I could do, so I went to bed and cried. I cried for being alone, and I cried for wetting myself.

The next morning, Charlene told me she had spent all night cleaning her coat, so her mother wouldn't see it. I apologised again. I'd embarrassed myself. For me, the end of '66 ended badly with my cousin Charlene.

This wasn't the only disaster. Grandma had problems with her bowels, and her pain was intensifying. She ended up in hospital again, just before Christmas time. Her stomach pains worsened, and the problem developed into a serious matter, causing her to have a bowel operation. Grandma had been having issues since 1965, and she'd previously had small bouts of hospitalization.

Aunty Connie and Uncle Oliver visited Grandma more often. Connie had bought Grandma some grey and grey-blue dresses to get her out of the black she still preferred to wear. We were all happy Connie got the upper hand now Grandma was ill. The only trouble was, Grandma became less interested in life and wanted to sit around. Also, she'd only eat her own cooking.

Mum was faced with the task of keeping a house. There was no way Dad was having Grandma placed in a nursing home yet. He was looking after his own interest-free rent. Dad wasn't prepared to start paying off bills at that time of his life, so Mum had to deal with the many difficulties placed upon her: housework, cooking, Grandma, and us.

Gradually, the whole house became just like Mum's bedroom: cluttered. We girls also had to help Mum with the dishes after our meals. I didn't mind, but Maxine would always weasel her way out of it. Mum used to do a weekly shopping order, but there was always something she'd forgotten, so she'd get one of us to do her shopping after school. Fortunately she had one honest daughter: me. Maxine always spent Mum's change, much to Mum's disapproval, so I usually got the shopping job.

The family doctor had told my parents that Grandma had been neglecting herself for years. This wasn't something that had just come over her. So, this year we never went away on holidays after Boxing Day. Aunty Connie and Uncle Oliver came to stay with us, as usual, over the Christmas period, and we decided not to have the family get-together, because Grandma was too ill.

Personally, I felt Grandma had let herself go around the time Dad and I were caught by Mum, when Mum wanted to buy a house in town and move away from Grandma. Around that time, Grandma started to conveniently get sick. Now she was really ill, and unable to look after herself or the house, but it was funny: after Aunty Connie's marriage, Grandma seemed to become even more ill, and she really wanted to stay in bed.

Gradually, the kitchen held piled-up clothes on the sofa, and dishes were left on the table. Nothing was ever put away. All those years Grandma slaved in that house seemed such a waste of time and effort. It was falling down around her ears, and it was like she was saying, enough is enough: just let it all go.

Despite all the mayhem surrounding us, there was one good thing that came out of this disarray; Mum could come out of her bedroom. After all those years she'd spent in her room, like a prisoner in her cell, she now had to manage this big house. She'd just lived in that one bedroom. This was the time I actually remember Mum being in our lives. She didn't have time to hide, and there was no need to. The wicked witch had gone to bed, and the princess could leave her cell.

I had questioned myself about my mother's reasons for hiding in her bedroom. What did she do in there? I would find the answers to these questions much later on. Funny, though; now Grandma was imprisoning herself in her bedroom. She'd imprisoned herself on the farm and took my young parents with her. Events change, and roles do too. Before the year was up, Grandma was back in hospital. She really wasn't well. The bowel operation had knocked her.

Chapter 36

Life Has Changed, And All My Friends Have Left

Regardless of Grandma being sick, Dad had insisted we still go out for the day. Gradually, he started to take us to places of interest. Sometimes we'd go to the car races. I didn't mind. I liked to watch the cars race around, and Gordon Knight was driving a TQ racing car at the time. The sounds of those cars racing around the dust was exciting. Best of all was seeing Gordon win, because we knew him, but my favourite reason for liking the races was the new Oak flavoured milk and ice cream we got. Mum and Dad befriended Hilary and Glen, who lived at Deep Gully Creek. On the weekends, we often went to visit them at their house close to the creek and picnicked with them. They had two kids a lot younger than Maxine and I. We didn't have much to do with them, however Barton found himself two new friends. Hilary and Glen also came out to our house when Grandma was in hospital. She'd had her operation, but she was still complaining of stomach pains. The doctors had been trying to rehabilitate her into developing better eating habits.

Dad also bought himself a portion of land on the mountain range in Booneville, a small hamlet near Spencer Shire. Glen would go with Dad to help him cut timber on this land. The two men were always scheming and trying to find ways to make money.

We went to their house and had a picnic on the bank of the creek. I'd be sixteen this year. I decided to wear my pink bikini. The women were cutting up food. I told Mum I was going for a swim. She nodded okay, as her and Hilary were having a deep conversation. The young boys and my brother were already there, swimming, diving, dunking each other and having water fights. In the water, I suddenly felt eyes watching me. Looking up, I saw something that scared me, so I quickly sank down into the water to hide my body. I got over it and enjoyed myself.

Later that day, Glen wanted to teach my sister and me to water ski. Maxine had her turn on the skis. Mum and Hilary were chatting on the creek bank, oblivious to everyone. I looked at my father and Glen. It was blatantly obvious that I was being talked about by them. I could feel their eyes going over my body, like I was some show-piece. I refused to go on the skis, left the men, and returned to Mum.

Maxine hadn't noticed. She had another turn on the skis and did pretty well. There and then I thought, no more exposing myself to these types of looks from men - and my father. All this wasn't adding up. I couldn't understand why this was happening to me. My own father - but Dad was always in awe of me from little, admiring my beauty as a child. This day he scared me so much, I felt like my mind was a child's mind, and my body was making me fear older men. I guessed it from my experiences with my father, and I knew what they could do to me, that they could physically hurt me. I'd learned this out of the magazines. This wasn't normal or natural, my own father acting like he did around me, and now with a stranger. I was frightened of their intentions. I did not want to face another situation in my life. It was not easy being pretty; it caused me so much pain. Men's eyes showed me something that was not normal.

February, 1967: back to school for my third year, with a promotion to a higher class. All good things come to an end. My fun times from last year had stopped, because most of my friends from fourth form had left, including Sherry, who had also moved to Rosemont. Vera and Polly were still with me. We grouped together and had some good times, but I was already fifteen, a year older than my class mates. As soon as Vera and Polly turned fifteen, they left school to do nursing. This meant I'd have to make new friends. I started to befriend the ethnic girls: Cornelia Hauser, Catherin Schulze, Jutta Koch, and the Burski twins, Adela and Nadia. I was making friends with the not-so-popular girls. These friends included Robyn Davis and Henrietta Marks. I really liked Henrietta, and sometimes I'd go to her house after school. She had her own bedroom, and a Siamese cat which only liked her. Henrietta had an older brother who I never met, because he was never there. He was quite a few years older than Henrietta. She was a very quiet girl and seemed more like an only child. All these girls had the same aim as me: to do well that year. It was the year before our final, so now I was hanging around with the more studious girls, and I refused to look at the boys.

My new friends were quiet and we'd mostly sit, sometimes talking and sometimes saying nothing to each other. Our worlds were different. Because I still wanted to have fun, laugh, joke, and mix with older people, some of the brainy girls from the highest classes in my year started to mix with me. Wanda Graham and Milly Sweeny and these girls talked a lot about a wider range of topics. I had both quiet and talkative friends.

The girls in the higher classes talked about going on to sixth form and gaining their Higher School Certificates. This was something I'd love to have done, but I knew my parents couldn't wait until my schooling was over. For the first time at high school, I was feeling under stress, and the only way to handle this was to be determined and knuckle down and study. I wanted to show the world I was capable of being intelligent, and not just a pretty face. I wanted to look older and be more responsible, so I decided to wear my uniform at its proper length. No more miniskirts at school for me. I wanted to give my full concentration to my schoolwork, so I busied myself, sitting up until all hours, studying and learning.

Chapter 37

Grandma Becomes Incapacitated

My home, as well as my personal life, was testing me. I had to face a lot of pain, and many times I hated the atmosphere and tensions at home. It was so tense, and I wanted to die again to free myself of these problems. Grandma was becoming sicker, and Mum wasn't coping with Grandma; she had her own problems with Dad. Mum suspected Dad and Hilary were having an affair. He was starting to come home late at night, and he seemed to be going to more meetings: union meetings. Mum was becoming frantic. She couldn't drive a car; she was stuck.

Grandma had another bout in hospital, and then returned home. She tried to help herself, but it was so difficult for her. I noticed her hygiene was slipping, and she was getting dirty. Dad also noticed Grandma's deterioration; he couldn't stand anything unhygienic or disabled. He told Mum she had to take over the household cooking. Grandma was upset at first; it was very difficult for her to give up what she'd done for

271

years and years. She knew she was getting tired. She was seventy-two years old. After a month, she gladly resigned herself to the fact that Mum would be doing the cooking and the household chores. However, Grandma wanted to cook her own meals. That was her one stipulation. It was agreed, but she ate very poorly, eating quick meals, and many times I caught her eating bread and jam, which upset me, making me feel sad for her. I started to cry for her, and I wondered why she did this, when there was plenty of food in our house. Grandma started to stress me, when I thought of how strong she had been, and now all was lost; her strong will was gone.

Sometimes, I'd watch her cooking for herself, and I noticed horrible behaviour. She always seemed to have had a runny nose in those days. Once, she was going to cook sausages, and mucus from her nose dropped into the frypan. She continued to cook the sausages. Either she didn't notice, or she didn't care. I was horrified. This wasn't the person I knew as a child, the person who was so clean and strong. Things didn't seem real any more. Our house was becoming a shambles without my former grandma.

Grandma was sent to the hospital, on and off, and the doctors told my parents the same old story. Her stomach problems were because of her poor eating habits. My parents explained how she wouldn't eat my mother's cooking. It was her last thread of keeping her own control on her life. So, the only option was hospital, to try and stabilize her eating habits. In later March, Grandma suffered the worst of all fates; she fell and broke her hip. This meant she was laid up in hospital for quite a few months. She'd become more frail, and when we went to see her in the hospital, it broke my heart. She'd really thrown in the towel. Mum was at least freed of Grandma, and there was some breathing space for a short period of time. Actually, it was so nice for my sister and me to have the bedroom to ourselves, because we were still sharing the bedroom with Grandma.

During these times on the weekends, my sister and I listened to re-runs of Chubby Checker on the TV. The audience were up and dancing; they made you feel like you wanted to join in.

I'd look at Maxine and say, 'Come on, let's dance.'

She'd get up off her chair, and we'd twist to his song, 'Let's Twist Again'. It was such a great feeling to dance along to the music. I loved to dance.

This new music was changing everyone. Even Mum was starting to like the new music. We could listen to the more modern radio stations for the pop music. We were gradually catching up to my cousins, who were years ahead of us with modern trends, but I guess being isolated on a farm and away from townspeople, you were not always able to be up to date. I liked Herman's Hermits singing 'No Milk Today', and The Beatniks' 'Can't Be Sad About It.' My favourite was Donovan's 'Mellow Yellow', and there was The Beach Boys' 'Good Vibrations', 'Wild Thing' by The Troggs, and 'Georgy Girl' by The Seekers. I loved the crazy 60s we were in, but we were not part of the real world. I was too young; all I could do was listen on the radio or watch the TV or read and act it out.

The news was showing us how it was in the Vietnam war, and it was a horrific tragedy. I felt it was a waste of young men's lives. I thought the old men creating the wars should have been sent to war, because they'd at least had a life, and they were the ones to start the war. The old were penalising the young for what they thought right. This war drew us into it, due to us being exposed to it on the TV. I'd watch it, but felt I wasn't affected by it because we didn't know anyone serving in it. When you know someone, it becomes more personal.

We were being influenced by TV shows like *Combat* with Vic Morrow. I guess they were accustoming people to war, and glorifying it with movie stars. It was one of our must-see shows through the week. I think the war in Vietnam did have an influence on us.

I had to think of a job I'd like to do, but I just couldn't work out what I could do, and there were only two people in my world who may have been able to help me to choose a career, if I'd been a more stable, confident person in the world beyond school. They were my sewing teacher, Miss Ferguson, who was constantly telling me I should go into modelling, and Aunty Connie, who also encouraged me to consider modelling; but I feared my body, and the consequences of owning such a body. I just wanted to be loved for me, not for my image. With Grandma in hospital, Connie and Oliver came out to visit us more often, so they could go and spend time with Grandma in the hospital. Aunty decided to regularly bring Grandma women's magazines, or post magazines to her. On one of their visits, Oliver brought along his two daughters, Peggy and Kate, and they spent two weeks with us on the farm for the Easter holidays. The girls were over from England visiting relatives with their mother. Barton's friend, Mike Long, had a big crush on Kate, and she also liked Mike. All of us loved the girls and their sweet natures, and the oldest one, Peggy, looked so much like her father. The girls were the same age as Maxine and Barton, so Oliver must have come out to Australia after his divorce from their mother. The girls lived on the Isle of Jersey.

Dad had some work to do on his property with Glen, so we took the girls with us to see Dad's property in Booneville. While there, I didn't feel comfortable around Glen. It was really great having the girls stay with us. We took them everywhere, but after the two weeks, they had to go. We were very sad to see them go, and they were just as sad to leave us. We never heard of or saw his daughters ever again after they returned to England with their mum.

Aunty Connie and Uncle Oliver also brought with them Oliver's nephew, Ryan. How he loved me, but Ryan was younger than me. He was fifteen and I was soon to be sixteen, and I couldn't stand to be with a boy younger than me or be seen going out with a boy younger than me. It didn't matter to Ryan that I was a year older than him, because for him it was love at first sight. Unfortunately, the feeling wasn't mutual, and to be honest, I didn't notice him that much. On his visits, he'd sit and stare at me. When he left to go home on his first visit, he asked me if he could write to me. I agreed to it with a shrug of my shoulders. For a young boy of his age, he wrote the most beautiful letters, expressing all the beauty he saw in me and the love he felt for me, and how he couldn't bear to live without me. To me, it was as if he'd given me a jigsaw puzzle, and his letters mystified me. I couldn't see anything he saw in me or between us. I couldn't understand him. He'd sent me a photo of him in one of his letters, asking me what he was thinking of. Puzzled, I looked at the photo, turning it in all directions and angles, and then put it away. I'd pull it out and look at it again, but I had no clue to what he was thinking. His letters talked about how beautiful I was, and how he wanted to be with me.

My aunty explained to me, on a visit without him, 'Christine, do you know that Ryan loves you so much, and he cries all the way back home to Rosemont when he leaves you. And all he does is tells us he wants to go back to you, Christine.'

To me, it was a joke, and I laughed. 'Does he? Why?'

'He loves you.'

Love to me was a word with no description or feelings; it only puzzled me. Wondering how he could love me, I'd stare at Aunty. Somehow I think she realised I was incapable of loving anything or anyone.

Ryan visited us a few times until I guess he couldn't face me anymore. I guess it must have been so hard for a boy of fifteen to love someone with all his heart, and not receive any love and admiration back; but I was so closed off to love and so unfeeling for any human being, even my mum, who I wanted love from. I'd never felt love, to give love. It was only nature that I felt any love towards.

Even though I refused to look at the boys, there were boys at school who were writing me love letters. Peter was one of them. His letters were also beautiful, but he was younger than me too. He wrote me a letter every day expressing his feelings for me, but it was all falling on deaf ears. It was wasted energy for these boys, as far as I was concerned. I had no feelings for him, although he was madly in love with me.

Cracker night was coming up on the Queen's Birthday, so my brother, sister and I went with Dad to collect firewood for the bonfire. As I lifted this big piece of wood, I disturbed a frill-necked lizard. It saw me and ran up my leg, probably thinking I was a tree. It frightened the life out of me. I ran screaming, pushing it away from me.

Dad came running over, singing out, 'What's up?'

Seeing him approaching me brought more terror. If he came close to me and Mum saw us, she'd really hate me. I became more scared of him than the lizard. Calming myself, I told him it was just that a lizard scared me. My sister and brother were near me.

Maxine asked, 'Are you alright? Did it scratch you?'

Looking at my leg, I said, 'No, it just frightened me.'

Dad said, 'Okay, go and finish fetching wood and be careful; move the wood with your foot first, and back away before you pick it up.'

They went off, but Dad came nearer to me. I freaked out, as he actually touched my breasts again. I pulled away and ran off. Again, I felt unsafe around him. My siblings didn't know the depth of anguish I was suffering, and I needed them around me always to feel protected and safe from Dad, without them being aware of it.

Everyone wanted something, but the other wasn't always able to give it, due to their own stresses or problems. I longed for Mum's affection, love and acceptance that she couldn't give me, but could freely give to Barton. She'd spend time with him, and sometimes I'd see them together and I'd wait to see if she'd do the same for me, but she never did. Many times when I saw them together, strange feelings overcame me.

Once I nearly fainted, going down on my knees, and as I did, I said in a fading voice, like my life force was being sapped from me, 'Muuum!' It was my last dying effort to reach out to her.

She came over to me. 'What's up with you?'

'I don't know; I felt faint.'

She took me into the kitchen and sat me down. 'Are you alright now?'

'Yes.' I looked at her, wishing she'd hug me.

'We'll go to the doctor tomorrow and have you checked up,' she said in a calmer voice, but she never touched me, just stood in front of me, speaking down to me as I sat on the old sofa in the kitchen.

I was taken to the doctor, and told there was a small goiter problem, but nothing to worry about. I felt it was just stress from feeling unloved.

Grandma returned home in July, 1967. She was to use a walking frame to move out of her bed into the living room. After the trauma of breaking her hip, Grandma lived in constant fear of falling again and re-breaking her hip. It was so hard on her, getting in and out of the bed. The doctor ordered her to be taken out of her bed every day. Mum was being faced with this burden of helping Grandma in and out of her bed, and we weren't allowed to help. Dad explained to us it was in case Grandma fell with us. He didn't want us to injure our young bodies.

As time went on, Grandma began to cry when she had to get up and go and sit in the lounge. Sometimes she'd scream at him, 'No, Max, please. I don't want to sit out there.' He'd make her, as if he was punishing her on a deeper level for past hurts. She cried when moved, and she was happy when put back into her bed. She also had to get up to use her commode near her bed. Mum would empty it. I felt Grandma did this to herself to hold us there, to rid herself of any responsibilities as far as the house was concerned. She got to the point where she wanted to be looked after, and to not be the one looking after others. Really, Grandma had more control over my parents, because now she was dependent on them, and she was guaranteed they'd stay with her.

Chapter 38

We Lose Our Bridge As Well As The Woman Grandma Was

This was the time of the big flood. Maxine and I just reached home as a torrent of rain broke free from the sky and sent buckets of rain down upon the land. The rain was heavy as I stood on the verandah, looking out at our cows. I could see they were trying to shelter near the outside toilet. The rain was so intense; I could hardly see the cows. The wind was blowing a gale, and the rain started to beat in on the verandah. We were so lucky to have made it home and not get caught up in the storm. Luckily it was Friday evening. It looked like it was setting in for a long while. The whole night the storm raged. I had some strange messages that day on the bush track - something about a meeting - and there seemed something eerie about the house. I knew there were others who looked after us on the other side, but this was deeper. I went to bed and fell into a deep, deep sleep. In the black of night, I had been suddenly awoken in my bed. All was silent and still. The rain and wind had gone.

This was the night I saw the ghost in my room, and got the message, *you're not grasping life and its experiences.*

The next morning, I woke to find that everyone was doing their normal things. Grandma was reading her magazines, and Maxine was stirring in the bed above me, but I had seen something last night that I wouldn't be able to talk about to anyone.

The rain and the wind were still raging. Last night there had only been silence when I was awoken. I lay on my back and pondered the night, trying to make sense of it all. The weekend ended up being one of our wettest ever. The rain continued all that week. The lagoon started to spill, and through the week, large volumes of water hurled over the spillway, flooding the road into town. We were lucky there were two roads into town, and we couldn't ever be blocked off because the second road was well away from the water.

Gordon Knight paid us an early morning visit on Monday before school to inform us the bridge was down, and we couldn't use the track any more to go to school. My parents would have to find another alternative for us to get to the bus stop. I was so sad to hear our bridge was gone. Gordon told Mum that the colliery wouldn't be building a new bridge, because it was closing down all operations soon. Only the pump house would remain in operation to supply our home with water, and Gordon would only be checking it now and then.

The bridge was gone, and it was the only bridge where I had no issues with co-ordination. That morning Gordon drove us to the T-section road going to Spencer Shire and Hastings Crossing. From there we caught the bus. We explained to our driver, Jim, that from then on we'd be catching our bus from there. He was a great old soul, and he was so kind. Many times, he waited for us kids, because we were running late.

We were so lucky we weren't actually on the bridge when it was swept away. On my last trip over the bridge, I had felt it swaying, but thought our bridge would never in a million years be washed away in a storm.

With the bridge gone, I missed our track, and its beautiful nature. I wouldn't be able to see the icicles forming in the winter time on the ferns that grew alongside the pipeline that ran off the bridge. Those icicles made imaginary figures and shapes and looked like fairy ice kingdoms. After all those years, the bridge stood through all kinds of weather all elements; as with all things, age makes things become weary with their heavy burdens, so they eventually succumb to the peace of death.

The rain continued for over a week, and both the lagoon and creek became very swollen. Our stray dog, Froggy, was missing. He was a beautiful boxer dog, with an endearing face that was so full of sympathy and love. We'd called him Froggy, because he had a silly way of sitting that made him look like a frog. We looked for him everywhere. Dad thought someone may have liked him and taken him home with them, as he was a very lovable dog. When we told Grandma about Froggy's disappearance, she thought he'd probably got swept away in the creek. That wasn't a good thought. I preferred Dad's reasoning. There'd been lots of townsfolk coming out to the lagoon to witness the big fish the lagoon was spewing over its spillways. I would be left wondering about Froggy, and many times we'd go search for him, never giving up on him, but we never found him, and had to concede that he was lost and would never return to us.

Our lagoon was a private sanctuary, which meant no one could fish in that lagoon, so it was protected for donkey's years, and the fish and eels that lived in there were free to grow and thrive, undisturbed by man. The flooded waters from the lagoon revealed its hidden treasures, and the secrets of the fishes' and eels' world in there. The fish and eels were up to six or seven foot in length, due to being untouched in their own environment. The townspeople were coming out to look at or catch these big fish, and some were taking them home to eat. Dad had also brought some up to the house for us to eat. He scaled and gutted them, and their innards were full of mud. He cleaned them, and Mum cooked them, but they weren't good eating. They were too muddy. That lagoon had many deep, deep, hidden secrets.

In September I turned sixteen, and Mum and Dad gave me some new shoes. My school days were productive, but I had a new dilemma with Mum; she was telling me all her concerns about Dad's infidelity. She thought Dad was having an affair with Hilary, and I thought Mum may have had some reasons to be concerned, because Dad was often away from home, even on the weekends, telling Mum he had to work.

All the magic was going out of our lives, and I wasn't going to the pictures as much, only now and then. I only got to see a few films throughout the year, including *The Graduate*, which I liked so much. Most of my weekends were spent at home. My sister was still playing sport, but she was staying in town at her friends' houses, either Linda's or Cathy's. I had no house to go to, because Jill and Melinda were busy with their working lives, but I still had nature, and spent a lot of my time with our dogs, Blue and Rusty. This was to be my pastime, walking around the lagoon or the creek. I'd watch TV, my favourite shows: Bud Abbott and Lou Costello made me laugh so much, and Jerry Lewis and Dean Martin. I was seeking out comedies. *The Bob Hope Show* was hilarious; so was *McHales's Navy*.

I still liked songs like 'Mellow Yellow' and The Byrds' 'Mr. Tamborine Man' and 'A Whiter Shade of Pale' by Procol Harum, and 'Guantanamera' by The Sandpipers, and 'Poison Ivy', but I didn't know who sang that one. Sandie Shaw's new song, 'Puppet on a String' and 'Light my Fire' by The Doors were favourites. I liked songs that had a message.

I wasn't an ordinary child; I possessed a strong will and mind, even though I didn't express myself like that. Deep within, I knew I was different and strong. To me, my mind was the only thing people could not ever take from me. My mind held my dreams and gave me the satisfaction that one day, I'd be able to do something good in the world.

I did really well in my exams, and soon we were off school for the summer break. At the end of school, I was promoted up into the next class for next year. I'd finally climbed from the third bottom class to the third top class, and I was looking forward to next year's classes. I would be in the class with all the girls I'd made friends with, and I'd received more books for my excellent passes.

Grandma was really unwell, and Aunty Connie and Uncle Oliver came home for Christmas, even though they'd been coming a lot that year. Christmas was knocking on our door, and it was time to buy some new clothes. Mum and I went shopping in Mrs Cooper's; she owned a dress shop for women. This was where we always bought our clothes each summer for the holidays. Mrs Cooper sold very good quality clothes; she had a keen eye for fashion, and many of the fashion labels she had weren't found in other local shops. One thing I can say about my parents, when it came to dressing us up, money was no option. Mum enjoyed this time as much as we did. She used to scan through the clothes, picking out what she'd like me to wear, and I picked the clothes I liked.

I couldn't believe she chose a white dress with black polka dots. As soon as I saw it, I didn't like it.

'No, I don't like that,' I screeched in horror.

Mum snapped back, 'Well, at least you could try it on.'

In a huff, I took the dress, headed into the change room and placed it on the hook, undressed, slipped the dress on, adjusting it on my Marilyn Monroe body. I looked at myself and thought I would stand out too much. I pulled a distressed face. It looked like something you'd see on Marilyn Monroe.

My body was already giving me problems. The problem was, my mind hadn't caught up to my maturing body. I came out from behind the change room curtain, and the women went into raptures.

'Oh, Christine, how beautiful you look, and your figure is so lovely,' said an elated Mrs Cooper, calling to others in the shop to come and look. I was infuriated by her announcement. The women goggle-eyed me and smiled in awe. I did get caught up in the glamour of the moment and twirled, allowing the skirt to flare, and I held the sides of the dress to gently lift the skirt, and put my head back, posing, raising and lowering the skirt from the front and back. I watched my reflection in the mirror as I did this. I turned to see the women's faces all smiling, and I smiled back at them, because what I saw in the mirror didn't look pretty. I looked at my mother, and her eyes were watery with astonishment at her daughter's beauty.

Remembering how it would attract the attention of men to me, I rejected the dress. 'No, I don't want this dress, and I don't like it.'

'What?' My mother craned her neck in disbelief.

Mrs Cooper couldn't believe my words either. In her frustration, she walked away and asked me to think about it. Other women in the shop shook their heads. Everyone went back to their first intentions when entering the shop, busying themselves working through the rows of clothes hanging on the racks.

'Christine, what's the problem?' My mother questioned.

'Nothing. I don't feel comfortable in it,' I pretended.

My mother was disappointed; I could see that. She should know why, without me having to explain to her. She knew my secret. In the heat of the moment, she'd evidently forgotten the one person we didn't want to attract.

This was the main reason why I didn't choose that dress. Dad had shown me he still hadn't got past touching me. The dress did look good, and being pretty, would cause too much pain, and I didn't want any pain, or to cause any aroused feelings in those who shouldn't be aroused.

Searching the racks for a more mature looking dress, I found the perfect blue dress. I went to the change room and tried it on. Perfect, and I felt comfortable in it. It was a plain, straight A-line dress, with a kick pleat in the middle of the lower skirt of the dress. It fell from the shoulders and had no waistline. It hid my figure completely. The neckline was very high, and it seemed to hide my bust line as well, squashing it down. No one would know what my figure was like in that dress. I felt safe, happy and mature in this dress; I felt like a different person. There'd be no attention given to me. Being self-conscious of my body, I denied my own body's beauty. My mother was trying to get me to reveal my body, while I wanted to hide it.

Christmas was spent at home with Aunty Connie and Uncle Oliver, and all the family were re-invited back out to the house, so my cousins and their parents rejoined us. There was no homemade Christmas pudding and no more trinkets, only a bought tin pudding; however, the festive season was still felt and loved by the family.

My siblings and I had many undeveloped talents, that lay dormant in us. Maxine would have loved to have played the piano. She did get to play sport, which she also loved. Barton was a whizz at taking things apart and putting them back together from the age of five; he would prefer to pull mechanical things apart instead of playing with them. There was an obvious need inside him for discovery; he only needed to be given the right instructions and know-how. It's a pity my parents weren't more open-minded, seeing us kids as people, and not kids that were to be kept out of sight. Maybe if they'd seen some of our gifts, they could have placed us into the correct activities to manifest our talents. If this had been done, maybe Barton may not have been so destructive with his toys. Maybe if he had been seen for his worth, and not humiliated for his slowness, he may not have got into trouble with the law in later life.

I loved to pretend I was a ballet dancer, dancing on my toes as if I knew what I was doing, and I loved to look at myself while I danced. I'd whirl, and while whirling, the relaxation gave me inner peace. We were never encouraged to develop any talents that were obvious. I'm sure we would have all benefited if we'd had our talents recognised and brought into a workable reality. As children, you were just there, and I had no idea what for. There were always the excuses we lived too far from town, Dad worked shift work, and Mum couldn't drive.

Dad got rid of the old pink plywood van and purchased a newer, aluminium caravan, but we wouldn't take any friends away with us, and we'd only go to local bays or beaches, due to Grandma being so sick. That year we spent a couple of weeks at Chider Beach. It wasn't the same without having a friend with us.

Chapter 39

My Last Year At High School

In 1968, I attended my last year at high school. As usual, we trudged the main dirt road to walk to the T-section to catch the school bus. I was so glad it was my last year at high school. This road was also a two-and-a-half mile journey, one way, and the road was dirt: not as picturesque as our old track. The difference was on our track we never passed a soul, but now we were faced with passing cars and dust. This road was exposing us to other people.

Many times we'd refused lifts in strange cars, preferring to walk. We'd encountered trucks that were carrying ethnic construction workers going to the big power-line-transmission construction going on in the area. They'd drive past us, wolf-whistling, and sing out to us. We'd turn our heads away, but I was curious about those men from other countries. It was a laborious trip, and somehow it took energy from us, and it didn't replenish us. There was one man who we were passing every day, and eventually we accepted his lift. I couldn't see any danger in him or any wrong; Maxine did, and if she was walking alone to the bus stop, she'd never go alone with him in his Jeep. She would always make sure either Barton or I were with her. His name was Derek. He wore a wide-brimmed hat; he had pitted skin from bad acne, and carried a distinctive, bad body odour. I was grateful for the lift.

The pump house had to go out of commission, and Mum and Dad were told when Grandma died or left the farm, the house would be demolished. This was sad news, but it was inevitable, because the house was willed to Grandma by Michael Davies, to live there until she died. Grandfather had died mysteriously and was loved and respected by Michael Davies, an industrial magnate who owned both Lachlan Vale and Fenton Collieries. Because Grandfather died in the service of the pit, in his will Michael Davies bestowed the house on my Grandma. Davies died before Grandfather; however, his will declared the decree prior to his death.

Now Grandma wasn't well, and the colliery people knew it, because the emergency calls for an ambulance were done through the colliery. Our beautiful old telephone was attached to the wall, and you had a handle with so many turns for dialling the phone. Three long turns and a short turn connected us to the colliery switchboard, and from there, they called the Hastings Crossing ambulance service to come out to get Grandma. To the colliery, it was just a matter of time. Dad didn't want to leave there yet; his ties were too strong, so he insisted on his mum being cared for at home, which our mum did. She never got any help or thanks from the sons and daughter of Grandma. Mum was the one who was the most hated by Grandma and was the one caring for her.

I wanted change; I was outgrowing the farm. I didn't want to carry on the same life circumstances as my parents. I was beginning to think on how I would raise my children. It would be completely different to the way my parents raised me. I would protect my children above all things and all people. If I did marry, it would be no earlier than twenty-eight. My biggest dream was to move into town. We should have moved into town years ago. Dad held on and held on, and Mum had been taken captive to be Grandma's nurse and caregiver, so he could stay longer. My only chance of leaving the farm would be when I started to work.

We lost our old horse, Bonnie. Dad was quite sad about her loss, because she was his horse. She'd had a long history with Dad, and Mum too, because she was their sulky horse, and she was my first mode of transport when I was a baby, until Dad got a car in 1953, after the birth of Maxine. Bonnie was a short, small-statured horse compared to her beautiful, tall daughter, Star. Bonnie had a shaggy type of coat, whereas Star possessed a short-haired coat that was both elegant and glossy. A bit like me and Mum; Mum was short and I was tall. Bonnie died in her usual grazing area of the paddock, which seemed to be the spot for all the horses and the cows to end their days. This was near the middle gate, close to the fence line, and this middle gate was close to the cow bails where the cows went through before they were sent off to market. Maybe they had a tie with that cow bail area. My dad told me a story about him, as a kid, and the cow bails. As a kid, he was once scared by something invisible at the middle gate. It is an eerie area, and something invisible rushed at him. There were many eerie areas in our house. To think of it, we kids seemed to avoid the cow bails as a play area, and only clamoured around them on market days, when the cows were being herded into the cow bails to be transported to the sales yards. I recall many events around the cow bails, like branding the beasts, marketing the cows, and even inoculating the cows, which was done by the vet as they were herded through the close aisles of the pens. Star was the only horse left, and she was around my age. We were born a few months apart; she was older than me.

Despite my confidence, I was still smoking, and doing it more often. I'd been smoking since seven. This time round, Dad was catching me out, or my siblings were dobbing me in. Sometimes I'd get belted for it, but that didn't stop me; I still smoked. I was also swearing, and again, he'd catch me out or I was told on.

Dad was in earshot when I was joking with Mum. He caught me swearing and said he was going to cure me of it there and then.

'Okay, I've had enough of this. Tell me every swear word you know, Christine.'

He was flabbergasted. He stood near the verandah entrance, and I was in the doorway of the laundry. I looked at him, raised my eyes to the ceiling, and looked back at Mum in the laundry. She was gritting her teeth, because we hadn't heard him coming. My siblings heard the commotion and came running out of the house to join in on the trial of Christine, the one who swore and smoked. I edged out of the doorway of the laundry for some distance and went and stood over near the old table. Mum was looking at Dad and Maxine was holding the kitchen door, waiting to see what I'd do. Bart went and sat on the chair near the old shoe box.

I blurted out, 'Bastard, bloody, shit, and fuck.'

He edged in towards me. 'You know it's not nice for a girl to swear like that,' he informed me. His body shook in exasperation.

Defiantly I thought, but you do.

He charged at me to smack me for each swearing word I knew. Mum was just watching. Maxine didn't say a word, she just jumped out of the way in a startled manner, moving back as if it were her being hit. My brother dived behind Mum.

I didn't cry; I just thought, you old bastard. I looked at Mum and thought, you old cheese, just standing there looking at me. I don't give a fuck what you all think. I know myself and I will be me, the way I want to be. My confidence was soaring, but I still couldn't tell them out loud what I thought of them.

After getting quite a few whacks, Dad imparted to me, 'Now I'm going to cure you from smoking, my girl. Carol, go and get me those cigars.'

Mum went inside. I was rubbing my bum. Maxine and Barton were just standing there with their eyes on Dad. Next thing, Mum was back out the kitchen door and on the verandah. All eyes seemed to divert to her and what she was handing to Dad. It was a packet of Midway cigars.

'Okay, my girl, let's see if we can't cure you once and for all of smoking,' he predicted with a grin, confident he'd already won the case.

He took the wrapper off the unopened packet and flipped up the lid, pulled up a cigar and presented the box to me. He was smiling. I took a cigar. With it in my mouth, I posed, waiting for a light. He struck a match. I rolled the cigar to taste its flavour, and it wasn't too bad. As the light was placed on the tip of the cigar, I drew in, and smoke swirled into my mouth. I knew not to draw back on this one, and I casually smoked it, liking it, which I informed him of.

'They're nice, Dad: not bad at all.'

He was flabbergasted and frustrated with me. He threw his hands in the air and said, 'That's it. I quit. Let her go. But, my girl, don't let me see you smoking near me.' He pointed his finger at me. Dad knew he couldn't win with me, and I was left to make my own choices, as long as he didn't have to witness them. He moved off into the house, and I was allowed to finish the cigar.

My brother edged in and asked, 'What's it like, really?'

'Good. Why?' I quizzed him. 'Do you think I don't like them?'

He smiled.

At this time, I'd had my hair styled in the Mia Farrow cut by my cousin, Charlene. I loved my really short hair; it suited me so well. I felt I'd made a mature decision to dress more grown-up, and to wear my hair really short. I'd developed another side to myself, a more acceptable side to my mum. At school, I started to enjoy sports, and loved to play vigoro. I participated in the track and field events on sports carnival days; I did really well in the long and high jump sections. At school, we had house sports teams. My house sports team's name was 'Eleanor House', and its colour was red.

I was starting to gain Mum's attention through amusing her. I was becoming a comedian and winning her over with dirty jokes. I learnt these at school. My personality was becoming stronger. I attributed that to being more resourceful the previous year at school and discovering my own hidden capabilities through my own determination to achieve. I was watching lots of funny TV shows, and this was bringing out a sense of humour I didn't know I had.

I was starting to like more pop music: The Monkees' 'Last Train to Clarksville' and 'I'm a Believer', and I liked Micky Dolenz the best. The Beatles were great with 'Hey Jude', and Blood, Sweat and Tears' 'Spinning Wheel'. Mum still had her issues, but I was diverting her away from the stress of it all.

I felt as if I was an old person in a young body, and just hadn't caught up with the older person within yet. My imagination and jokes had Mum and others in fits of laughter, and at this stage of my life, making people happy is all I wanted to do. This was also the time I forcibly took my small mum into my arms and kissed and cuddled her heaps. She couldn't escape me, and I'd kiss her on the lips, roughing her up, and making her laugh.

I was telling my family and my Aunty Connie that in the year 2000 I would be forty-nine. They looked at me strangely and laughed at me. I guess they couldn't think that far ahead. I could see a future, but what was in the future, I didn't know. I knew there was one place I had to get to, and that was Victoria Falls, in Africa, to find the Fountain of Youth, and sit by it and sip from it every day. I told them.

Mum said, 'Where do you think up such nonsense from?'

I laughed. 'I don't know; it just comes to me.'

There were many thoughts coming to me about a new life, having a car and freedom. I wasn't as easily hurt any more by other people's words. However, there was a nagging question I had to ask my mother, much to her horror and bemusement. I always waited for the opportune moment to present my questions; I'd learnt to use tact with my mum. I knew when the appropriate time was to ask her questions, so she didn't snarl at me. I'd learnt how to ease her moods and approach the wild beast of unpredictability in her.

'Mum,' I'd say in a sweet, but not too sweet voice, to the point of irritation, 'was I adopted?'

She'd look at me strangely, saying, 'No, you're mine and I birthed you. No one else did.'

At sixteen years and nine months, I was given my first car by Mum and Dad, a little Standard 10 with a semi-automatic clutch on its gear stick. It was a blue and white car. I loved it, and I was so happy with my car and I couldn't wait to learn to drive, so I applied for my L plates. This car meant freedom. Living out on the farm, eight miles from town, with no access to public transport, only a school bus we had to walk two and a half miles to catch, with one service in the morning and one in the afternoon, Dad realized we needed a car. When we started working, we couldn't keep walking the dirt road and get to work on time via the school bus. I got my L plates; I had three months to learn to drive the car. Of course, Dad had to teach me, and I couldn't be alone with him, so if Mum wouldn't go, I'd beg my sister to come along. She was pretty good, but she never knew why I asked her to come. In payment I told her I would take her out when I went out. This helped me clinch her company.

While learning to drive, there were some funny incidents; Dad almost jumped out of the car a few times. He held onto the door handle through most of the lessons. I don't know why, because I considered myself a good driver.

In the September of 1968, I turned seventeen, and in the first week of October, after Labour Day, I went for my licence at the local police station. It was a very funny day. I went in, and I had this big, fat, older policeman giving me the test. He almost jumped out of the car like Dad did. I think he gave me my licence in case he got me for a second test. It would have been too much on his nerves to face me again. After the road test, there was an oral test in the station. All the policemen gathered around me as I did the test; I was stared at throughout the exam, and that made me nervous. They were younger men, nice looking, but I wasn't interested in them. I was just there to get my licence. I got my licence, and I could drive to school. This gave me more freedom and self-confidence and personal power, and with this, I was losing my shyness. I loved the freedom. Carmel, who had humiliated me at school, wanted to be my friend. My car won her over. I had a car, so she found me interesting. I was accepted by my former enemy. We actually became best friends, and her friend, Dawn Sheppard, accepted me as well. I reasoned this was how life is, but they would never really know me, and it was to my advantage to have them in my life, because now I had a place to stay in town, at Carmel's house. To me, I had no home really, and the less I was around, the better.

Time healed things between Carmel and me, and she had a lot of novels in her room. I'd never read a novel outside of the required school novels. She told me she loved to read. She offered me some of her books to take home to read. She read books on strange events or topics I knew nothing about. She had books on Hitler. I took one of them to read. It was an eye-opener as I read of the atrocities he had committed to the Jewish people. This book fascinated me; it was quite graphic, describing how the surgeons in the regime experimented on Jewish women, and the book detailed some shocking experiments done to women's wombs. What fascinated me was how lamp shades were made out of human skin. Even though this was new reading for me, I wasn't shocked. Nothing seemed to shock me; all I needed was to understand the world I was living in.

At this age, I started to realise I didn't have to be accountable to anyone other than myself. I was given lots of freedom, and never questioned on where I was going or what I was doing. The only thing I wanted from my home life was to be accepted and loved by my mother.

Carmel, Dawn, Maxine, Henrietta, and I went to many places together, and we often went to the beach on the weekends. Driving around, I did some pretty stupid things in the car. I was a real daredevil. Sometimes Carmel and I went out at night, but we never told our parents the full truth of where we were going. The next day, to win my mother over, I used to volunteer the information to her. I wanted her to know what I was doing and who I had met. I wasn't always telling the truth; I wanted to make my life exciting, to amuse her, and to win her love.

My sister and I sometimes went out to the local disco in Hastings Crossing, because Maxine had a boyfriend, Collin. Peter, who had been writing me love letters every day, was Collin's best friend. Maxine and I were out at one of the discos when Peter approached me.

Nervously, he asked, 'Chris, can we go out together?'

I looked at him. 'No, Peter, you're younger than me.'

He was upset. 'It won't make any difference.'

'It will to me; I'll feel like your mother.'

He was visibly hurt as he stood in shock, staring at me for a moment. He walked off holding his chest, going back over to Collin and some of the other boys, who weren't too far away from us.

I watched Peter talking to Collin. He was really upset, but on my part, there were no feelings for him, and I wasn't going to force myself to be nice to him for his sake. Next, Peter was bending over, clutching his chest, Collin was worried, and took him to a friend's car and they drove off.

Collin came over and blasted me. 'Christine, do you know what you've just done?'

I was upset, seeing Peter holding his chest. But I said, 'No, Collin. What? What did I do, and what was wrong with him?'

'Pete's having an asthma attack, and he has to go to hospital.'

'I'm sorry, Collin, but...'

Collin walked away.

I sang out, 'Collin, I…'

He rushed to his car and off to the hospital to see Peter. It was so hard to feel any love for anyone; I'd received so many love letters from admirers but couldn't accept any of them as a boyfriend. My fate was already mapped out with another man that I hadn't met as yet, and I couldn't stop my spiritual journey, which I had no idea I was on.

I knew my mother had it hard at home, especially as Grandma was becoming more bedridden, refusing to get out of the bed. Mum had to do everything for her in the bed, including toileting her. She changed her sheets while Grandma was in the bed. Mum had virtually become her nurse. Dad did try to teach Mum to drive a car, but she was too nervous. This had been one of her biggest problems, not being able to drive a car to escape the house now and then. She coped with her life by taking sedatives like Valium. I'd come home from school and try to make her happy by telling her lots of dirty jokes. She'd react with, 'Oh, Christine,' as she laughed.

I'd grab her, holding her tight, and kiss her hard. At home, I was becoming more of a daredevil. This was a time I felt a great sense of strength, because I was breaking into new parts of me, breaking my old barriers of fear, as well breaking her barriers towards me. What I wanted from my mother, I was starting to take from her or demand it from her, but it had to be done in an appropriate way, through fun and joking. All was beginning to work out for me. I was learning how to get my needs met from her. My freedom was allowing me to voice my feelings, and this gave me a sense of power, and the ability to take from her.

There was still that nagging question that had plagued me all my life.

Every now and then I'd ask, 'Mum, was I adopted?'

'No, you weren't, I assure you,' she'd insist.

I'd look at her and wonder, because I never felt I belonged with this family.

'What do you keep asking me that question for, Christine?'

'I don't know,' At this stage of my life, I was feeling more and more that I didn't belong to this family, or even to this earth. I felt like a stranger in both worlds of the family and of the earth.

I'd been smoking for a long time. I was at a party in town and was having a smoke outside the house, while talking to Mitchell and Susanne, a couple of friends. I'd lit up a Rothmans cigarette and was smoking it as I spoke to them. All of a sudden, I became faint, and nearly fell over.

Mitchell caught me and asked me if I was okay. I told him it must have been the cigarette, so I squashed it out and that was it. I never touched another cigarette after that. I gave it up, because I had to be in control of my life.

I completed year four, and even with all my freedom and my wild nature ways and trying to voice myself, it never interfered with my studies. I excelled in my last year of high school, getting very good passes in all my topics: an advance, two credits, and three ordinary passes. I was happy.

Mum asked me, 'What do you want for doing well in your exams?'

I said, casually, 'A bag of dried apples and apricots.'

Shocked at my answer, she asked, 'That's all?'

I'd surprised her. She didn't really understand my request. I answered again, 'Yes, that's all I want.' I never was a materialist person, and, really, I had no great wants for material things. My biggest want was freedom.

School over, and there was a lot of spare time, so I'd go to Carmel's place more often. We'd go to the Claire Point Beach for the day. We met this guy, Alf, who was a surfer, and his mate, Mike, and his girlfriend, Donna. Alf owned a panel van. He invited us girls into the back of it with Mike. Donna, Carmel, and I were game, and we got into the back of his van. Sometimes there were dangers in what I did, but I was seeing everything as fun, and not dangerous. We were all chatting away, and I started to act like I knew what I was doing and voicing my opinions on life.

Suddenly, I was confronted by a very angry Alf. What I said had upset him. Next thing I knew, I had a knife to my throat. I wasn't shocked and showed no fear at all. I remained calm. He lowered the knife. Carmel, Mike, and Donna backed away, and Carmel wanted us to leave there and then, so we did.

When I got out of the van, I looked at Alf with no fear, as if he had lost and I had won, announcing to him, 'You don't scare me.'

He was still sitting in his van. He looked at me sternly, as if I was a weirdo. Carmel pulled me away, and we left the two men in the van. I felt like I had a built-in safety net, and always felt safe. This led me to do as I pleased, and no one scared me. I was a changed person, with no fears. This was my first test, and as I think of that day, I can see my naivety, and my inability at grasping the true nature of some people and their outlook on life, and how not all of us were kind.

Maxine and I went into the Wentworth disco, if I was at home. She and I had some good times in there, and we met some really nice people. We met an Aboriginal guy and his friends, who were from Cape Fletcher. One of Maxine's friends, Frances, really liked him, but I think he liked me. I was still not interested in boys. Many times, Carmel and I would go into Wentworth as well, but it wasn't enough for Carmel. She needed to go further afield, so we'd sneak down to the Dawson Hill disco, called the Crazy Dancing, but it was boring, and I wasn't really into these places. Carmel suggested we go out to the Claire Point Beach Club. So, we told our parents we were going into Wentworth, and then went to Claire Point Beach.

That night there was a cabaret. This place had lots of older guys. They weren't like the boys from high school. Even though I'd left school, I was still being asked out by some of the boys from school. They weren't exciting enough for me.

That night I met Brook, and Carmel met Glen. On our first meeting, Brook was so quick. He seemed to be all over me. That was too quick for me. I told him no way was I giving up my virginity before marriage. He backed off. He still liked me. He asked us to come and visit them, so on most weekends we'd go to Claire Point Beach. Brook and Glen were two surfers. Brook became very interested in me, and Glen was interested in Carmel, but of course Brook wanted to touch me and have sex. I kept telling him no.

Brook revealed to me, 'Chris, I won't marry a virgin.'

Even with those words and the thought of him leaving me, I couldn't allow him near to me, so I refused his advances.

I was wild and free, and not going to lose my virginity before marriage, and I didn't even want to get married or have sex. I had no idea about the sexual act, because it was never discussed in my family, or by my girlfriends. I didn't talk about it, nor did they. It was so strange; the only man I ever wanted to go further with me was my father. When I was a child, he'd take me around on the back verandah. He would play with me, which caused something inside me to stir up, and that was something no other man so far could do.

All I wanted was to have fun. I didn't give in. No one was going to touch me again. It was painful to be caught out after being exposed by my mother - and of all people to find us, my mother. Oh, my mother, she was so devastated, and I lost her love due to my father's insistence on touching me. Only in marriage would I allow intimacy, and marriage seemed to be the only right thing to do to make it decent and right. That concept would come with a price. In marriage, I would be imprisoned in my body, and placed in a box, a house, to rot in my own private hell, to lie there sleeping until the hour came when the two princes, my two sons, could move out of the castle. For me to be freed in my own sexuality, will be when I'm me in contact with those who will open my many doors for me to seek myself.

Brook and Glen informed us they were going to Jacksonville for a year. Brook asked me, 'Chris,' as he gazed into my eyes and leaned his arms over my shoulders, 'can I write to you, and will you write back to me?'

Smiling at his roughly handsome brown face, brown eyes encased in weathered skin that seemed older than his years, due to the harsh sun and sea, I said, 'Yes, I will write.' I then broke free of him and wrote out my address and handed it to him.

On our last day, we spent the whole time cuddling and talking. He was the first guy I allowed into my life on a slightly intimate level for a long period. About a week after they'd left for Jacksonville, I received my first letter, and he confessed his love for me. I liked him a lot, but I wasn't in love with him. He wrote to me faithfully every week. I loved receiving his letters, and I wrote back to him.

Christmas holidays were spent at Cape Fletcher. A week after Christmas day, we went away, leaving Aunty Connie and Uncle Oliver at the farm so they could visit Grandma. Grandma was back in hospital. This gave Mum a much-needed break. Mum and Dad took our newer aluminium van to Cape Fletcher, and Barton, Maxine and I drove up in my car. Dad had instructed me to put air in the tyres of my car. I hadn't been shown how to do that yet.

Driving up to Cape Fletcher, we called into Gordon Valley, stopping at a petrol station. I got petrol and drove the car over to the air hose, and asked Barton if he had any idea how much air I had to put in the tyres. Of course he didn't know; he was only thirteen. I decided to put in seventy pounds; this had come up on the gauge while I was filling the tyres. After putting seventy pounds in, I couldn't get any more in. I didn't understand the gauge reading either. All four were filled, and I paid for the petrol. We made our way to Cape Fletcher to join our parents.

As I drove the car, it seemed strange, bouncing all over the road, and it was so hard to handle. The road up there was a narrow, cut-up, tarred road. I was used to driving on dirt roads, because our roads were dirt roads, but the car was acting strange. We kept going, and eventually we got there. At the caravan park, we found Dad and Mum. Dad was very happy, and close to being really drunk. He was sitting out front of his annex having a beer with the neighbour, with his typical Cheshire cat, silly-looking grin on his face.

'Did you put air in the tyres?'

'Yes, Dad,' I replied, 'but the car seemed to be bouncing all the way up here.'

'How much air did you put in the tyres?'

'Oh, I saw seventy, and couldn't put anymore in there.'

'What? Seventy?' He wriggled in his seat.

'Yeah, Dad. Why? What did I do wrong?' I stepped back from him as he stood up.

Doing a circle, he said, 'God bugger me, girl; it's a wonder you didn't explode the tyres.' He went and got the gauge out of the boot of his car, sat back down, clutching his lower stomach, wriggling more, and tossing himself from side to side as he did when he was nervous. He stood up again and went to the car, bent down, and looked at the tyres.

I asked, 'Why? What did I do?'

Unbelieving, he asked me again, 'You put in seventy pounds of air?'

I nodded yes.

'That's what you put in a truck,' he informed me, releasing the air from the tyres.

Barton and Maxine started to laugh, and it was hard for me to keep a straight face as well. The neighbour was over with Dad, inspecting the car tyres. They were astonished; Dad was telling me that on the gauge were pounds. It was a bit of a joke as others were listening.

I wasn't upset, and said, 'But Dad, I didn't know it was pounds in the air hose, and you didn't tell me how much to put in.'

He looked around, and seeing others' faces with smiles, he became really good about it, and changed his mood. A few beers works wonders in an angry man. The caravan neighbour being there helped as well. Dad let out the excess air, and I was told to put in no more than twenty-eight pounds of air per tyre. I was so happy I had stood my ground, and I wasn't hurt by any embarrassment. Actually, I wasn't embarrassed one bit.

This holiday was such a great holiday. It was only the family, and none of my school friends. On the site was a big community hall where activities were played, and there were competitions held throughout the day. They even had a TV set up there. There were games for the older boys who like billiards. On the caravan site, there were lots of young people. Maxine and I met Gillian. She was a most beautiful young girl who had older parents. Her parents seemed protective of her, but they allowed her to hang out with my sister and me.

Gillian told us she was an adopted child, and she had Polynesian background. She was extremely gentle and sweet, and both Maxine and I liked her so much. We befriended her, and she became our companion. Gillian was sixteen, in between my age and Maxine's age. At night time, we took her out with us to the discos. We ran into the cute Aboriginal guy, Steve, and he still had Frances, and she was keeping a close eye on him, not letting him out of her sight. This time I actually got to speak to him. He asked me if one day I'd like to go out on a date with him. Smiling, I declined, because he already had a girlfriend, Frances, and other than that, I wasn't really interested in boys.

New Year's Eve was celebrated at Cape Fletcher, and Gillian's parents entrusted their daughter to Maxine and me. I didn't want to go to the disco, and I suggested to the girls that we go to the Country Club in Newton Bay; the girls immediately agreed to go, and we were very excited. It was to be our adventure, but we weren't to tell our parents, so on New Year's Eve we went off to the club. As far as our parents were concerned, they never stipulated a time or curfew for us, but they may have disagreed with us going to the club. I was seventeen, and the other girls were under that age. We went, and we got in, and had the best time ever. At the club there was a big party on, with lots of dancing and fun. We met these guys who were all friends with each other, and so we each had a partner, three for three.

On the countdown to twelve o'clock on the threshold of New Year 1969, everyone waited, and then the whistles blew, and the sirens went off and the song 'Auld Lang Syne' played, and everyone started to kiss. Before you knew it, everyone was kissing everyone. The guy I'd met, he and I were having a long passionate kiss. He released me and went off to kiss someone else. Then someone else kissed me. I didn't see who it was. Whoever he was, he was the most beautiful kisser I had ever kissed, and when he released me, I still had my eyes closed. On opening them and looking around, I couldn't work out who it was. Wow!

The New Year didn't stop there. We all agreed to go and watch the sun rise when the club closed. Maxine and Pete, Gillian and Hayden, and Jeff and I went to the waterfront. We sat and got into some heavy kissing as we waited for the sun to rise. There was no thought of returning to the caravan, and my parents wouldn't worry about us, because we were all together, and Gillian's parents knew she was safe with us. These guys were really nice guys. They didn't try any funny business with us. They were happy to bring in the New Year with us.

Finally, the sun rose, and we watched it come up and bring with it another glorious day. The guys were a bit older than us, and after the sun rose, and a few more kisses, it was time to go home to our caravans. I think each of us didn't want to go, but these guys weren't from our area and were from Rosemont, so we said goodbye forever, and headed to our vans. At the caravan park, no one was up, and so we all went to our vans, and Gillian would tell her parents she was in our van with us if they asked. Maxine and I crashed on our beds in the annex. We slept for ages.

Later on, we met up with Gillian. Her parents hadn't heard her coming in, so nothing was said about her lateness. We girls pondered on the boys we'd met and wondered if we'd ever see them again. Over the rest of our holiday, we didn't run into them at all. So now there were two guys I actually liked and allowed into my space, but not to keep in my space for too long.

I could distance myself from others. No one really got very close to me. I wanted to be responsible for my life, maybe because my mother seemed so immature and irresponsible. I was sick of her childlike ways and

I didn't want to be like her. All my life, she'd been trying to place me in an adult's role, to support her by listening to her woes. I'd felt more like her mother than she was mine, as I'd listened to her problems and dealt with her outbursts of anger and pain. Many times, there was no sense in her ravings and complaints. Who were all these people in my life? There were many characters playing in a game that I didn't want to be a part of. Sometimes these games sounded frightening and made me feel old and way too responsible for my years. Sometimes I'd close down on feeling my body, and I felt like I was only a set of eyes, and not a body. It felt separate to me. It was heavy, and I didn't live for my body; it was just there to house me and carry me around. It would have been nice if someone could have explained and reassured me that it was a good thing to have a lovely body. Maybe then I could have coped better with it, but no one cared to or saw the need, so lacking understanding and knowledge of my own physical self, I lacked knowing the advantages of owning such a body. This body was mine and only mine, and not for sharing with others.

PART TWO

Chapter 40

Knowing My Future Before It Arrived

There was a significant dream in my childhood, and I will never forget this dream, because it was around the house of the Farrows. The Farrows lived near the top of the hill, before you walked down to the main road to catch the bus to school on our last leg of the track we used to walk, before the bridge was washed away. Also, Mr Farrow and Alex Norton rode around the property to keep an eye on the lagoon. They were the Special Constables, and this was part of their job. They often rode through our land, stopping at our fence to have a chat with Grandma or Mum. Little did I know that one day they would become connected to my family.

In my dream, I was inside the Farrows' house, and I was looking outside through their window into their yard - and their house was surrounded by wolves, and these wolves were just waiting. They seemed to be waiting for me, but I was too scared to go out to them. I could never understand that dream. It wouldn't be until later in my life, I would be able to understand

and connect to the reason for that dream. That family would be connected to my family through marriage, and the wolves were the protectors of the family, and the pathfinders, and I would one day be as they are, a protector of the truth of my family. I would be a pathfinder for my family. They were letting me know I had a journey, like they did. We don't realise how we are directed in our early childhood into what we should aim for in our adulthood. Back then, I knew nothing of energy. Energy is always in motion; in that motion we are lead to clues to show us our way through various people, or through dreams, through movies, through books, etc. Many of us shrug off these clues to our life, and this is part of the mysteries of life, the clues.

If only I'd known about these clues in my childhood. I would have loved to have known about such things as intuition, guides, meditation; and to know I was being guided by my intuition to understanding myself and others, this would have made life easier to understand. I had no idea of intuitions or a higher self or guardian angels, or even God and angels, for that matter. We were never educated on the unseen or unknown or God. I knew things like we never died. I laughed in funerals, and wondered why people cried at them. Knowing these things, I still had fears around them, because in my life I would fear the unknown things, invisible in me, and many other things in my life. It wouldn't be until I was much older, in my late thirties, I would start to learn about life, understanding it, but still fearing it. At this age, through books, I would start to find out about the unknown. I feared to find out; however, it was all the unknown locked up inside me. Many will try to suppress my potential and my powers, and I will have to dig my way out of other people's holes that I allowed them to dig and place me in. I will have to search and experience through many people, who will be gifts to me, opening doors to my inner world and awakening me. I had no idea an inner world existed. I was so unaware of my spiritual self. I knew there were many things beyond this world, and death was not the end, as I said, and we come back. I don't possess the words to describe my inner thoughts. I was seeking knowledge, and wanted to learn so much. Finally, I'd find my knowledge in books hidden from us as children, and from the TV, but I wouldn't learn from my parents. I found out bits and pieces of our family history and knowledge from my grandma. In questioning her on the family, she shared some knowledge, but was guarded with her answers, giving me what she wanted to give out. There was always more behind her words, and I'd look at her with searching eyes, and she'd look away from me.

Finding the self is part of my life's purpose; I just didn't know we had to seek ourselves. My life to date revolved around people lost in their sadness, resentments, regrets, grief, pain and sufferings. It would have helped me so much if my parents knew that life was a journey to discover the self, and if they did, they could have nurtured me through, helping me to develop my mind, and lead me to the right books to feed my hunger for knowledge and understanding of life.

If only they could have seen the potential of all their children, not only me, and guided us all in our endeavours to find ourselves, and allowed us to make choices for ourselves and didn't ignore us, seeing us as just there to be fed and watered in silence, with no interaction or conversation on a higher level. No wonder I had so many problems with my mother's futile conversations that amounted to nothing. It seemed so senseless and demeaning to her as a person.

My parents were married too young, but I didn't want to get married, or maybe I'd marry at the age of twenty eight. Somehow I knew, when I did marry, it would be to a foreigner, and my firstborn son would be called Julian. I only wanted boys, no girls. I couldn't get a lot of information on foreign countries and the people from foreign lands, except through the TV or movies.

My favouite myth was the story of Jason and the Golden Fleece, and my favourite songs as a child were 'My Bonnie Lies over the Ocean' and 'Johnny's So Long at the Fair'. All these will haunt me, and they will be connected to my life and my dreams, and will be connected to the Farrows' house, but why? And the name Julian: why? Time will answer my questions, but while I'm living through the experiences, I will have forgotten these moments and times of connection.

I felt I was connecting to other realms in my dreams, and the visions and dreams were trying to tell me parts of my future. Dreams are cryptic, and until we become aware and have higher understanding and knowledge, we don't understand the true messages they are trying to communicate to us. We walk in the dark of our shadows. We are so conditioned by our parents, and trust them above all. Nonetheless, I was being prepared for my future. We are all being prepared for our future, but few of us recognise it. We must live our dreams, or bring the dreams into reality.

I'm the one in our family who will be the pathfinder, to release family patterns that the family is unaware of, and that they have been re-living for maybe centuries. I wish to release the taboos in my family, and any curses placed on us. I will not only find out about myself through the experiences of this family, but I will be placed on many different roads that will lead me to other parts of myself, in my memory of myself in far off and distant times.

Messages and directions are also given to us through dreams, people, places, events, movies, books, and meditations. Children receive all their knowledge between the ages of zero to seven, and if only parents realised this, and watched their children's drawings and listened to their stories and thoughts, we could nurture and guide our children on their true paths.

When your children tell you about strange stories, feelings, thoughts or experiences, please, parents, please don't dismiss them as trivial and irrelevant, because they do have significance. As parents, we need to open our own minds to understanding our children, and as your children are developing, they are helping you to understand your world and its phenomena. Most parents reject their children's dreams, visions, stories, events, and say they're silly and it's all nothing. False. Those encounters are something, there to help us understand ourselves and our world we live in, as each of us has a different perception, and each lives in a different world. Each other's minds are so different. We are like chalk and cheese. All is a clue, guide and direction to know our desires, or what it is we need to address in this lifetime to help us become fully-fledged adults, safe in doing what the soul has intended on the physical plane in our physical vehicle. They are secrets from your Essence that resides at your heart, and where your inner knowledge was put from your God within, working through your intuition, and through your third eye of knowing, and in the brain through the mind of God, where all is connected to the higher self that watches over you, and lovingly waits for you to recognise it and respond to it, to start your journey within; and then your story will unfold, and the mystery of you will be revealed.

As children, we are so connected to these higher places of self, our wisdom and knowledge within us, but as we move along in life, both in a family or in a community, town, or city, we lose connection to our higher self, and then something sparks in some of us to remind us to begin our journey. We re-seek what was missed and lost in childhood, that something we yearn for. Is this our re-connection to our soul, our source of power that is beyond all things and time?

We don't know what it is, but the pull is greater than the flesh, and the flesh must succumb to the soul's purpose, and if not, woe to the flesh that disobeys its soul's purpose. Many of us will be thrust into situations to do as we are to do, and many of us will become ill to stop us, so we will listen to our inner voice and take heed as to what is required of us.

If a child's imaginings, dreams and desires are not fulfilled, they will haunt the child into adulthood until realised, or at least accepted. We all possess so much talent and potential, but many will say some of us have none. It's not that some of us have no talent or potential, it's that for some of us, these weren't allowed to manifest or be brought to the surface and made recognisable to the child. Without self-awareness, how do we know what we possess within?

Many children are actually living out their parent's lives and dreams that they didn't accomplish or fulfil. Parents do this to their children, enforce a career or dream on them that may not be to their liking, and because parents are supposed to be their guides and their elders, children often respect them and do what they want, to their own detriment, stifling their own lives and dreams.

All that is untouched within us will die with us, never to be understood or known of, and we may not or will never understand who we are, or know our true selves; and in death all can be lost and never experienced.

I am always trying to find out about life and to understand life, and to understand the ones I lived with. I am a seeker, a seeker of the self, my true self seeking to connect to my God within and my higher self. The ones I lived with, I felt, had no idea of life or themselves, and I thought they lived in a closed house, and never went outside their boundaries. This was me. What you fear or think about your parents or others is within you. They are also there to help you to unfold the mystery of you. This may seem contradictory, as I say my parents didn't see our potential and nurture it, and made us live their unfulfilled dreams, and now I'm saying what you fear and think of your parents is within you.

This is for the child like me, who is totally left alone and not loved, and with limited bonding. I feel my parents never loved me or saw me, and what I'm saying is that I never saw who I was, never loved myself, and I was always afraid of the unknown, but now I know I'm not afraid of the unknown. What I was afraid of was the unknown parts of myself, and my power and potential. I was a self-educated person who hungered for knowledge, but it's not until now that I know all the knowledge I needed for this lifetime dwelt in me. I was always looking outside myself for the knowledge, but with time and maturity, that knowledge came through to me.

I had to understand my family and its idea of being a family, but the information was too scant, so I had to piece the puzzle together slowly over years, and dig deep into myself for the answers.

The answers are within us always, if we wish to delve into our lives and our struggles. This is not for all people. Some won't want to go within and dig up all their baggage, place it on a table before them, look at it, own it as theirs, and deal with who they really are.

As an adult, I have journeyed and discovered many things I never thought I could possibly do in this lifetime. All my dreams seemed unattainable, but they weren't, and my soul drove me to seek my life's purpose, once I became aware of my soul and my will was determined enough to achieve the goals of my soul.

My road is long on the journey, but I'm truly glad of the journey to find my true self in all the mistaken information I was fed as a child, and took on as real, and to see the lies and denials I've created of the self, and to rid myself of these deceptions that I have taken on. These can cheat me out of a secure and loving life.

As we are taught, so we teach ourselves through what we perceive as a truth, and it's in our perceptions, that all our failings start.

In all communities, town, cities, religions, political states, and in all other areas of life, this is the one thing that separates us and causes us so much trauma, suffering, pain, grief, trouble, hatred of our fellow men, wars and mayhem: *our perceptions*, which are based on beliefs from our families, and other peer members and role models in our lives, and how we perceived what we saw and learned through our eyes.

Unfortunately, as a child I had a brain like a sponge, and absorbed everything that came my way. I'm not referring to knowledge of the world, but the family information. My fertile mind planted every seed of thought into it: the good, the bad, and the ugly. I took on all the roles of my peers in my family, and played out all the roles displayed to me and owned them as mine, and made them my own reality, in unawareness. Now for the first time in my life, I'm truly happy and feel complete, and have come back to my true self by doing a complete cycle. In my completion, I truly have no need to take on others' roles. I can stand neutral in a situation where I would have lived out the other's pain, suffering and struggle, not realising it wasn't mine, due to being so used to doing so.

Now I can stand with other people and feel nothing of their pain and anguish in me. While standing with the others, I truly feel compassion and love, without words or judgement about the situation being played out in front of me. I'm truly in touch with my own inner light and Essence.

I will tell you my story and how I went about doing this. My first aim was to break destructive family patterns I had no idea of as a child. This is part of my mission in life, to recognise these family patterns we've all carried through generations, in unawareness. My story will tell you about how I unravel other parts of myself, and how only my soul knew of this, but showed me visions, when I was in the appropiate places, to unfold that knowledge from within, and with the appropriate people to do it with.

My stories are not to condemn my family, my stories are to show how I saw the family I lived with, and how I will unravel the drama I created.

To be continued...

Life

As I stare out into the crowd
I am free
Freedom is the basis of the truth to life
One must be free to express one's feelings and thoughts.
Angels, Angels walk with me
Free me of fears, and desperation the world reflects to me.
Give me the strength and courage to let
me see those reflections in me
For fears and desperations I see in you are in me
The world is safe and I am full of your Grace
to walk the earth that bounds me not
Only man bounds himself
For I am part of the Greater plan
So are they who journey with me.
Give them memory, for they've just forgotten.

Christine U. Cowin

About the Author

I grew up on a farm in Australia. I was one of three siblings. In my young childhood, I encountered sexual abuse by my father. My mother found out when I was eleven and seemed to think it was my fault. This caused me a lot of pain and isolation. I found it very difficult to make friends. I went through high school experiencing some good times and some difficult times. In my last years of high school, I decided to discipline myself and studied hard to pass with good marks. I would have loved to have continued on at school; however it was not in my parent's vision.

I married early, had two children reared them, and they made their way in life. I divorced my husband to realise my life's dream. I wanted to travel but I never thought I could financially.

I worked, bought my own home, and had many, many friends. I was always helping others but I couldn't solve my own issues.

I studied at the Esoteric College in my home town. Here I had the opportunity to open myself fully to my spiritual self. Through this college, I was able to journey overseas to study in Italy.

When I was making arrangements to go to Egypt, before we went to Italy, I remembered where I had to go: Turkey.

In 1984, after seeing this fishing village in Turkey in a magazine, I thought I had to go there. The memories came flooding back and so I went to Egypt and to Italy, left the group and got on a train from Rome to Brindisi in Italy to catch a ferry boat to Samos, then on to Turkey. On touching Turkish soil, I knew I'd come home.

After a long month travelling around Turkey knowing it like the back of my hand, I sold all I owned in Australia in 2002 and went back to Turkey to live, not knowing what would unfold for me there. I just followed my spirit and went.

There I re-lived my life, awakened. In Turkey, I didn't feel lost, misunderstood or angry. I felt I had purpose and direction. I learned to feel and be in my body, and I was not sailing through life. I had many experiences, met many people, and formed strong friendships. I was very popular there and learned many things.

I learnt I had to write my life story. I had to re-live my life, from age 7 through to my present age at that time, to write this story. Later on, I had to either study to get my Celta Certificate to teach English, or go home. Because I was short of money, I decided to return home. As I prepared to return home to Australia, I began to get angry.

In 2008 I returned to Australia and all those lost, misunderstood, and no-direction feelings, and feelings of unhappiness, returned. Now I had to unravel myself on a deeper level to unlock the secrets within me that were holding me back from stepping into the life I should be living.

That process would take me another 10 years. In 2018 I unlocked an unknown mystery that had me chained to fear, stopping me from moving forward, achieving my dreams, and living my true life's purpose.

My books are a series. I invite you to walk with me as I journey into my secret self, expose those secrets, move into my truth, and live my true life.

My website contains my Bio, links to purchase my books and reviews:

Website: www.christineucowinwriter.com

Email address: christine@christineucowinwriter.com

Amazon Central Authors Page:

www.amazon.com/author/christineucowinwriter